How to Stop
the One You Love
from Drinking

How to Stop the One You Love from Drinking

I Know Because Intervention Worked for Me

Mary Ellen Pinkham
with Families in Crisis, Inc.

G. P. Putnam's Sons
New York

Copyright © 1986 by Mary Ellen Pinkham and Dale Ronda Burg
All rights reserved. This book, or parts thereof,
may not be reproduced in any form without permission.
Published simultaneously in Canada by
General Publishing Co. Limited, Toronto

Library of Congress Cataloging-in-Publication Data

Pinkham, Mary Ellen.
  How to stop the one you love from drinking.

  1. Alcoholics—United States—Family Relationships.
2. Alcoholics—Rehabilitation—United States.
3. Alcoholism—Treatment—United States. I. Families
in Crisis (Clinic: Minneapolis, Minn.) II. Title.
HV5132.P56 1986   362.2'92   86-17021
ISBN 0-399-13158-2

Typeset by Fisher Composition, Inc.

PRINTED IN THE UNITED STATES OF AMERICA
1 2 3 4 5 6 7 8 9 10

Acknowledgments

I hope you already know who I am, but I would like to introduce you to some of the other people who helped make this book possible. They include the three founders of Families in Crisis, the Midwest's only Intervention counseling clinic:

Nels Schlander—Nels graduated from the University of Minnesota as an alcohol and drug abuse counselor. He has worked with adolescents and their families and was on the staff of the Adult Chemical Dependency Program at St. Mary's, the Minneapolis institution renowned for dealing with chemical dependency. He has been in private practice for several years, working both with individuals and human resources administrators at major corporations.

Mary McMahon—Mary worked with many corporations and schools when she was associated with the Johnson Institute, the first Intervention center in the U.S., from 1971 to 1980. She has been with the St. Mary's Rehabilitation Center 1980 since and has spoken around the world at seminars in the field of chemical dependency.

K. D. Dillon—K. D. spent fourteen years on the staff of the St. Mary's Adult Chemical Dependency Program. She has worked in industry as an employee assistance counselor and entered private practice in 1982.

I would also like to acknowledge the assistance of *Mary Brown*, marketing director and Intervention specialist at Families in Crisis. Mary has nine years of experience in the field of chemical dependency.

The authors are indebted to Vernon Johnson and the Johnson Institute for their pioneering work in defining alcoholism and helping alcoholics and their friends and families deal with the disease.

And of course I'm truly grateful for all the help I get from my partner Dale Burg, who worked with me on my book *Mary Ellen's Help Yourself Diet Plan* and is my collaborator on the columns I write for *The Star* and *Family Circle* magazine.

*This book is dedicated to
my husband, Sherman F. Pinkham, Jr.
He gave me the freedom to be who I was
and the support to be who I wanted to be.*

Contents

How to Stop
the One You Love
from Drinking

Introduction

It's okay to love an alcoholic. But it's not okay to let him keep on drinking. And there's a way—a loving, caring, kind way—to get him to stop.

When there's a drinking problem in a family, time and time again people avoid facing up to it. No matter how much chaos it's causing, either they refuse to put the blame on the alcohol or they say, "I've learned to live with it," "It isn't that bad yet," or "If there's a real crisis, I'll do something." They hold on to the hope that something will happen to stop the problem or that it will just go away by itself.

No doubt something will—a job loss, the breakup of the family, perhaps a jail term for a DWI, maybe even death. Ninety-seven percent of alcoholics die of alcohol-related symptoms. If you really care about someone, you'll get help for him or her and get it *now*—while there's still something left to lose.

I don't care how discouraged you feel, I don't care how many remedies you've tried before, I don't care how unwilling to change the one you love is. Even when previous treatments have failed, even in cases that appear hopeless, I can assure you there *is* a way to get him or her on the road to recovery and to have a full and exciting life for yourself.

I understand your concern, your anger, your pain, and your frustration. Chances are, the alcoholic you love is feeling a lot of pain, too. I know this because I've looked at it from both sides now. I have friends and family who are recovering alcoholics. I am one myself.

I expect my alcoholism will come as news to the millions of readers of my helpful hints books. They probably thought Mary Ellen Pinkham really had her house in order. Well, I may not have had any cobwebs in the attic, but I had more than a few in my head.

In March of 1984 they cleared briefly, long enough for me to realize I was in trouble, and I checked myself into a treatment center. Two weeks later, I called my collaborator. She knows I have a habit of writing from personal experience. "One thing you can count on," I told her. "I'm not going to turn this into a book."

I did not plan to grow up and become an alcoholic and go into treatment, nor did I intend to become a best-selling author and then put the icing on the cake by writing about my alcoholism.

That certainly wasn't my goal when I made that phone call. I was halfway through treatment then and still ashamed to admit that I was an alcoholic. Shortly afterward, I reached a turning point in treatment and realized I was wrong to feel ashamed.

By the time I'd completed treatment, I was ready to come out of the closet about my alcoholism. Having accepted what I had been told—that alcoholism is a disease, and that part of recovery is having a good support system—I knew I had no other choice. To create a support system, I had to start by telling everyone the facts.

Amazingly, I had to fight for the right to call myself an alcoholic. Everyone tried to convince me it wasn't so. "You weren't that bad," they said. Only when I told them *everything* did they let me own up to my disease.

I was in high school when I had my first drink. It was the old story: Someone's mom was out of the house, so my friends and I got the booze out of the cabinet. We each took a drink, gulped it down to get the effect, and then refilled the bottle with water.

Unlike many alcoholics, who always remember the effect of their first drink, I don't recall if I got drunk that first time.

I do know that I liked acting as though I were drunk. Whenever I drank afterward, I always tried to make myself look more intoxicated than I was. There was a lot of glamor, I thought, in being intoxicated. It had a great deal of fascination for me.

Besides, I had adolescent skin troubles and a weight problem. Alcohol was a great discovery, because after a couple of drinks, I felt better. I felt special. I had always been outgoing. I could have been the life of the party even without the drinks, but when I had them I felt prettier. I acted prettier. People paid more attention to me, or so I thought. Now I realize that I paid more attention to them. The drinking gave me the courage to talk and say what was on my mind. It made me feel powerful, in complete control. The hangovers didn't bother me. Feeling good was worth the price. I didn't realize the price I'd eventually pay was much, much worse than a hangover.

Personally, I always thought my drinking over the years stayed pretty constant. That wasn't so, but nobody told me anything different. In every relationship, I got the green light on my drinking. And in my business, drinking's part of the normal routine—going out to lunch, meeting for cocktails. I don't remember being confronted about my drinking too often.

Besides, I enjoyed it, though I enjoyed it less as time went on. If those who drink or use drugs didn't have fun from using them, they'd stop sooner—because they'd crash sooner. So maybe eight out of ten times were fun for me. But it became scary when I started to lose control. I was always walking on a tightrope.

The call—the addiction—is very powerful. It's terrifically, almost unimaginably, exciting. That's why trying to persuade a practicing alcoholic or a drug user how happy he'll be when he gives up alcohol or drugs is like telling someone who doesn't believe in God how much he's going to enjoy the afterlife.

The alcohol creates such a strong illusion that I thought *it* was what made life wonderful. Now that I'm sober, I realize that only in my mind was I better off when I was drinking. When I was drinking, I felt I couldn't fail. I was Suzy Parker and Dorothy Parker rolled into one gorgeous, brilliant package. In reality, at least some of the time, I was a self-centered, opinionated know-it-all. A bore.

My delusions helped the drinking get worse. I'd say, "If I'm so great after three drinks, imagine what I'd be like after five!" So I'd go for five. Then I wasn't making any decisions at all any more. I was completely out of control.

I can't tell you how many times I went out planning to have only one or two drinks. But after a while, a team of wild horses couldn't have pulled me from the bar. I know that's a tired cliché, but I really mean it. The urge was that strong. I didn't stop until I was intoxicated. But, being a smart cookie (maybe a rum ball), I didn't crumble. Instead, I became totally preoccupied—thinking about how I wouldn't drink or about when I would drink next. If I stayed away from it for a week or two, it consumed my thoughts entirely.

On the day I took my last drink, I went to work all dressed up. My associates knew that when I came in all decked out, it was a pretty good clue I'd skip out of the office around noon and not return until the next morning—probably with my dark glasses on.

That particular day, we'd all been under pressure and I decided to play the great boss, taking everyone out and telling them how much I cared about them. At 11:30 I went into my sales manager's office and told him to put on his coat. Fifteen minutes later, six of us were seated in a nearby restaurant.

My drinking started slowly. It usually did. I ordered a glass of wine instead of my usual Dewar's, because I intended to go back to work. Besides, I'd been putting on weight, so I planned to cut back by mixing the wine with seltzer and drinking it slowly.

The minute I took a sip, I knew I wouldn't be able to stop with this single drink. It felt very warm going down. Almost instantly, I felt its effects. Lunch dragged on. I stayed in the restaurant, drinking, until about 5:00 P.M.

When I drove home, no one was there. The details of the early evening are foggy. I know I continued to drink, but I wanted companions. I called around, and since I got no answers, I decided to visit an aunt and uncle who lived about fifteen miles away. I knew they'd have liquor. I drove there intoxicated.

I don't remember anything more of that evening. I awoke in my aunt's house, dying of thirst and full of guilt about the events of the night before. On top of that, I remembered that my husband and my son were leaving for Florida that morning.

When I came into the kitchen, my uncle looked at me and nodded. "Kid, you're something else when you're drinking." I hoped he wouldn't say anything else. I couldn't bear to hear the details.

I drove home, praying my husband and son hadn't left yet, so I could say goodbye. Their luggage was in the hall. I had planned to drive them to the airport, but in my absence Sherm had made other arrangements. My parting words were, "I'm so sorry. Something is very wrong with me. I don't think I'll be home when you get back."

I crawled into bed, threw the covers over my head, and spent the day there, trying to block out memories of the night and day before. I tried rationalizing: It was the wine; scotch wouldn't have made me so crazy. I wasn't the only one drinking; my co-workers and my aunt and uncle were drinking, too. I drifted in and out of troubled sleep.

Early Sunday morning, I was agitated and desperate to talk to someone. I called Anne, a friend and business associate who agreed to meet me at a local diner. As I drove there, I thought about how much trouble I was in. I'd even been seeing a psychologist and, just two days before as she was leaving on vacation, I had promised her I wouldn't drink while she was gone. Yet look what had happened.

When I entered the restaurant, Anne's face showed her concern. I started to tell her I needed help but I backed off. I could handle it myself. Hadn't I done a pretty good job of taking care of myself and everyone else until then? Maybe I just needed strict rules to stop my drinking. I told Anne, "I'll just quit. I'm resolved. I've done it before, and I'll do it again."

Anne looked me in the eyes. "You need help, Mary Ellen. You're fighting an alcohol problem, and I'll do anything to start you in the right direction." She took a brochure for a treatment center from her purse.

Suddenly, my drinking was in the open. Anne knew I had a problem. I had acknowledged it. I made arrangements to check myself into Hazelden, a treatment facility near Minneapolis.

The day I went into treatment, I was a broken woman. I had reached bottom. Life seemed meaningless, and all I knew was that something had to change or my life was going to come to a sudden or unhappy end. Thoughts of suicide started to creep into my mind. Some of my closest relationships were on the rocks. People I had loved dearly were getting to the point where they'd had it with me. I sensed this, but I was confused. Since no one had pointed out to me what my drinking was like, I wasn't aware of my behavior.

I felt that people had turned on me, but in reality they'd just gotten tired of coping with me, with the sarcasm and insults I heaped on them when I was drunk.

I called my collaborator to tell her I was going into treatment. "That's great," she said. "Then you'll have nothing to hide. Then nobody can move you around the chessboard of life anymore. Mary Ellen, sober, you have more confidence than anyone in the world. But when you drink, you become needy. You turn from a dynamo into someone I'm uncomfortable with, someone I don't even know. I haven't seen you drink many times, but the few that I have, I saw the difference in you." Somebody loved me enough to level with me, tell me her feelings, offer me support. That made me feel wonderful. That was a ray of hope.

Once I sobered up, I had to face the fact that many of the people closest to me, including my immediate family, had serious alcoholism problems of their own. And I wanted them to understand that there were options other than living as an alcoholic—or with one.

I knew it was going to be tough to get them to accept help. I knew what a hard time I had given the very few people who were brave enough to confront me about my own alcoholism. Luckily, I crash-landed in treatment. Other people keep using alcohol until they wind up in insane asylums or cemeteries. The drug winds up controlling them.

Having no control over your alcohol (or whatever your drug of choice, from cough syrup to heroin) is one symptom of chemical dependency. That's bad enough.

What's worse is that alcoholics and other chemical dependents won't recognize that they have a disease. Like the people around them, they either refuse to see alcohol as the main problem, or they tell themselves the situation isn't so bad, that some day they'll do something about it. That's why you have such a hard time getting them help. Before you have any hope of dealing with the underlying disease, you must penetrate that denial.

If you've been living with an alcoholic, you know how tough this is. An alcoholic will never ask you for help. He loves his alcohol; why on earth would he ask you to take it away?

It was a revelation for me to realize that an alcoholic doesn't have to ask for help to get it. You can give it by initiating an Intervention.

Maybe you've heard of Interventions, but I'd be willing to bet you can't describe one. I've discovered that even people who believe they've been involved in an Intervention may not understand the process very well. In the past, many people who led Interventions were ill-equipped or ill-informed to conduct them properly.

An Intervention is not a confrontation. It is not a blaming session. It is a loving and carefully rehearsed way of telling the person you care about exactly how use of alcohol or drugs is affecting his or her life—and yours. You don't tell it one-on-one (as you've probably discovered, such efforts fall on deaf ears), but together with other concerned family members and friends. The goal of Intervention is to get the one you love into treatment, which is the first step to recovery.

Exactly how it works is what this book is about. All you need to know at this point is that it does work where other "solutions" have failed.

It worked on my husband. It worked on my sister. In fact, Families in Crisis, the Minneapolis organization where I found the three wonderful counselors who helped me with my family's Interventions, told me that they have been successful with 95 percent of the cases they have seen. In the overwhelming majority of cases, the people on whom an Intervention is initiated go directly from Intervention into treatment. The rest go within 48 hours.

They go because during the process of Intervention, they come to realize at last how their alcohol use is affecting their lives. They come to understand that if they don't go for help, their families, their jobs, and anything else precious to them are in jeopardy. Their alcohol is all they will have left. Or else they go simply to get everyone off their back. The reason isn't important. What's important is that they go and get help.

In a small number of cases an Intervention may fall short of its goal, but no Intervention fails. Once the problem has been brought into the open, no one involved in the disease—the person affected or those around him—can ever retreat into denial again. I suppose it is possible that they may convince themselves the Intervention never happened; but if they follow the advice they are given, they will not be able to hide behind denial.

Why isn't everyone doing Interventions? Why, as a matter of fact, had no one done an Intervention on me?

The answer is fairly obvious. To begin with, most people don't have the least understanding of the disease of chemical dependency, and they have even less information about Interventions. I myself learned about them only in the course of my treatment. Then, when I looked for help, I was fortunate to find Families in Crisis. Its three principals, Nels Schlander, Mary McMahon, and K. D. Dillon, all had years of experience in initiating Interventions. Not enough people have the resources I did.

Out of curiosity, I tried to find a book about Intervention, but I could locate only a pamphlet or two. The few books that listed the word *Intervention* in the index mentioned it only briefly and generally described it (completely erroneously) as a confrontation.

In general, books I read about alcoholism weren't helpful. Most of them read like a college text or what I call a "drunkalogue"—someone's sordid story of how alcohol sent him into the gutter. Who can relate to this? A minute percentage of alcoholics are on Skid Row. Most are nice people who manage, for the most part, to be functional both at work and at home. They are people whom other people love.

One exception among the books I consulted was *The Courage to Change*, which includes case histories of alcoholics and their decisions to recover. Still, the big question it raised for me went unanswered. What gives someone the courage to change? How do I give that kind of courage to someone I care about?

According to 1985 statistics from the National Council on Alcoholism, there are 12.1 million alcoholics in the United States, a 14.3 percent increase since 1980. The Council estimates that each of these people has a direct affect on the lives of four other people. That means over 60 million people (and I believe the real figures are even higher) are intimately involved with alcoholism and its consequences.

When I discovered this, I couldn't get it out of my head: So many people in so much pain, so many people headed for big trouble. The irony is that there *is* a solution available to them. They just don't know about it.

There was one way to spread the word, of course. I knew I'd be taking a risk, but finally I made up my mind. I dialed my collaborator.

"Forget what I said," I told her. "There's a book we've got to write." This is that book. A book about Intervention. More accurately, a book about miracles.

A Note Regarding Drug Abuse

Most often in this book, I will be referring to alcoholism, since alcohol abuse, not drug abuse, is what I am most familiar with. But the problems are the same whether it's scotch or cough syrup the one you love is drinking by the gallon. He or she is just afflicted with a different form of the same disease: chemical dependency.

I'm always amazed when people say, "Mary Ellen, you were a drinker, not a drugger, so why do you think you have something to say to people who are dealing with a drug problem?" The fact is, if I started taking other mood-altering chemicals—anything from sleeping pills to heroin—I would be very likely to become addicted to them just as I am addicted to alcohol, for reasons that will be clearer once you read about the disease. (By the way, there are plenty of dual dependants. Alcoholics often get into using cocaine because it increases their tolerance for alcohol.)

If you read my diet book, you know I saw a lot of quack "diet doctors" before I discovered that the only sane way to lose weight was a combination of diet and exercise. My diet doctors loved to prescribe uppers, or amphetamines. Each time I started with a new prescription, I immediately escalated my use and needed more and more pills. Within a month, I would become totally preoccupied with the pills and have to stop using them cold turkey. I actually became addicted to them.

Unfortunately, too many doctors are unintentionally pushers—not only of amphetamine for weight loss, but also of other drugs, such as tranquilizers. I know that because I'm addictive I shouldn't take many kinds of medicine. I have to watch my chemical use very closely. Even coffee zonks me out.

Although many doctors are becoming more aware of this sort of thing (in Minnesota, for example, they now have to take some training in chemical dependency), many still don't quite understand. When they offer me pills, I explain that I'm a recovering alcoholic, and they say, "Fine, but do you want pills?" without realizing I could get hooked on them. My brother, who is a recovering alcoholic like me, went so far as to have surgery without painkillers!

Occasionally, when I was offered marijuana or cocaine, I always refused. I knew I would probably like the stuff too much and I never wanted to find out for sure. I felt I had enough problems without a habit that might send me into the streets at two in the morning trying to score some coke. You wouldn't believe the number of attractive, intelligent, successful men and women doing just that. I met them at the treatment center, and I found that I often had more experiences in common with them than with the alcoholics. We sat and talked about our substance abuse and discovered it was exactly the same.

What is typical of alcohol abuse is just as characteristic of drug abuse. Read these pages and you'll find that what I say about alcoholism is completely relevant to your loved one who is dependent on drugs.

Most important, the solution I'm suggesting to anyone concerned about an alcohol abuser—an Intervention—is as appropriate, and promises to be equally effective if your loved one is a drug abuser.

1/
Giving Your Problem a Name

If you bought this book, I'm 99 percent sure the person you're concerned about is an alcoholic. At this point, however, you may still have your doubts.

I've noticed that people who have to deal with someone with a drinking problem tend to fall into two categories.

There are people who are familiar with alcoholism and alcoholic behavior, people who may even know a great deal about it, but who do nothing. Either they don't know where to go for help or they just haven't been able to get their heads out of the sand. Children of alcoholics with alcoholic spouses, for example, are so accustomed to living in an alcoholic home that they are simply stuck. They compare their alcoholic spouse to their alcoholic parent and decide he isn't nearly as bad. If you know the problem in your home is alcoholism, you may skip ahead to chapter 2.

On the other hand, you may know that something's wrong but you can't identify the primary cause. You're not sure what you're dealing with. Or maybe you're just unwilling to put a label on it. I see people with their lives crashing around them who just can't bring themselves to say, "I'm living with an alcoholic." One of the counselors at Families in Crisis says that to this day his dad can't bring himself to admit his son is an alcoholic. He just says, "My boy is doing a little better these days because he isn't drinking."

But whatever category you fall into, you are reading these words because there is someone in your life for whom you suspect drinking is, or will become, a major problem. I think you deserve a pat on the back. Many people in your situation have given up hope. Others haven't the courage to examine the facts.

Avoiding the label

There's a funny prejudice we have about the word "alcoholic." In 1956, the American Medical Association recognized that alcoholism was a disease. Even people who know this for a fact—even I who *am* an alcoholic—still in their hearts tend to regard alcoholism as a moral issue.

I lie in bed sometimes, on bad nights, and say to myself, "If only I hadn't done this or that, I wouldn't be in this situation." I forget the fact that, as an alcoholic, I had no choice.

And I resent it when people think that blaming the disease gives me an easy out. When I admitted to being an alcoholic, someone actually said to me, "Oh, Mary Ellen, this is the greatest thing in the world for you. Now you can blame everything on the alcoholism." Well, that's true. I wouldn't have gotten into some of the messes except for the alcoholism, and I suggested to this person that he keep his mouth shut until he knew what he was talking about.

Think of it this way. Everyone knows that a diabetic isn't responsible for the fact that his pancreas doesn't produce insulin. What he *can* take responsibility for is controlling his intake of sugar. Similarly, I can't help what alcohol does to me. But that doesn't mean I'm helpless. Now, knowing I have a disease, I can make a choice: Drink or not. Ignore the problem or take care of myself.

Still, I know I take a risk admitting I'm an alcoholic. I wonder, "Will people like me anyway?" I love the mail I get from readers, and I think to myself, "Will this disappoint them? Will they think less of me? Will some of the publications I write for decide not to renew my contracts?" Public opinion is a lot more sympathetic than it was even a few years ago, but there's still a stigma attached to the label "alcoholic."

I fall into the trap myself. I read books about Elvis Presley,

Joan Crawford, Errol Flynn, and many others, and I find myself saying, "What jerks!" And then I catch myself and I realize that these stars had a disease called chemical dependency. How sad it is that the people around them didn't know what to do to help them.

When someone repeatedly abuses alcohol, instead of simply acknowledging "She's an alcoholic," we say she has no self-control, that she's weak-willed. We blame the person, not the disease—as if the person is naturally stupid or bad. Why else would she do some of the crazy things that users do?

Or perhaps you're not convinced that the underlying problem is alcoholism. You're not sure you've got an alcoholic husband (or wife, or child, or parent, or friend). You think: If only he had a better job, he wouldn't drink. If only we had more money . . . If only he had fewer responsibilities . . . If only the kids would behave better . . . If only I were a better wife . . . If only I'd let him join that church choir when he was in eighth grade (yes, I actually heard this one!), then he wouldn't be hitting the bottle.

If the person you're concerned about drinks and you are having problems, I would say the chances are very good that you are dealing with an alcoholic, but I understand your hesitation. Not only is facing up to the label hard, but it also seems to lead you down a blind alley. If you do admit someone you care about might be an alcoholic, then what?

Well, there's Al-Anon. But maybe you're a non-joiner; you can't figure out why talking to strangers about your problems will help. Maybe you've heard bad reports about Al-Anon. Maybe you're just not ready to take your problems public. And if you're not absolutely convinced that the primary problem is alcohol, you're not even sure this is where you belong. That's normal at this stage of the game.

So you try and find some information on the subject that may help you. What's out there—at least most of the material I've seen—often seems irrelevant and cold, if not outright frightening or embarrassing.

When I was in treatment at Hazelden, I bought a book about drinking. I took one look at the picture of the woman on the cover, and I said to myself, "No wonder this woman drinks!" She was pathetic looking. Even today as I'm writing this—and I've been sober for two years now—I'm embarrassed to identify myself as an alcoholic if that's what an alcoholic looks like. I can't relate to it—not on my good days, anyway.

Look for professional help, and too often you find that the main issue is being avoided. Psychiatrists and psychologists, who should recognize that certain kinds of behavior are the result of alcoholism, treat the symptoms instead of the primary disease.

The people at Families in Crisis always say that since the first goal of any psychiatrist is to help people to get in touch with their feelings and emotions, the first thing he or she should insist on is that the patient be chemically free. That means using no mood-altering chemicals while you're going through family or marriage counseling or one-on-one therapy. According to what I hear from friends and acquaintances in therapy, this isn't always the case. Yet if the counselor demands abstinence and the patient can't comply, he ought quickly to recognize a serious chemical dependency problem.

A friend and her husband (the husband was, in my judgment, an alcoholic) were seeing a marriage counselor. In all the time that they saw him, the counselor never once spoke about the husband's alcoholism, though of course drinking was mentioned many times in the course of their discussions. My friend once tried to bring up the possibility that her husband should be seeking help for alcoholism. "What!" the counselor said. "You want to send your husband to reform school?"

If trained people have trouble recognizing—or perhaps simply giving a name to—alcoholism, it's certainly understandable why you might.

Looking at your situation

At this point, I won't ask you to look for the symptoms of alcoholism in the one you love. I filled in plenty of those questionnaires myself. You know what? According to every one of them, I wasn't an alcoholic. (The folks at the center where I went for treatment certainly would have been surprised to hear that.)

The point is that I've always been good at beating the system or ignoring the facts. So are most alcoholics until they get help.

"Do you drink in the morning?" the questionnaires ask. I didn't. Well, wasn't that proof I wasn't an alcoholic? I could convince myself even if there were ninety-nine other questions and I answered yes to every one of them. As a matter of fact, I had an alcoholic friend who *did* drink in the morning and she passed the test! Her position was that 11:00 A.M. isn't morning.

I spoke to another friend who told me he wasn't an alcoholic because he jogs 5 miles a day. This proves nothing, of course. Many early and middlestage alcoholics are in topnotch physical shape: Look at all the professional athletes using drugs and alcohol. The coaches and managers around them don't deal with the problem because the athlete is their meal ticket. The athlete may be alcoholic, but he's bringing in lots of money. Besides, even a coach who wanted to do something probably wouldn't know what to do, or how to do it. Everyone just hopes the problem will go away.

I've been reading about one attempt to handle drug abuse in professional sports. Without any warning, the athletes are subjected to a urine test. I believe if anyone suspects a player of having a problem, most likely he has one, and it makes more sense to me to deal with it in a loving manner, with an Intervention, than by catching him off guard and handing him a cup. (These are the wrong guys to pick on anyway. The guys on their way into the floors of Congress and the judges' chambers and the operating rooms should be getting the cups!)

A lot of people convince themselves they're not alcoholics because they're doing well in business. That's one of the myths I hung on to. I'd seen plenty of examples to the contrary. But I told myself I wouldn't be doing so well in my career if my drinking were really a problem.

I actually made a point of taking on lots of jobs, everything offered to me, as a constant affirmation that Mary Ellen was okay. I believed that as long as I was welcome on shows, as long as I could turn a buck, everything was fine. How could I have a drinking problem if Gary Collins wanted to talk to me on television?

All the while, of course, even in business, I was messing up. Sure, I had money, but I made foolish choices. I took chances I might not have if I'd been more in control. I lent money to people who were bad risks. I wasn't watching as closely as I should have. I was doing a lot of things that—to a counselor trained in chemical abuse—spelled trouble.

I frequently hear people convincing themselves that someone they love isn't an alcoholic just because he's kept his job. Or because her friends drink more than she does. Or because he's stopped drinking, maybe for months at a time. They're denying other indisputable evidence that the person has an alcohol problem.

Now that I'm more aware of these things, I've gotten to the point where I can read between the lines: When I hear about a family in other kinds of trouble, I always wonder if there's an underlying drinking or drug abuse problem.

The fact is, certain kinds of problems and disruptions— social issues, family matters, legal, financial, and job-related issues—are typical of families in which someone is chemically dependent. So what I want you to do, with the help of some questions I've prepared, is to focus on what's going on in *your* family.

It is possible, even probable, that the person you're concerned about might answer some of the questions in a different way than you would, or might even say they don't apply. Your task is to answer these questions from your own personal point of view. It's not necessary at this stage to make any kind of judgment about alcoholism.

SOCIAL EVALUATION

Have you been receiving fewer invitations?

Have you stopped accepting invitations?

Do you entertain less than you used to, or less than you'd like to?

Do you see your friends changing?

Are you hanging out with people who drink heavily?

Are you leading separate lives: you with your friends, the person you're concerned about with his?

Would the person you're concerned about ever choose to eat in a restaurant that doesn't serve liquor?

Does the person you're concerned about make excuses to avoid functions where alcohol won't be served?

Do you ask the person you're concerned about to control her drinking before you go to a party?

Does the person you're concerned about routinely have a couple of drinks at home before a party starts?

Does the person you're concerned about exhibit personality changes at parties? (Become the life of the party? Flirt? Ignore you? Launch into crazy conversations? Initiate arguments? Do silly things like dance a hula on the hostess's table? Insult the hostess or another guest without realizing it?)

Has the person you're concerned about displayed behavior at a social occasion that wouldn't be tolerated if he weren't "high"?

Do you feel trapped at parties (You want to go home; he doesn't)?

Have you ever left him to find his own way home?

Is the person you're concerned about always the last one to leave?

Or is she the first one to go home (so she can drink alone)?

Or does she want to stop for a nightcap after the party's over and everyone else is ready to go home?

Is the person you're concerned about always the one who suggests another round?

Have you ever called the hostess to apologize for this person's drinking?

Has the person you're concerned about dropped previous hobbies?

Have community activities, sports, or other interests been curtailed or stopped completely?

Has the person you're concerned about been involved in a lot of arguments?

FAMILY EVALUATION

Is the person you're concerned about rarely home?

When he's home, is he either distant or angry?

Have you stopped doing things as a family?

Is everyone in the family less active than they used to be—cutting down on social or athletic activities?

Is everyone going his separate way—either staying out or remaining in his own room?
Do the children avoid bringing friends to your house?
Is your sex life in trouble?
Do you think there's "someone else"?
Are you losing a lot of sleep?
Is there a lot of arguing between family members?
Do you have reason to believe you're being lied to?
Are you physically afraid?
Are you afraid of being yelled at?
Are you worried that the person you're concerned about might be suicidal?
Do you not trust your kids alone with the person you're concerned about?
Is one or more of the kids doing badly in school?
Is one or more of the kids a model child who has taken over some of the adult responsibilities?
Is one or more of the kids taking on the role of mother or father?
Are you seeing a marriage counselor or family therapist?
Are there frequent threats of divorce?
Are you being insulted for no reason?
Does the person you're concerned about accuse you of things that aren't true?

FINANCIAL EVALUATION

Are you always short of money?
Has money gone to alcohol that should have gone elsewhere?
Do you know how much was spent on alcohol last month?
Is there always enough money for partying?
Is the person you're concerned about plunging into bad investments?
Is the person you're concerned about spending as though there were a hole in her pocket, then complaining constantly about being short of cash?
Is the person you're concerned about always borrowing or lending?
Do you know how much he makes?
Will he discuss money with you?
Will he discuss money with you without getting angry?
Have you taken over paying the bills?

Have you gone to work because you had to?

Are you paying legal fees that are the result of drinking (DWI, divorce or child support from a marriage that failed due to drinking)?

Are you paying repair bills that are the result of carelessness while drinking (a burned sofa, a car accident, unusual amounts of dry cleaning)?

Are you paying medical bills that are the result of drinking (a broken leg from a drunken fall, a car accident)?

Are you paying for marriage counseling, psychiatrists, or psychologists for any member of the family?

Are the bar charges a significant part of your restaurant bills?

LEGAL EVALUATION

Has the person you're concerned about been arrested?

Has the person you're concerned about had one or more DWIs?

Has the person you're concerned about been a principal in a divorce or child custody case that may have been the result of drinking?

WORK EVALUATION

Does the person you're concerned about miss a lot of work due to sickness or other excuse?

Do you find yourself covering up for the person by phoning his company (or school) to report phony diseases?

Is the person you're concerned about frequently absent on Mondays or Fridays?

Does he often get to work (school) late?

Does he often leave work (school) early?

Does she seem unreasonably resentful of her boss or co-workers (teachers, other students)?

Does she avoid the company of her co-workers (students)?

Is he hanging out with a different crowd at work (school)?

Does he complain that he is criticized a lot?

Does he seem to overreact to criticism?

Does he have a record of on-the-job accidents?

Is she concerned about being fired (failing)?

Has she failed to be promoted?

Is he contemplating quitting (his job or school)?

A friend of mine filled out this questionnaire. She's a wonderful woman with a nice husband who just happens to be an alcoholic, though she won't acknowledge that. Still, she was amazed to discover that many of these questions perfectly described the circumstances in her own home.

I hope I've helped her become aware that what's happening to her husband is part of a pattern. Perhaps she'll listen to that little voice in her head saying, "Maybe it's not the stress or the job loss or the difficulties with our child. Maybe it's the alcohol itself that has to be dealt with."

As I look back, similar things were happening in my own family. I wasn't the only one with a drinking problem. As is fairly typical, I married a man with a drinking problem too. That's one of the things that brought Sherm and me together. Sherm's behavior pattern was different from mine, but the things he did were covered in the questionnaire.

In our early years, we might not have had enough money for a chair or a couch that we wanted, but there was always enough for a round at the bar. I remember going to the mailbox and getting stacks of past due bills and overdrafts from the bank. When Sherm was out with his checkbook with him, he'd write a check for anybody's alcohol. He didn't realize what big trouble he was in. His attitude was, "I'm not making enough money; I've got to work harder." The fact is, he was making enough. He was just spending it badly.

There's a joke about the guy who comes home on payday and has to confess he's spent his entire check in a bar. Just as his wife is about to lay into him, he yells, "Wait: I didn't tell you. I bought something for the house." That stops her short. "You did? What'd you buy?"

"I bought it a round."

That's less funny than it is sad. I don't think people realize how much money goes to the booze. I bet at one time it was consuming a fourth or more of Sherm's paycheck. In treatment, they sometimes ask you to come up with a financial accounting for the drinking years—the bar bills, the medical bills, the legal bills. Even with that evidence, people have a tough time admitting the problem is alcoholism.

Whether the major problem is financial, social, or whatever, if you recognize your family patterns in the preceding questionnaire, I don't think you ought to waste much time considering whether the person you're concerned about is really an alcoholic. Assume that he or she is, and recognize that you must find a way to help.

Even if he is not drinking much now or getting into much trouble at this point, I can assure you that sooner or later he will be. That's in the nature of the disease. And if you don't know a lot about alcoholism, now's the time to find out.

The Disease of Chemical Dependency

The moment I accepted the fact that I had a disease was the moment I was ready to begin my recovery.

Instead of feeling, "Poor me. I'm a victim," I felt incredibly relieved. I saw that all the mistakes I'd made weren't my fault. Once I was free of the load of guilt I'd been carrying around, I was ready to make some changes.

And I wasn't alone in feeling this way. I have heard other alcoholics say that until they finally believed they had a disease, they couldn't find their way to recovery.

It seems to me that no one—not the person afflicted by the disease nor those around him who are affected by it—can begin to cope with problem drinking until they understand something about the disease. I know that the counselors at Families in Crisis spend part of the first session with any concerned person explaining exactly what they're dealing with. I think that's where you should start, too.

What is chemical dependency?

The disease of chemical dependency is the addictive, abusive, and (eventually) destructive intake of mood-altering chemicals. The chemical of choice may be alcohol, it may be a drug (anything from sleeping pills to heroin), or it may be both alcohol and drugs. Soda isn't the only thing alcoholics are mixing into their cocktails. They're combining alcohol with amphetamines, meperidine, methylphenidate, and all sorts of other drugs. Many of the people I went through treatment with had dual addictions. They may have started out alcoholic, but eventually moved on to prescribed medications and wound up drug dependent. Today there are fewer "pure" alcoholics going through treatment centers than ever before, but more people are addicted to alcohol than to everything else combined.

Anyone who drinks is a potential alcoholic. Still, only a very small percentage turn into the stereotyped derelict. And an even smaller percentage are the headline grabbers, the rich and famous who all seem to be coming out of the closet these days and revealing their chemical addictions.

While that's good for raising public awareness, I think it may also be creating another kind of confusion. Punk rockers and movie stars haven't cornered the market on being chemically dependent. Most alcoholics are nice, middle-to upper-middle class people who are in the house doing the laundry, taking care of their kids as best they can, getting their jobs done. Some of them can be very successful (plenty of chief executive officers are alcoholics), but basically they're just regular folks who happen to have a serious problem that is interfering with the whole of their lives. They're suffering from a disease and they are probably unaware that they have it.

Is chemical dependency really a disease?

In 1956, the American Medical Association recognized that alcoholism was a disease. This was enormously helpful because it meant that alcoholics could at last get help in a hospital setting. It should also have helped to change public opinion and end the moral issue that historically has clouded the subject. Because alcoholism was viewed as a moral problem, few people could find help to recover; and because so few did, others assumed that people who drank excessively were lacking in character. They believed that by simply diagnosing the problem—"You're an alcoholic"—they could expect the afflicted person to recover spontaneously or cure himself.

Yet despite the fact that information about the disease of alcoholism is widely available today and that a great deal of effort is spent disseminating that information, most people still don't seem to know that alcoholism is a disease—or they simply can't believe it. That's because we tend to think of a disease as something that's caused by a germ (like flu) or that's the result of some system in the body that has gone berserk (as in diabetes or cancer).

Doctors, however, take a different approach. They say a disease is something that is *primary, progressive*, and *chronic*. Alcoholism meets all these standards. So it doesn't matter what your mother has to say or what your friend's opinion is; if the person you care about is alcoholic, he is suffering from a *disease*. It's as likely to afflict you or the guy next door as a rock singer, a movie star, or a President's wife. Therefore you have the right and the obligation to be just as concerned about the person and just as caring as if he or she had cancer.

By *primary*, doctors mean that the alcoholism is a disease itself rather than a symptom of some greater social, emotional, or physical problem. Now, a lot of psychologists and psychiatrists who should know better still ignore this fact. Their attitude is, "Before a person can get help with his drinking or his alcoholism, we have to discuss what his problems are."

One of my friends experienced this attitude when she went for psychological help. On the form he gave her, the doctor asked that she list five reasons for being there. The first she listed was stress. The second was problems with her husband. The third was business problems, and the fourth problems with her son. She finally got around to her drinking—in fifth place. She knew that drinking was the real reason she'd come, but she couldn't own up to it.

She never had to, either. Two thousand dollars' worth of talk later, the psychologist had still never addressed the fact that she had a chemical abuse problem. Of course, my friend knows now that she couldn't stop the drinking problem by working on the marriage or her son's behavior. The drinking was causing the other problems. Any solution that doesn't deal with the alcoholism itself is no solution at all—it's like wrapping a blanket around someone who's got a chill and believing that you're treating the fever. It's unreasonable to treat the symptoms of alcoholism and think you're curing the disease.

By *progressive*, doctors mean that the problem's going to get worse. The fact is, it will inevitably lead to insanity or death. Oh, you may not see the word "alcoholism" on the death certificate, but 97 percent of alcoholics die of alcoholism (via alcoholism-related diseases or accidents while under the influence). Only about 3 percent get help. According to the National Council on Alcoholism, it's the direct or indirect cause of about 95,000 deaths a year. Cirrhosis of the liver alone causes 30,000 deaths.

My own dad died of alcoholism when he was forty-eight years old, but in his case they called it heart failure. Since that's what my mom would prefer to believe, she's convinced herself it was so. A few years ago she told my brother he ought to be very careful about his cholesterol because there was heart disease in the family. What he really has to be careful about, of course, is drinking.

Other serious diseases associated with chronic alcohol abuse are cancer of the liver, larynx, esophagus, stomach, colon and breast, and malignant melanoma. It also leads to high blood pressure, stroke, and heart attack; damage to the brain, pancreas, and kidney; stomach and duodenal ulcers, colitis, and irritable colon; birth defects and fetal alcohol syndrome.

Chronic alcohol abuse also may be a cause of impotence and infertility, premature aging, and other problems such as muscle cramps, lowered immunity, sleep disturbances, and edema.

After I'd been in recovery a while, a friend of mine who didn't know that I had an alcohol problem said to me, "Mary Ellen, you know, you're not as sick as often you used to be." Until he pointed this out, I hadn't even realized how often I'd complained of being ill when I was drinking. My brother, who as a recovering alcoholic knew the real nature of my problem, later said that he'd never met a woman who had her period as often as I did. Every week I complained of "cramps"—my coverup for hangovers. Even if I wasn't hung over, most of the time I really didn't feel well. And I was one of the lucky ones: I stopped drinking before I developed any serious problems.

I've read in National Council on Alcoholism literature that alcohol-related diseases account for about 20 percent of national expenditures for hospital care, and in the *New York Times Sunday Magazine* that 30 to 50 percent of all hospital admissions are alcohol-related. Doctors estimate that chemically dependent persons will die fourteen years before their normal life expectancy. If they don't die prematurely, they'll go insane because of damage to the brain cells. While the death of a person you love usually causes great pain, I think you sometimes suffer more when you have to watch him or her slowly disintegrate, either physically or mentally.

The progress of alcoholism isn't always steady. Very few people become full-blown alcoholics the moment they start drinking. I suffered few consequences—other than hangovers and some embarrassing behavior that seemed minor compared to the rewards of drinking—until I was really into heavy drinking. In my case, the switch came quickly. There's no pattern to it. You don't wake up one day and say, "Today is the day I think I'll screw up my life with alcohol," and start on the downward spiral. Usually, in fact, an alcoholic follows an up and down pattern—some good periods interspersed with some bad.

It may take five years or it may take fifty, but eventually it will happen: The alcoholic will hit bottom.

By *chronic*, doctors mean exactly what you would expect. There is no known cure for the disease. You can, however, control it. Alcoholism is the most treatable—and yet the most untreated—disease that exists. With help, an alcoholic may lead a happy, meaningful, and fulfilling life. I'm proof that it can be done. And there are many recovering alcoholics like me.

Why do people deny that alcoholism is a disease?

I think that those afflicted, and the people around them, deny that alcoholism is a disease because it's not unlike being diagnosed as having cancer or any serious illness. The first reaction is usually denial. Everyone feels that if he ignores the facts, the problem will go away.

With chemical dependency, shame is also part of the picture. Like the cancer patient, the alcoholic may think, if only

I'd taken care of myself, this wouldn't have happened. The alcoholic's family circle takes on blame as well: Dad and Mom believe they weren't good parents, the wife thinks she hasn't been loving enough, the kids feel they haven't been dutiful.

I also think that people want to protect their own social drinking by ignoring the disease potential, just as smokers like to deny the evidence and point out that at ninety George Burns is still smoking cigars. It's generally acknowledged that smoking causes lung cancer and other diseases, and it's foolish to continue the habit. Similarly, if you acknowledge that drinking can lead to alcoholism, it's kind of foolish to keep using alcohol. But drinking is a habit few people want to give up.

Who becomes chemically dependent?

The staff at Families in Crisis counsels people who say, "I'm a professor," "I'm a doctor," "I'm a lawyer," "How did this happen to me?" "I should have known better." Once you accept that alcoholism is a disease, you have to acknowledge something else. A disease is very democratic. It does not respect age, sex, race, color, creed, or class.

Nobody knows exactly what kind of environmental or psychological facts send you over the line from social drinking to alcoholism. Some experts believe that research will eventually reveal that there is no distinction (a "heavy drinker" is just an alcoholic at an earlier stage), and I tend to agree with them.

No one has ever been able to pinpoint a "typical" alcoholic personality, but everyone seems to agree that metabolically, alcoholics are different from non-alcoholics. The difference is due either to genetic predisposition or just to the effects of heavy drinking.

I don't like scientific language any better than you do, but I think it's important that you understand a few specific things about the way the disease works in the body of an alcoholic. Personally, I found this information amazing.

In a pamphlet called "The Disease Concept of Alcoholism," Dr. David L. Ohlms explains that a Houston, Texas, scientist doing brain research just a decade ago was one of the first to note the different way in which alcohol affects alcoholics. In order to get fresh tissue for her studies, the scientist made arrangements through the local police to study the brains of derelicts who had died the night before.

In the course of her work, she happened to mention to her colleagues that she was surprised to discover that the derelicts were also heroin users. She based this assumption on the fact that in the brains of these chronic alcoholics she'd found certain substances closely related to heroin.

Her colleagues pointed out that the derelicts, who could barely afford a bottle of cheap wine, were extremely unlikely to be using drugs. That realization tipped the researcher off to a new area of investigation, and she began to explore the effects of alcohol on the brain.

She discovered that in the bodies of normal drinkers, alcohol breaks down into a toxic substance called acetaldehyde. Then it breaks down into carbon dioxide and water, both of which are passed off as waste products.

In alcoholics, the system doesn't function as well. Not only does the alcoholic's liver produce more acetaldehyde, but also, according to Dr. Charles Lieber of the Mount Sinai Alcohol Research Center in New York City, it doesn't produce enough of an enzyme that eliminates acetaldehyde in the normal drinker.

When it remains in the body, acetaldehyde travels to the brain, where, according to some animal experiments, it becomes a powerful, morphine-like substance called THIQ. This substance has some interesting properties. THIQ occurs only in the brain of an alcoholic drinker. THIQ is so potent that when it was tested for use as a painkiller during World War II, it was rejected as being too addictive.

Certain strains of rat that refuse to drink anything alcoholic even in the most diluted form immediately prefer alcohol to water when injected with a minute quantity of THIQ. You might say that they become instant alcoholics. Dr. Ohlms reports that when THIQ is injected into a monkey's brain, it remains there for years. He links this fact to the progressiveness of the disease. It may explain why someone who's been sober for years suddenly starts drinking again at the same intensity and with the same behavior patterns as years before. The THIQ level in his brain has remained constant.

Why do some people's bodies deal differently with alcohol? Test results on animals and humans seem to indicate that a malfunctioning enzyme system precedes the onset of alcoholism. Such a chemical flaw might be inherited and might explain the fact that children of alcoholics, according to various studies, are three to five times as likely to be alcoholics as the general population.

Another possible genetic link has been explored by a researcher who discovered that even after months of sobriety, some 80 percent of alcoholics tested had abnormal brain waves. These resulted in memory impairments and a condition called anhedonia—an inability to experience pleasure and to respond appropriately.

This researcher suspected the problem might predate the alcoholism. He tested children of alcoholics, boys who'd never been exposed to alcohol even in utero, and confirmed that they had a higher incidence of these abnormal brain waves than the general population.

I met an alcoholic who was adopted and who could only start making progress toward his recovery when he'd traced his biological parents and discovered they were both alcoholics. At that point, he could accept the fact that he was the victim of a disease.

Another friend whose parents don't have a drinking problem became an alcoholic himself. When he started recovering, he thought back to the stories he'd heard about his grandparents and realized they'd both died of alcoholism. No one acknowledged Grandpa was an alcoholic. What they said was "Grandpa worked real hard. He had a real good job. Oh, every once in a while he beat up Grandma, but you know, she kind of deserved it because she got 'mouthy.'" They didn't talk about how much he drank.

Some alcoholics with no family history of alcoholism may develop the disease, possibly later in life than people with alcoholic relatives. Researchers suspect that these people are born with deficient levels of endorphins, opiates that the body produces naturally. They may be predisposed to drink in order to feel normally good.

Other research indicates that some alcoholics have a metabolic irregularity that causes alcohol to stimulate pleasure more than in normal people (so they become dependent) or that they may be neurologically supersensitive and so use alcohol as a protection.

Since heredity is at least part of the picture, I'm grateful to know all that I do about the disease. I want to prepare my son, Andrew, for the consequences of his behavior if he decides to drink. Many children of alcoholics don't become alcoholics themselves, after all.

Genetic predisposition or no, the only way you become an alcoholic is by drinking. It's learned behavior. One of my friends comes from northern Minnesota, a place where people work hard—and play hard. It's just taken for granted that after work you stop off at a bar for a few drinks, perhaps every night. Drinking separates the men from the boys in certain circles; drinking is macho.

Until it's considered socially unacceptable, drinking will continue. A friend thinks social drinkers are becoming more aware of what a horrible habit it is because of what it does to your body and your mind. He predicts that someday having a drink will become about as socially unacceptable as a runny nose. I hope he's right. I know I started drinking because it seemed an attractive thing to do.

I wish the companies that make the stuff would stop glamorizing it. Instead of a beautiful woman lying on a velvet couch, the liquor ads ought to show some of the characters on the Bowery. That's the real story. And even if you're not there in the flesh, when you're alcoholic you're there in spirit.

What's the progress of the disease?

The first time I broke into the liquor cabinet with my friends, I was starting what specialists in the field call the *learning* phase of alcohol abuse. This happens either as a result of experimentation (as in my case) or accidentally, as when a doctor's prescription hooks someone on a drug habit. I learned that alcohol worked for me. It was as though it had been waiting for me. Once we connected, we became close buddies.

Experts call alcoholism "the feeling disease," since it progressively affects the emotional life of anyone dependent on it. They explain that the range of human feelings goes from pain to euphoria, with normal feeling in the middle. In the learning stage, you feel euphoria while you're using alcohol, and after use you return to normal.

When I went into what they call the *seeking* stage, I started to look foward to alcohol. At this stage, you're not really upset if you can't get to your chemical of choice, and you still return to normal after the euphoria of using. Lots of drinkers stay at this stage. But the conservative estimate is that one in ten will become an alcoholic at this point.

When you get to the next stage, you've crossed over the line from social drinking into *dependency*. You're hooked. You begin to display the classic signs of alcoholism (which I'll review later). You escalate from feeling euphoric to going out of control. Instead of feeling normal after drinking, you may begin to feel some pain.

If you don't get help, you go right to the last stage—*drinking to feel normal*. You start drinking when you're in pain (which, because of all the other problems that have cropped up in your life by now, is virtually all of the time). Afterward, you're in pain once again. If you're confronted about your alcoholism, you'll rationalize your use (blaming it on other problems), project unpleasant feelings (you hate yourself, so you turn that hate on others), and deny that you have a problem with alcohol.

From what I understand, it normally takes from ten to fifteen years to pass through the different stages. You use (or learn) anywhere from six months to five to seven years, abuse (or seek) for three to five. It takes only about two years of dependency until you cross right over to the last stage. When they can speak truthfully, people close to the alcoholic, particularly the spouse, say they suspected the problem was alcoholism for at least seven years before they reached out for help or could even admit the situation.

I have read another description of the stages of drinking which includes many of the same milestones, although it groups them slightly differently. According to this description, the early stages (most typically the person affected is twenty to twenty-five) are characterized by blackouts, increasing tolerance, sneaking of drinks, and guilty feelings.

The middle stage, in which the drinker is perhaps twenty-five to thirty-five, finds him still trying to keep a grip on his career, social life, and family, but seeing deterioriation in all those areas. He begins to experience loss of control, becomes preoccupied with drinking, and often winds up hospitalized for alcohol or an alcohol-related disease.

The hospitalization may precede the chronic phase, which includes obsessive drinking, deterioration of moral and ethical behavior, and physical symptoms such as psychomotor problems, (i.e., being unable to tie his shoes).

What are the signs of alcoholism?

Occasionally, someone with a drinking problem will come right out and admit, "Yeah, I'm an alcoholic." This is the trickiest of all manipulations. This admission keeps you, and the alcoholic, completely stuck. Diagnosing the problem doesn't make it go away. No one will be cured without help.

More typically, alcoholics (and the people close to them) try to convince themselves they're just social drinkers. Either they don't admit the amount of alcohol they drink or they convince themselves they're in control of it. Even if they've read and heard that it's a disease, even if they *believe* that it's a disease, they don't want the "alcoholic" label. For one thing, it would require them to deal with it—by stopping drinking.

To me the definition of a social drinker is someone who decides she wants a martini, goes to mix the drink, discovers there's no olive, and decides to forget the whole thing. It's someone who goes to a party whether or not there will be liquor. If you *must* have a drink to be social, you're not a "social drinker."

But the final criterion is that when people are just social drinkers, alcohol isn't causing problems for them or the people around them—specifically, the kinds of problems that were covered in the questionnaire in the previous chapter. If that questionnaire has led you to acknowledge that there may be a chemical dependency problem in your home, and if I've managed to convince you that alcoholism is a disease, maybe now you're ready to move to the next step: identifying the symptoms of chemical dependency.

It is generally acknowledged that alcoholism is characterized by four main symptoms, all of which have become evident by the dependent stage. These symptoms are the only characteristics common to all alcoholics.

Preoccupation. This includes the anticipation of drinking at certain times of the day (watching the clock for lunch break, waiting for the end of the work day to go home and drink), and/or as the primary factor in other kinds of activities (for example, waiting for a party or weekend when a lot of drinking will take place, or planning a vacation that is anticipated as a drinking binge). It also means the growing need for alcohol during times of stress, whether it's work or family-related, or times of celebration. It includes taking precautions never to run out of a supply of alcohol.

Rigidity around use. The alcoholic will have set times during the day or week for drinking. I was a binge drinker, and Wednesday was my big day. Some people never drink on workdays, so they don't believe they have a problem. Some people binge only one month of the year. What is important is that if they're alcoholic, they won't tolerate interference with their drinking. If the original reason for drinking doesn't materialize (a party is canceled), the alcoholic will find another way to drink at that particular time.

Rigidity may involve the kind of drink (scotch and water only, or a particular brand of beer) or the place for drinking (a favorite bar, a friend's home). Some alcoholics won't drink when the kids are awake, or in front of their spouse or parents. My own rigidity involved being dressed up when I went drinking.

Because of his rigidity, the alcoholic will limit his social activities only to those that involve drinking. He won't go anywhere where he might be without a supply. If he doesn't have sufficient opportunity to drink his "quota" in public, he may begin to drink alone.

Growing tolerance. Alcoholics develop the well-known "wooden leg" syndrome, and are able to hold liquor without showing it. As the disease progresses, they need more and more to get the euphoric effect, of course. So they also find ways to take in larger amounts without being obvious. They may gulp drinks, order stiffer drinks, order the next round before the present one is finished, act as the bartender at parties, drink before a social engagement, buy alcohol in greater quantities. They begin to use alcohol medicinally.

Loss of control. This includes everything from morning to

binge drinking, drinking more than planned, and increased blackouts. The loss of control due to repeated chemical use results in harmful consequences. The alcoholic may drive while drunk, drink while pregnant, subject others to verbal or physical abuse, and violate his or her own moral standards with actions such as adultery or stealing. (Many of those consequences were covered in the questionnaire in the previous chapter. Now you may understand their cause.)

I personally would include a fifth symptom common to all alcoholics: *defensiveness*. The alcoholic defends his drinking or blames it on others. (I got drunk because I didn't eat lunch; I drink because I work too hard; I'm under too much stress; I hate you.) He resents advice and avoids people. He lies about when and how much he drinks or comes up with countless excuses and rationalizations.

By the fourth phase—drinking to feel normal—tolerance is usually reduced. Your body is in such poor physical condition that it can't handle large amounts anymore. But all the other symptoms are present and heightened. The alcoholic has lost all power over his use, becomes paranoid, guilt-ridden, self-hating, lonely, possibly even suicidal. If you can see many obvious signs that he's in trouble, you can help him before he gets to this point.

3/
Spotting the Signs of Alcoholism

Despite what you may have heard from people who are uninformed or naive, an alcoholic's behavior is very predictable. Even a nonprofessional can diagnose alcoholism with a fair degree of accuracy. Once you know what to look for, the cork comes off the bottle, not only for the alcoholic, but also for you. The secret is out.

In the previous chapter, I mentioned the four main symptoms of alcoholism—preoccupation, rigidity, increased tolerance, loss of control, and what I consider a fifth, defensiveness. As I look back on my last days of drinking, I realize that I exhibited all of them. If you are trying to analyze the behavior of the person you are concerned about, you might want more specific examples of how these symptoms are manifested. That's why I've included another questionnaire at this point. Go through this section once without answering any questions. Read through them all. Then, on a second reading, see which might be applicable.

Preoccupation

1. Does the person sneak or hide liquor?

If the imagination that alcoholics use to hide their supplies were applied to other fields, I'm sure some of them would outcreate Leonardo da Vinci and Thomas Edison combined. I know a guy who can't operate his toaster but managed to rig his windshield wiper fluid container to hold booze. Instead of shooting onto the windshield, the tube ran into the car and right into his mouth. Another man I know fixed his garden hose to hold alcohol. When he went out to "water the lawn," he took a few shots. I know of women who've filled their perfume bottles with gin and who've hidden liquor in hat boxes or kitty litter boxes. One of my friends confessed that she had her housekeeper fill empty baby food jars with vodka and stowed them in her purse. She'd be at the church bowling league and step into the bathroom or the parking lot every so often, taking little nips from a little nipper's jar.

Alcoholics are so clever at this sort of deception that their families may never figure out what they're doing. They know only that no matter how controlled the situation appears to be, the drinker disappears briefly yet returns drunk.

My own sister kept a case of Cold Duck stashed in the trunk of her car. One winter day the bottles froze and exploded. It didn't seem at all strange to her to be mopping out her trunk with her ski parka on. Normal drinkers, of course, don't keep alcohol in the trunks of their cars—or in the garbage, or the basement, or the bathroom.

I don't intend to pass along any hints to drinkers, but the fact is that toilet tanks are perfect for holding bottles. Some people hide their vodka or gin in white vinegar bottles and bourbon or scotch in bottles that formerly held apple cider vinegar. My friend Mary used to pour booze into the orange juice carton since no one in the family liked juice. They assumed she was hitting the carton because she was low on vitamin C.

Some alcoholics will drink anything that contains alcohol—including mouthwash and Nyquil. One of the gals in treatment said if she was out of scotch, she'd have Scope on the rocks. She claims she actually liked it, and what's more, nobody figured out what was going on.

Lots of people carry booze to work in a thermos. And they sneak around to buy it, too, because they're ashamed of how much they're getting. Many people wouldn't dream of using the local liquor store as their source. Or if they do, rather than pick the stuff up themselves they'll have it delivered. Plenty of alcoholics drink in public only when they're out of town. My brother Johnny had a major drinking problem, but no one in his family had ever seen him take a drink.

Alcoholics hide the empties, too. They're the ones who volunteer to take out the garbage so no one will see what they've been up to. They may even toss the bottles in a neighbor's garbage. To avoid having the sanitation men take notice, or the possibility that a dog might overturn the trash can and expose the evidence to the neighbors, they even drive around until they find a dumpster in which to toss the bottles.

My friend Paul would push a cart around the liquor store and stock it like a housewife doing weekly grocery shopping—even after his wife left him due to his drinking. (Finally he lost everything else, including his friends and his business.) Paul was a rarity: Most people will sneak around rather than face comments about their booze purchases.

I used to claim that I never snuck drinks. But when I was in treatment, I had to own up that whenever my meal companion made a trip to the john or the telephone, I'd quickly signal the waiter for another, whether or not I had half a drink on the table already. If there wasn't an opportunity to reorder, I'd water my drink to make it last longer. An alcoholic is like a pessimist: He never sees the glass as half full; to him it's always half empty.

Also in treatment, I remembered the time during my drinking days when I had a lunch date with a dear friend to discuss her own recent treatment. (I had been shocked to discover she was an alcoholic since I'd never seen her drunk over the years I'd known her. It turned out she did all of her drinking at home, alone, until one day she broke her leg while drunk and her family did an Intervention.) I told the waiter that I didn't want to offend my friend, who didn't drink, and so (this was sneaking, of course) I arranged for him to add a shot of vodka to the glass whenever I ordered a club soda and lemon (at the time I believed vodka had no telltale smell).

After *he'd* been in treatment, my husband confessed that

he used to instruct waitresses to add a shot of brandy to his cup whenever he ordered coffee.

You should suspect sneaking when the person you're concerned about always volunteers to be the bartender at parties. It's not just goodwill that's motivating him.

2. Does the person use liquor as a reward?

In my life, I've accomplished quite a few exciting things. My first book was number one on the *New York Times* Best Seller List for a whole year. When I made the list, it was normal for me to celebrate over a drink or two with friends. It was not normal to celebrate the same accomplishment with a drinking party fifty-two weeks in a row.

If there is no such thing as a celebration without alcohol, that's a warning signal. And if everything that happens becomes cause for an alcoholic celebration—T.G.I.F. becomes T.G.I.M., T.G.I.T., T.G.I.W., and so on—that's a warning sign, too.

When I sold a second book, I called a friend and said, "Let's take the day off and go partying." He said, "Why don't you just go out and buy yourself something you've always wanted? You deserve it for a job well done."

I didn't see it his way. Whatever I might buy could wait. It was more important to reward myself with alcohol. He didn't see it my way, either: Why would anyone choose to drink when she could go shopping?

Social drinkers may drink at times to reward themselves, but not over and over again. And drinking is not their exclusive means of celebration.

3. Does the person anticipate and plan drinking situations?

An alcoholic may be very clever about handling her disease. If I knew I would be someplace where everyone else would be drinking moderately (such as a business-related cocktail party), I sometimes didn't drink at all. I knew I couldn't count on stopping after just one or two and, at this sort of party, my behavior would stand out.

Though I didn't go in for big benders, like the alcoholics

who check into hotels for a few days or a week expressly to drink, I was a binge drinker. I'd start at lunch and carry the binge through the afternoon. Or I'd get going at dinner. Binge drinkers, of course, are in as much trouble as those who drink steadily morning, noon, and night.

In the early stages of my disease, Friday night was a big deal, the night out with the girls. Our stated purpose was to eat dinner (in other words, fill up on the free hors d'oeuvres) and meet boys. Actually, I was more interested in an encounter with Jack Daniels or Johnnie Walker than with any Tom, Dick, or Harry.

I may have led the pack, but everyone did a good amount of drinking—yet never once did we acknowledge that we were meeting specifically to drink. Only later did I make dates "to have some drinks." (If we'd been really accurate, we'd have made dates "to get drunk." That's a level of truthfulness that I'm not sure anyone has ever achieved.) By then, more and more of my time was consumed with thoughts of drinking: when, where, and with whom? I spent days anticipating it and even more time trying to recover from its effects.

I did make some occasional efforts to quit. So instead of thinking about drinking, I was thinking about *not* drinking. Like someone on a diet who's fixated on cake, cookies, and rolls and spends hours figuring out how to avoid them, I thought all the time about what was forbidden to me. Then I'd start feeling sorry for myself for being denied my pleasure, or else I'd start feeling okay about my using (after a month of sobriety, you feel you have control) and eventually, I'd give in to temptation.

What I'm trying to point out is that someone who can manage his drinking at certain times does not necessarily have control over it. The alcoholic husband of a Families in Crisis counselor was a professional who knew that being seen drunk would have a very negative impact on his career. He never drank in the bars in the community. He wouldn't get drunk at parties, either. But he'd go out of town and drink alone, or he'd plan a vacation with people who drank heavily or permitted him to do so. Similarly, a buddy of mine, a teacher, was specifically told by the school board that he couldn't be seen in bars. No problem. He started drinking at home.

Some alcoholic doctors arrange their schedules so they won't be on call when they're drinking. If you're a woman, just pray you don't get one of these as your OB. The wife of an airline pilot told me her husband refused a job promotion because he'd be on call. Suppose they needed him when he was drunk? I have a New York friend who refused to move to Los Angeles because he'd have to drive if he lived there. In New York if he drank too much he could always get home by taxi. It was so important for him to be able to drink as often and much as he wanted that he turned down numerous job offers. The point is that an alcoholic may manage his drinking, but he won't stop it—no matter what the consequences. That's another of the differences between alcoholics and normal, or social drinkers.

I myself planned my drinking. When I was touring to promote a book, I wouldn't touch a drop. I made an exception once in Chicago, and I partied the night before a big show. I not only felt ill, I was paranoid. I thought my props would fail me and I was sure the host would show me stains I wouldn't know how to remove.

I vowed never to repeat the experience and I didn't, but I still had plenty of time to get into trouble. I was only on tour about two months of the year, and I always had my weekends free.

At the beginning, when I was using drinking to celebrate, I really did have a lot of fun. But the fun vanished as I began to use alcohol indiscriminately—not only if things were going my way, but also if they were not. My husband asked me to marry him over a bottle of champagne, and we had our first major argument over another bottle. We gave parties to celebrate our business successes, but also our failures, as when Sherm was fired from a good job with the Minnesota Vikings football team. There was really nothing to celebrate about that.

In the early and middle stages of alcoholism, you associate liquor mostly with the good times. Unfortunately, those memories have a way of overriding anything else and they keep the alcoholic going until he can't turn back.

4. Does the person drink to avoid painful realities?

"Relief is just a swallow away." We alcoholics medicate our painful feelings with booze. When you drink constantly to get relief, you're no longer a social drinker.

Heavy drinkers are almost always depressed because alcohol itself acts as a depressant. Alcoholics believe booze will help their depression, but actually it's the cause of the depression. Even if he hasn't contracted a serious disease yet, the alcoholic may be miserable because he's suffering from some related ailment—insomnia, lethargy, paranoia, apathy, anxiety, sexual dysfunction, even thoughts of suicide. When an alcoholic or drug user says he's going to get "blasted," he probably never realizes he could eventually wind up putting a gun to his head instead of a drink into his mouth.

Alcoholics tend to attribute their drinking to "stress." You better believe life *is* stressful when you're a practicing alcoholic. When I quit, I went virtually overnight from a Type A personality to a Type B (well, maybe a B plus; God is still working on me).

Alcoholics and their families are convinced that their problems cause their drinking, but in fact it's just the reverse. If with this book I convince you of only that, I'll feel I've really accomplished something. Once you stop the denial and acknowledge the alcoholism, things have a way of getting better. Naturally I didn't know that until I went in for treatment. When I was drinking, the more problems I had, the more I wanted to drink. Of course, the next day, my problems were still there—and I had a hangover besides.

Rigidity

5. Does the person feel uncomfortable in nondrinking situations?

When I was drinking, you wouldn't have spotted me at any family-style restaurants. I wasn't spending much time at church or school activities either. And I didn't get together with many friends who didn't drink. I preferred drinking situations, and I tended to avoid the others entirely.

I particularly avoided situations in which I knew only one drink or two would be served—where the bar would shut down once dinner was started. I remember being very indignant whenever that happened. What I did was gather a group of friends to go out clubbing. If they can't gather a group, other alcoholics just go out and drink by themselves. Some prefer it that way.

When you're trying to analyze someone's problem, look at social situations in which only a few drinks will be served. You will probably find that the person you're concerned about will leave early and continue to drink elsewhere.

In my drinking days, if there wasn't a good party to go to I'd throw one myself. I'd meet my guests at the door, their favorite drink in my hand. I've cut out a lot of that, and I find I don't anticipate the parties as much. I don't spend my week waiting for party day to arrive, since I'm busy doing other things. And when I do go to a party now, I remember everything that happens.

I don't lose days to hangovers anymore. I visit more friends—both drinkers and nondrinkers. And I even enjoy being by myself. I've taken up needlepoint; life in general is just much more peaceful and fun. It took a few sober years for me to realize how many of the activities I claimed to enjoy were just excuses to drink—watching football games, going to card parties. I remember clearly how much such drinking meant to me.

I was reminded of it at a funeral recently, when the best friend of the deceased didn't make it to the cemetery. He told everyone his car had stalled, but the truth was that he'd gone drinking. He knew there was no chance of his getting a shot at the cemetery. It was so sad. I know this man loved his friend, but his alcoholism prevented his being around for the final farewell.

Someone with a drinking problem can find a thousand flimsy excuses to avoid a nondrinking situation—everything from "I've got a cold" to "I don't like your parents." Or he'll agree to put himself in such a situation only provided his stay will be brief.

6. Does the person drink alone?

You don't have to be in an empty room—though house-wives and the elderly often are—to be drinking alone. You qualify if you're the only one in the group with a drink.

Nels Schlander told me about a group of friends who felt it was time to initiate an Intervention on one of the guys in their card-playing group because they realized that, time and time again, long after the others had switched to coffee, he would still be drinking alcohol. That, too, is considered drinking alone.

At lunch one day, a friend told me that his wife had ac-cused him of being an alcoholic. He insisted he drank just to relax, but she'd said the fact he couldn't admit he was an alcoholic made him one. Her hunch was right, but her ap-proach was all wrong. You can't ever expect an alcoholic to admit to his alcoholism. You just have to try and collect undeniable evidence of the disease. As my friend laughed about his crazy spouse, ordering drink after drink while I sipped club soda, he gave me plenty of evidence. He was drinking alone. I told him the title of this book and I added, "You're someone I love, Tom." He looked surprised, and said, "Really?" And then he ordered another drink. Alco-holics are tough nuts to crack.

I used to believe I never drank alone. Then I thought back on all those times I'd pour myself a drink and start telephon-ing people. Drinking while you're making phone calls is an-other way of drinking alone. It is also a nice way of making a fool of yourself. God bless the people who put up with some of those conversations from me.

A friend from way back called after I went into recovery. She began insulting me and my family, and I realized that she was drunk. As the conversation went from bad to worse, I just said to her, "You're drunk, and I'll be happy to talk with you some other time, when you're sober." I haven't heard from her since then, but do I feel for her! If she remem-bers the phone call, I'm sure she's full of guilt—though while she was drinking, she surely thought what she was doing was okay.

Here are some other examples of drinking alone:

· Having drinks while getting dressed for the party is drinking alone.

· Having a few drinks at a bar by yourself is drinking alone.

· Having a few drinks while waiting at the bar for your guest to arrive is drinking alone. (Erma Bombeck says, "Patience is not always a virtue. Often it signifies a drinking problem." Is she right!)

· Drinking while watching television is drinking alone.

· Drinking while preparing dinner is drinking alone.

I think most alcoholics find it relieves their guilt to have someone drinking along with them, so they'll coerce others—"Come on, Joe; join me, will you?"—but if they can't find a partner, they'll do it by themselves.

7. Does the person drink in the morning?

My dearest friend from Hazelden, an enormously successful businessman who was in the chronic stages but still doing brilliantly at his job, started each day in the shower with a drink. You know those soaps you can hang around your neck with a cord? If this guy had been into drugs instead of alcohol, he'd probably have been in the shower with "Dope on a Rope."

My sister avoided the "drinking in the morning" label by saying she never had her first drink until lunch, but she had lunch at eleven! To me, that's morning.

In my drinking days, a friend who models told me a morning drink would cure a hangover, so I tried one. I just about died. My system couldn't take it. This gal would have a quick belt in the morning and within an hour she'd be pulling a designer outfit over her head. With the same quick belt and in the same amount of time, I'd be pulling the toilet seat up over mine. Nevertheless, we were both rip-roaring alcoholics. (While drinking in the morning is a sign you're an alcoholic, not drinking in the morning doesn't prove you are not.)

Some alcoholics start drinking in the morning to calm themselves or get into a state that they've learned to consider as "normal." You'd never know they'd been drinking. I think it's so sad to see cars lined up outside bars early in the morning. Personally, I hadn't gotten to the point where I was drinking in the morning, but I don't have any false pride about it. That's just another wrinkle that's waiting for me if I choose to drink.

Increased Tolerance

8. Does the person gulp drinks?

A lot of people have the wrong idea about this one. "Gulping" doesn't necessarily mean chug-a-lugging. It means drinking a lot. Sometimes a lot means a large quantity of drinks (alcoholics don't need "a drink," they claim to need "a few" quick ones), and sometimes it means fewer but stronger drinks. Alcoholics prefer to mix their own when possible. And in restaurants, they always have one in reserve. There's a half-finished drink on the table, and they've already placed an order for the next. If someone ate desserts the same way, everyone would comment on how strange it was.

A good cocktail waitress usually picks up the empties quickly, but even if a fresh one had arrived, I'd always keep the former drink, even if it contained only ice and a sip or two. Alcoholics won't leave a drink behind. There could be a fire starting in the bar, but they'll drain the glass before they leave. Or they'll take a "roadie" along with them.

A full 10 percent of the drinking-age population drinks over 60 percent of the alcohol in the United States, a figure that nearly coincides with the percentage of alcoholics in the total population. (If all the alcoholics got help, the gross revenue of the alcohol industry would be cut in half.)

In the early stages, alcoholics often tolerate a large quantity of liquor. They may be the ones who are just starting to party while everyone else is passed out or ill. They may even be the ones who comment about someone else, "Boy, he just can't handle the stuff." They may be the ones who drive everyone else home. The ability to drink a lot and stay out of trouble just motivates the alcoholic to drink more. If social drinkers drank as much as we alcoholics on any given evening, they'd probably be dead.

Loss of Control

9. Does the person lose time from work due to drinking?

I lost a lot of time from work because of my drinking. I found myself lying to my employees. I'd call in sick with some of the craziest stories: I had PMS, I had Asian flu, African flu, and for all I know, I may have called in one time with Atlantis flu, hoping no one would remember Atlantis sank.

If you're an employer wondering if your employee has a drinking problem, Families in Crisis says look first at the size of the file. The thickest ones belong to alcoholics or people living with an alcoholic. Along with a higher rate of absenteeism for colds, flu, gastritis, and cramps, they have lots of insurance claims for therapy and accidents.

As his disease progresses, an alcoholic employee goes out for lunch and doesn't return. He or she starts coming to work with a hangover, leaves early, is excessively tardy (especially on Monday morning and after lunch), and is often absent, particularly on Monday and Friday. Either someone calls up and makes excuses for the person, or the absence is unexpected and the next day explained away as an "emergency," with increasingly improbable stories.

On an elevator, I once overheard a woman telling a co-worker that she missed a day of work because she'd drunk too much the night before. I knew she wasn't an alcoholic, because she was too open about it. An alcoholic would make up any excuse rather than admit he was drunk.

As anyone who has ever held a job knows, you can lose work time even if you're physically present. If you're sitting at your desk with a hangover, you're not exactly productive. If you're frequently absent from your post, taking long coffee breaks and running over to the water cooler pretty regularly, you're also losing work time. Someone who's alert to signs of chemical dependency knows these are clues that you have a problem—whether or not you're drinking on the job.

Many alcoholics are so good at their work that a lot of this behavior is overlooked. In most cases, they try to cover up because the job is the one thing they want to hold on to. On the other hand, many alcoholics run through jobs like Sherman through Atlanta. As a young adult, I loved to party. Sometimes now I wake in the middle of the night and look at the clock and think how in the old days, at this hour I'd just be coming home. I'm grateful to be home in bed.

I got away with missing a lot of work because I was good at my job, but I know how many days there were when I wasn't feeling so hot and my job performance was down. Way down. I wonder who would have hired me when I got really bad.

10. Is drinking jeopardizing the person's job?

Even though I've had a lot of success, I know without a shadow of a doubt that my drinking jeopardized my career. The longer I'm sober, the more I realize just how much of a negative effect it had. I had to come out of the closet before many business associates were honest with me. I can just imagine what will happen once this book gets into the stores.

Just the other day, my agent, Aaron Priest, received a phone call from a woman who is a bigwig in publishing. She wanted me to know she was thrilled and happy for me that I was writing this book. I guessed she must have known I had a drinking problem or else she wouldn't have been quite so effusive. Aaron said I was right. She told him that a boyfriend of hers who'd worked with me years ago had once said, "Sometimes Mary Ellen sounds weird on the phone. I wonder if she's drinking." I now realize that his concern may have jeopardized my relationship with him and his company. If it did, I'm sorry.

Employers have their hands full with alcoholic employees, who tend to be grandiose, aggressive, or belligerent on the job—and may be drinking besides. Someone who is drinking regularly will have trouble recalling instructions and details and handling complex assignments. His work will be uneven. A period of low productivity may be followed by a period of high productivity.

Alcoholic employees are famous for empty statements and

lack of follow-through. They borrow money from co-workers, exaggerate their accomplishments, and hold unreasonable resentments toward the people they work with and for. They are prone to lie, and they will overreact to real and imagined criticism. On top of that, their performance is often affected by domestic problems and embarrassments such as money difficulties, which lead to garnishments and other legal measures.

Even if you don't know exactly how the one you're concerned about is doing at work, you probably have clues. What is he saying? Does he have lots of complaints about the way he's treated—either by management or by his fellow workers? If he makes a move, is it only lateral? Is he passed over for promotions? Do you get the sense he feels that he may lose his job? All those facts are clues that his alcoholism has caused trouble at work.

11. Is the person less efficient since he or she started drinking?

Sometimes people who are alcoholic do manage to handle their careers brilliantly. They become not only alcoholics but also workaholics—and either can be a killer. Still, until it catches up with them, they can be a boss's dream employee.

Meanwhile, they're shortchanging everyone outside the job. In particular, women alcoholics who try to juggle work and family have a real dilemma. I'll tell you who gets cheated—first the kids, then the spouse. The job is the last to suffer, since it's the area we tend to hold onto in order to prove how well we're doing.

It takes a lot of smarts, lots of scheming and planning, to keep the disease going. Those same qualities also help in the business world. But eventually everything catches up with you. There are so many alcoholics who give so much to their work but are finally shown the door without knowing why. They don't realize their secret is out.

I would guess that the majority of alcoholics aren't doing a great job, and I was among them. I prided myself on the fact that I was working, but I wasn't operating at the top of my form. As my disease progressed, I started not being able to concentrate at all. Whereas in the beginning I could sit down for an eight-hour stretch of work and get something finished, my attention span got shorter and shorter. I think it was down to about ten minutes by the time I entered treatment. I started doing everything by telephone because it was just too much effort to get a letter out. I mostly just pushed papers around. This book certainly wouldn't have been written if I hadn't stopped drinking, and not just for the obvious reason that I wouldn't have had the material.

In the late stages of my drinking, not only couldn't I work, but I also couldn't manage my employees. Instead of telling someone, "You are a rotten worker, you're fired," I would try to make everything okay. For one thing, I felt I could control the behavior of others and had the power to get them to shape up without really doing anything. For another, I felt so guilty about my own behavior that it was hard for me to be critical of anyone else. I was afraid that if I told off an employee or fired an incompetent accountant, he'd cut off my complaints by saying, "Well, you drink." That may just have been a paranoid thought, but it sure affected my efficiency.

Because alcoholics can be very manipulative, they cover their inefficiency by getting others to fill in the gaps. I spent lots of money on advisors to do the jobs that I couldn't do myself. Each year I picked up a few more accountants, writers, attorneys, and secretaries. At one point, I really didn't know what was going on in my professional life. I made the deals, but after that everything was up for grabs.

People are hired to take over the alcoholic's chores at home as well. Or the family members take on additional tasks. The kids or husband do the household chores, or the wife takes over the lawn duties and odd jobs that used to be the husband's responsibility.

When I was drinking, a housekeeper came in three times a week. One night, after I got out of treatment, I was up late scrubbing the floor and feeling good about it. Suddenly, I had a flash of insight about my career. Before I went into treatment, I felt that if I had to read or test another household hint, I'd scream. That night I realized, "No wonder you stopped caring about this stuff, dummy. *You* weren't doing the work, so what difference did it make to you whether or not a product worked."

I didn't have time to shop when I was drinking. I didn't have time for hobbies, either, and I couldn't concentrate as I had in the past when, for instance, I'd made every single decoration on our Christmas tree. (Some alcoholics, however, hold onto their hobbies: I know some seamstresses who nip and tuck, handymen who get a buzz on and saw.)

Since I wasn't the world's greatest mother when I was drinking, I had to cover my bases in that department. Sherm and I had a vicious cycle going: If I was drinking, he'd be both mother and father, and if he was, I'd take over. In the later stages, we rarely drank together. If Sherm knew I was out, he'd take Andrew to a movie. We became efficient at covering for each other, but as parents, we really weren't efficient at all. When we quit drinking, Andrew finally had both a mother and a father—and he knew which was which.

Frankly, I don't know how I got anything done when I was drinking, and the fact is my life was quite limited. Today I live a more balanced life. As a matter of fact, it's so full, I still have a hard time getting things done. Time sure flies when you're having fun!

12. Does the person promise to cut down or quit, and then start drinking again?

There's a myth that says that a person who can control his drinking some of the time isn't alcoholic. Alcoholics may go on the wagon; some even become what we call "dry alcoholics." They have all the symptoms of alcoholics but just aren't using the booze. The fact is that they haven't really made the choice never to drink again. They haven't really accepted the fact that they have a disease.

13. Does the person appear remorseful after drinking?

As a social drinker or nondrinker, you can't imagine how awful you feel the day after you've let liquor get the better of you and either behaved badly or can't even remember *how* you behaved.

If you're alcoholic, once you start drinking you say things and do things you'd never dream of doing sober. You wake up the next day and say, "How could a nice person like me ever do that?" I remember once waking up in my hotel room and wanting to jump out the top-floor window. I literally had to hold onto the bedpost and pray. I really thought I was going to jump. I managed to get out of the room and into the coffee shop, thank God. If I'd stayed there alone with my thoughts about what a bad person I was, I wouldn't be writing these words today.

I got so paranoid that even when I behaved A-okay—even if I'd had a great time the night before, and was drinking an acceptable amount—I was remorseful. I look back and shudder at those mornings when I wept uncontrollably and begged Sherm to tell me I was okay. I cried, sometimes over nothing, just because remorse and fear are part of the package, especially as the disease progresses.

When you're in this state, your behavior can get really excessive. You may call (or ask someone to call on your behalf) to apologize to the hostess. You avoid seeing the people you were with. You keep a low profile. You find yourself sending flowers and candy. Before he recovered, Nels used to buy his wife new furniture to make her happy and keep her from nagging when his drinking got out of hand. From Nels's recollections of the frequency of his binging, I assume the place probably looked like a showroom warehouse.

Another buddy used to clean her house after a bad bout and prepare a wonderful meal for her family to make the guilty feelings go away. What I did was be extra nice to Sherm. I'd take the day off and ask him to go somewhere with me, maybe to a show. Eventually, the only time we did anything together was when I felt remorseful. Sherm looked forward to those times, when I needed him, when I wasn't as self-sufficient and busy as usual. This is how the disease takes over the family.

Another way I handled my remorse was by overeating. Many alcoholics can't eat a thing the day after a binge, but I felt starved. I've read that drinking dehydrates you, and along with water your body loses a lot of nutrients, so you overeat to make up for them. (I used to wonder why, if it was short of nutrients, my body wanted chocolate chip cookies.) I also believed that eating relieved my hangover, but I think it really relieved my guilt. I've observed that many alcoholics seem to have eating disorders.

Other alcoholics handle their remorse in other ways. Some just go into retreat. They become very quiet and skulk off alone. Many cover up their remorse by rationalizing their behavior:

· "Everyone was drinking too much."
· "Everyone gets carried away once in a while."
· "Without me, the party would have been nothing." (Probably. If you hadn't been there, the police might not have showed.)

14. Does the person spend money on alcohol that should be going elsewhere?

Did you ever see anyone sit down at a coffee shop counter and order a round for the house? It happens all the time in bars. An alcoholic knows that if you buy someone a drink, he'll most likely buy you one in return, so you will have a lot of drinks coming to you. Besides, making a grand gesture like buying a round is one way alcoholics compensate for their low self-esteem. Finally, drinking is the only way an alcoholic knows how to celebrate. If there isn't a party going on, he'll create one.

Alcoholics drop an awful lot of money in bars. Take a look at the expense accounts of executives with drinking problems compared to those who drink normally. Aside from the amount you spend on the liquor itself, you lose plenty on the deals you make after you've been drinking. I wish I didn't know about that firsthand.

15. Does the person show a personality change after he or she's been drinking?

I personally don't believe that people drink because they like the way it tastes. People drink for one reason: to change their mood. One of the earliest signs of alcoholism is how effectively it changes a person's feelings: Alcohol usually makes you feel good instantly. I've read it's the most effective stress-reducer that exists. If alcohol were invented today, it would be front-page news. People would label it the wonder drug.

Although people claim alcohol makes them better company, I have met only two men whom I feel were more likable under the influence. One never talked at all without a drink. The other was practically comatose while sober, but with liquor he was a live wire. Once in recovery, people like these two need some help to open up.

Unlike a normal or social drinker, an alcoholic may say or do something under the influence of alcohol that is so contrary to his personality or moral code that he would never do it in any other circumstances. Even when the alcohol gets you into trouble and the consequences of your behavior become painful, you can't resist chasing that wonderful (if only temporary) feeling alcohol gives you.

While I used to appear competent and socially secure when I was sober, I didn't really feel comfortable unless I was drinking. Then (people tell me) I became opinionated and self-absorbed. I had to have the spotlight. I had to be complimented. At my worst, I was desperate and needy. I'd lean over to some stranger at a bar and say, "What do you think? Do you think I'm a good-looking woman?" I thought this was flirting. I *felt* as if I were in complete control. Booze fills you with false courage and the ability to say things that you couldn't without it. That's why people go to bars for pickups and not to coffee shops.

My best girlfriend's father repeatedly told her, "Jean, don't drink until you get married." He knew that one of the consequences of drinking was that it helps you compromise your morals. A friend from AA says the day he felt he had hit bottom was when he woke up in a hotel room with strange arms around him and a voice murmuring, "I was made for you" and opened his eyes to discover he was in bed with the Wicked Witch of the East.

If the person you're concerned about has been drinking a long time, you might have a lot of trouble spotting a personality change. But you should try to look back and remember what he or she was like before the drinking got bad.

Some alcoholics drink every day and in some cases all day (even on the job) yet they seem to be functioning. The family is used to their alcoholic state, finding them angry and hostile, and generally worse to deal with, when they're *not* drinking. Such a person is drinking to be normal—to stay steady, maybe to avoid the shakes.

Some people overcome their shyness by drinking, becoming Romeos, real charmers, very lively and sociable. Others become depressed and passive. But whether the personality change is for the better or the worse, the person you're concerned about is dying. He needs help.

16. Has the person forgotten things that were said or that happened while he or she was drinking?

"I drink to forget," alcoholics say. If you only knew how accurate that statement is! It describes an alcoholic blackout.

An alcoholic blackout does not require hitting the floor. It is not the same thing as passing out, sleeping it off, being in a stupor, or having a seizure. It is a period of amnesia. During a blackout, the alcoholic seems to everyone (including himself) to be fully aware and in control of what's going on. He may not even appear to be drunk.

While most blackouts occur during heavy drinking, some alcoholics can black out after only a single drink. Alcoholics may not experience blackouts until after they've been drinking heavily for years, or they may experience them the first time they have a drink.

A blackout can be as brief as a minute or as long as several weeks. The drinker can be lunching with the girls, bowling with the boys, borrowing or lending money, driving a car, dancing or working—but the next day he or she will be unable to recall the event. Pilots have flown airplanes, doctors have performed surgery, and grooms have proposed during blackouts. I'm told that many people in jail can't recall the crimes they've committed because they were in blackout.

Following a blackout, you may repress the episode. This is a defense reaction, a way of not remembering and reexperiencing shameful or painful events. Or, if you don't have a total blackout, you may later experience euphoric recall, which distorts your memory. You remember how you felt while you were intoxicated, but not how you acted.

The experts say that there are three types of memory: remote, which permits you to remember details from long ago; immediate, which allows you to recall things for up to a minute; and short-term, which is the period in between. They believe that alcohol in the brain interferes either with the formation or the storage of short-term memory. So your behavior may be normal while you are in an alcoholic blackout, but your ability to remember the situation is affected.

Blackouts are why alcoholic dads agree to take their kids to the circus and husbands go along with plans to visit the relatives over the holidays, then don't deliver on the promises or deny they ever made them. They're not lying. They just don't remember.

Delusionary memory explains why an alcoholic will remember only that his wife rejected his pass but not that he was aggressive and threatening in approaching her.

I like to share my success, and I loved the people who worked with me. But money became an issue with some of my staff to the point where they began to annoy me. I suspect that I promised a few of them raises while blacked out and never followed through, so of course they became angry.

To me, blackouts were the worst consequence of "the morning after." Before I entered treatment, I was having them almost every time I drank. I didn't forget the whole day, just bits and pieces of it. Once I went to the garage and my car wasn't there. I still remember my feeling of panic. On another occasion everyone in the office was talking about the Christmas party held the night before. They brought up things I didn't recall. I pretended I did, of course. I baited people to get information out of them.

Many alcoholics consider blackouts to be the price you pay for drinking, but I could never reconcile myself to them. Nor did I believe, once one had passed, that I would experience another. I was great at putting my head in the sand. Besides, most people try to avoid direct confrontations and so help the alcoholic minimize the situation. Instead of saying, "Mary Ellen, you were drunk last night and you called me a tramp," the person might say, "Mary Ellen, you said some cruel things to me last night," which doesn't seem half as bad.

Some alcoholics not only expect blackouts but also prepare for them. A friend kept a pad and pencil by the phone to write down the names of anyone who called while she was drinking so she'd remember them the next morning. Of course, unless she recorded the entire conversation she wouldn't know exactly what was said. Other people play it safer and simply take the phone off the hook.

There is no way you can tell if anyone is having a blackout. In treatment, I saw someone in the middle of a group discussion stop suddenly and wonder aloud where he was. He had just come out of a blackout and hadn't the slightest memory of flying from Los Angeles to Minneapolis to check in for help. Another who checked in during a blackout thought he was still on a fishing trip he had taken three weeks previously. Also in treatment, I saw one fellow go to the refrigerator for soda pop, open the door, and yell, "Where are all the Miller Lites?" Not in the treatment fridge, that's for sure.

One friend sold a book for half a million dollars and told her alcoholic husband about it the minute she got the news. Weeks later, he mentioned that no one had ever told him the details of the sale. Well, it's kind of hard to forget a number like $500,000 unless you're Howard Hughes and that's petty cash.

If the person you're concerned about doesn't remember something significant that he or someone else said or did, and his reaction is surprise, denial, bewilderment, or fear, you can assume he was in a blackout. But you may see this sign only occasionally, because even chronic alcoholics don't necessarily have blackouts every time they drink.

17. Does the person drink and then drive?

These days more than ever, with all the public outcry against drunk driving, you have to be a lunatic—or an alcoholic—to get behind the wheel after a night on the town. Social drinkers don't get drunk and then drive.

I could never sleep at night until Sherm got home. Early in our marriage, I'd wait for him in anticipation. As time went on, I waited in fear. He was drinking. I hoped he wouldn't be stopped by the police. Then, once I'd gotten help for myself and knew the score, I prayed that the police *would* stop him. Maybe that would precipitate the crisis that would lead him to go for help. The police never stopped him, so finally, with an Intervention, the people who loved him did.

I can now admit that I too drove while intoxicated. If I had been stopped, I'm sure there would have been a coverup. My friends would have come to my rescue and put the blame on the police. They would have said, "They're stopping everyone these days, even little old ladies," or "It could happen to every one of us," or "Every cop I know drinks. Who do they think they are?"

Healthy people are outraged at the idea of someone driving drunk; they don't help that person minimize or deny it. I think attorneys ought to think twice about defending people for drunk driving. I've seen a case where people were hoping to get someone committed to treatment because of habitual drunk driving and the attorney said, "His license has been taken away, and he's not hurting anyone." The judge's position was, "He's not doing anything, he can't be committed." In my opinion, if suicide isn't allowable under the law, neither should people be allowed to continue drinking without any restraints. That's suicide too—and it might also be homicide.

Alcoholics continue to drink and drive in the United States because the consequences of a DWI are so minimal. I saw a cartoon of a blindfolded guy, labeled an alcoholic, holding a loaded gun. He was moaning, "Isn't it terrible? If I kill someone, I lose my license for a whole month."

Alcoholics Anonymous of Totowa, New Jersey, compiled a list of DWI laws from other countries. Here are some penalties for drunk driving in:

• Australia: The names of the drivers are sent to local newspapers and printed under the heading "HE'S DRUNK AND IN JAIL."

• Malaya: The driver is jailed, and if he's married, his wife is jailed, too.

· United Kingdom, Finland, and Sweden: Automatic jail term of one year.

· South Africa: A ten-year prison sentence and the equivalent of a $10,000 fine, or both.

· Turkey: Drunk drivers are taken 20 miles from town by the police and forced to walk back, under escort.

· Bulgaria: A second conviction results in execution.

· El Salvador: Your first offense is your last. Execution by firing squad.

Recently, *USA Today* devoted a whole page to the custom that attracts many problem drinkers to bars across America. The opening line was, "They call it the 'happy hour,' but there is no happiness in the tragedy that it brings." The article continued, "Across the U.S.A. this weekend, bars and restaurants will offer cheap booze to lure people through the door. Happy hour draws young drinkers, those between 18 and 24 years of age."

It concluded, "If we keep pushing drinks and winking at drunk driving, the grim reaper will be the only one laughing when the happy hour is over." The three-column picture in the center of the page showed happy young people at the bar with Death leaning over a shoulder and saying, "I'd be happy to buy your last rounds."

"Happy hour." Whoever dreamed that one up must have had quite a sense of humor.

18. Is the woman drinking during her pregnancy?

With all the data being reported about fetal alcohol syndrome—it affects one in 750 live births, is the third leading cause of birth defects and *the only preventable one*—I would say it's a safe bet that if a mother-to-be is abusing alcohol (and let's be honest: wanting a drink isn't one of the usual cravings of pregnancy), she has a serious problem. So might her baby. There's some new evidence that even one or two drinks a week can be harmful to the fetus.

I've heard all the rationalizations ("My doctor says it's okay." "My mother drank when she was pregnant, and nothing happened." "What about all those women in France and

Europe who drink wine with every meal?") Normal drinkers don't rationalize their drinking when they are pregnant. They don't rationalize their drinking, period.

Eleven years ago, I was pregnant and happy about it. But I wasn't so happy to discover that, pregnant or not, I couldn't give up alcohol. I searched textbooks to find evidence of any link between pregnancy and drinking. In those days, I couldn't find anything that recommended against it (and of course I probably couldn't have stopped anyway), so I felt I had a green flag. Today, you can't go into a bar in New York without seeing a sign that cautions you that drinking may cause birth defects. I did come across a statement that advised against drunkenness during pregnancy, but I never planned to drink until I became drunk. I am an alcoholic, though, and despite my intentions, I did become drunk occasionally when I was pregnant. Not a lot; and not willingly. But it did happen.

Now I realize I didn't have any choice, given my lack of information about my disease and my inability to take control of it, and that absolves me some, but the entire experience is still painful to look back on. After it happened, I would be on my knees at the foot of my bed, asking God for forgiveness. Then after a few weeks, I'd feel in control enough to drink again. Sometimes I would have just one drink. Often I couldn't stop.

When I first held Andrew in my arms, I just stared at him. I couldn't get over the fact that my baby was normal. When I was alone with him in the hospital room, I gave thanks to God over and over again.

A close friend was drinking when she was pregnant each time I saw her, and when I commented on it, she explained that this was a rare occasion. But I saw her often. She had a horrible time delivering the baby. And though many people voiced concern, they did it behind her back. They didn't really understand what a terrible thing she was doing or how it might affect her child. Her problems in delivery were blamed on the doctor or the hospital.

I've seen babies with fetal alcohol syndrome. I've held them in my arms. If you want to cry, all you have to do is look down into one of these tiny faces and realize how the life of this little being has been ruined by its mother's drinking. If you know someone who is pregnant and still continues to drink, this is the one case where there is no question about your moral obligation to get help and to initiate an Intervention.

19. Does the person drink more than he or she intended?

There are some alcoholics who drink daily and get drunk every time, but for most of us, this isn't the case. On occasion, we may drink just a little. More often we plan to drink moderately but don't stop until we're drunk or the bar closes. This is characteristic of loss of control, and I believe it's the major difference between heavy abusive drinking and alcoholic drinking.

An abusive drinker says, "I wanted to get drunk. It's my right. If someone doesn't like it, tough." He's probably a sociopath. He doesn't care about the consequences of his drinking. His attitude lands him behind bars.

An alcoholic will drink more than he ever intended to and get drunk at a time and place he never expected.

Father Martin, a recovering alcoholic priest who lectures throughout the country, puts it nicely. An abusive drinker is an immoral person who is choosing to be a jerk. An alcoholic is a moral person who because of his disease has lost the power to make the choice. Frankly, I'd rather be labeled an alcoholic than an abusive drinker.

Most of us alcoholics have been able to go on the wagon temporarily, sometimes even for an extended period. The real test is whether you can control your drinking once you've started. Even if an alcoholic has managed to cut down to a drink or two, at some point he'll lose control and get drunk.

As my drinking progressed, I got smart. I never took even one drink unless I knew I was someplace where I could keep drinking without terrible consequences other than personal ones. (In other words, I would experience guilt, remorse, and shame, but could be fairly certain I wouldn't wind up going into business with the Mafia.) That was how I managed my unpredictability. I knew that once I started, no matter how many promises I had made to myself I couldn't stop. Let me tell you, it's spooky not knowing whether this will be the night you have just two drinks or if you're going to lose complete control.

After I sobered up, I went over to the house of a friend who didn't realize I was recovering, and she offered me a drink. "No thanks," I said. "You don't have enough in the house for me."

20. Has the person missed planned family or social activities due to drinking?

I have never before admitted this to anyone. I missed my father-in-law's wake because I was home in bed with a hangover. I blamed my absence on Sherm's kids, but the blame is now put where it belongs—on the alcoholism. I loved Sherm's dad, but I was just so sick that day I couldn't get there. It's a sad thing to look back on and own up to but alcoholics typically miss all sorts of important things because they are too sick—or because they know drinks won't be served.

Sometimes there is just nothing compelling enough—not dinner guests, a child bundled and ready for a visit to Santa, even a bride at the altar—to take you away from the drinking. Those are the times when, once you've started drinking, you can't stop—no matter who you're hurting.

21. Has the person been treated for mental or physical problems that are due to drinking?

You wouldn't believe the number of people who have been put in jail for driving while intoxicated and still don't believe they have a drinking problem—even when they've had two or more offenses. And these are people who act and appear to be normal! One woman told me the only reason she got into trouble is because she's so thin that one beer makes her drunk. I don't believe her, but even if it were true, why does she drink even one beer if it causes problems?

Somewhere along the line, most alcoholics have been in a hospital or institution because of drinking, but they don't put the primary blame where it lies, on the alcohol. For example, a good percentage of accidents occur while someone is under the influence. If you don't believe me, just try hanging out in a hospital emergency room for a day. Jason Robards, the actor, is a recovering alcoholic. In his drinking days, he had a severe auto accident, and it took a team of plastic surgeons to put him back together. He was drinking before the stitches healed.

The mental wards, too, are full of alcoholics. My dearest friend from AA attempted suicide and ended up at the state mental hospital. When he was sent to Hazelden, the treatment center, he thought it was just another institution until he got into the program. I know of another recovering alcoholic who spent four months in a mental institution before counselors understood he had a drinking problem.

Not only alcoholics, but also their spouses, may wind up in mental institutions. I know of one alcoholic's wife who was hospitalized for two months until everyone realized that her husband had convinced her she was crazy.

I'm always amazed by the fact that most people prefer to think a loved one is nuts rather than alcoholic. And yet an alcoholism problem is so much easier to treat. A chemical dependency counselor I know has a daughter who had everything going for her until last year, when she suddenly became depressed, paranoid, and unable even to hold down a job. "If she only had a drug or an alcohol problem, I would know what to do," her mother said. "By comparison, those would be simple."

I was lucky. I didn't land in an institution or a hospital, but I did sometimes notice a few black and blue marks on my body and couldn't remember how I'd gotten them. And I did have a close call early in our marriage. Sherm and I had been drinking with friends and talking about high school days, when I'd been a pep squad leader. I decided to do a few splits for old time's sake. I ran from the kitchen and jumped from the step going down into our sunken living room. I landed in a perfect split, all right. I crawled into bed that night and stayed there for two days. I'm lucky I didn't wind up in traction or in surgery.

If you think back on your alcoholic's life, I'm sure you'll

remember medical emergencies that wouldn't have come up if drinking hadn't been involved.

22. Does the person neglect his or her family because of drinking?

Verbal and physical abuse are obvious signs of alcoholism. Most alcoholics aren't physically abusive. The ones who are usually have to get additional help once the alcoholic problem has been dealt with. There are, however, other kinds of abuse that are more subtle.

I've found, for example, that most alcoholics think they're pretty good parents. I know I did—until I dug deep inside myself and realized I was a horrible role model to my son and Sherm's children from his previous marriage. I was a hypocrite. I would lecture Andrew about not using drugs, then I'd drink and drive or have friends over and get high with them.

When they think about family welfare, a lot of women think about how comfortable they keep their homes. I have noticed that the last thing to deteriorate may be the housework. A housewife will hold onto that (just as an alcoholic who works will try and keep the job intact) to convince herself that if she has a clean home, she's a good mother. Meanwhile she does her family harm in so many less obvious but more damaging ways.

One friend cooked to cover up her drinking—hitting the bottle while she was alone in the kitchen. Offered a constant supply of baked goods, her son became obese. Other people pacify their kids with food to keep them occupied while they drink. "Go watch TV and have a bowl of chips." Kids who have an alcoholic mother or father are probably only too willing to comfort themselves with food. Plenty of them have weight problems.

I know of a woman who landed in the hospital with a drinking problem, but the kids didn't know the reason. Their dad told them she was there because she couldn't cope with their bad behavior. What a trip to lay on them! Andrew heard this story and was troubled by what the children had supposedly done to their mom. When he confided in me, I said, "Andrew, does Mrs. Smith drink a lot?"

"Yeah, mom," he replied, "because the kids are bad."

"No, Andrew," I said. "She drinks a lot because she's an alcoholic, like me." Andrew is squared away, but those poor kids are still walking around with a cloud over their heads.

I've seen alcoholic mothers put their kids in day care so they could drink or get them in bed early so they could hit the bottle. Other alcoholic parents spoil their kids out of guilt. In my drinking days, I'd buy Andrew anything he wanted. He didn't have to earn it, either. Buying things made me feel okay as a mother. I wasn't involved in what was going on at school or with his social life, and buying made me feel I was being a good parent. Kids want you there: at school, at games, with the family. Alcoholic parents usually aren't there. That's what I call being careless of your family's welfare.

I've seen wealthy alcoholics install all kinds of fancy equipment (VCR, pool table, the works) in so-called "family rooms," in which of course a family never appeared. They tell themselves they're wonderful parents because the kids have "everything"—everything, that is, except a parent who listens and nurtures and shares.

Since my sister quit drinking, she has had her son in counseling. The counselor told me that what her son treasures most is that she now says no. He confided this to the counselor with tears in his eyes: "I know my mommy loves me because now she says no."

Unless they're given permission to speak about alcoholism (which happens only when the problem is out in the open), it's unlikely kids will say anything. But they know what's going on and they will try desperately to engage the parent in another activity so he won't drink—they will, that is, until they give up and become very isolated.

And what about your spouse? He or she is "family," too. Alcohol can start off as a sexual stimulant because it relaxes your inhibitions. But if you're an alcoholic, you may lose interest in sex. You can't wait for your partner to get into bed—so you can hit the bottle while he or she sleeps.

If you drink, you smell. You are not very lovable. You are

worried only about your own self-satisfaction. As time goes on, the only thing an alcoholic man may be "up" for is another drink. The disease causes a great deal of sexual dysfunction, and that's ironic considering that lots of us started on alcohol because it made us feel so desirable.

In the alcoholic's family, the broken promises are endless. The price the other family members pay is enormous, but because many are used to the situation, they don't even realize how great it is. As long as there's abusive drinking, the liquor and not the family will be the number one priority.

23. Has the person violated his or her own moral code?

Not all, but a large majority, of practicing alcoholics, particularly men, sleep around. That's part of the disease. It's part of loss of control. While most spouses find this hard to deal with, it is nevertheless a fact. Because there's so much cause for concern about venereal diseases (including AIDS) today, you must recognize that you're at risk if your spouse is having extramarital sex. There's no point sticking your head in the sand about this.

Chemical dependents are just as clever at hiding their infidelity as they are about concealing liquor or drugs. All the alcoholics I have talked to about their sexual exploits regret them and are horribly ashamed of them. They didn't plan what happened, and once they're sober, they rarely take up a swinging life-style. Now, don't be a dope and worry about *who* your spouse is sleeping with. That's not the problem— the booze is. The infidelity seems to go away once the alcoholic gets help.

Since booze and drugs cost money, some chemical dependents may resort to stealing or embezzling. They have no choice. They can't ask for help, and they need money for their habit. It's a vicious cycle.

I have never met a recovering alcoholic or drug addict who doesn't have a basically good character. Each of them hates what he did when he was using. How would you come to hate something if you truly enjoyed it? That's what makes this disease so sad, to me: You lose your ability to choose.

Defensiveness

24. Does the person avoid or get defensive at suggestions that he quit or cut down?

Many alcoholics have never been advised to cut down or stop. They may, however, react negatively to the idea of organizations such as AA, MADD (Mothers Against Drunk Drivers), SADD (Students Against Drunk Drivers), drunk driving laws, bars that have a policy of not serving anyone who seems intoxicated, and books like this. They say things like, "AA is full of wimps," "Treatment centers exist only to make big bucks," and "It's a free world—it's no one's business what I do."

When I used to see public service announcements about drinking on TV, I would switch channels. I avoided all the literature. I didn't want to know what was going on.

My minister recently gave a sermon about alcohol—not just its abuse, but its use. He said that kids are in big trouble because of using drugs and alcohol, then asked the congregation, "Why are *you* still drinking? What kind of role models are *you?*" The nondrinkers applauded him and the drinkers resented him horribly. I know I would have too, in the old days. In fact, I'd never have been inside the church if I were drinking.

There are some alcoholics who aren't bothered about this kind of thing at all. Those are the ones whose denial is so strong it doesn't even occur to them that any of these things relate to them.

25. Does the person defend or lie about his or her drinking?

"The best defense is a good offense." Alcoholics defend or lie about their drinking because they don't have the ability to stop it, and they perpetually feel guilty and ashamed about it.

· "You'd drink, too, if you had a husband like mine."
· "Everyone has a bad day now and then."
· "It's a free country."
· "I'm not an alcoholic. I drink only beer." (Beer's alcohol,

too, folks. It's just as effective as scotch in turning you into an alcoholic.)

· "I have it under control." (I knew a guy who "limited" himself to five drinks a day. He was caught driving while intoxicated and had an unbelievable amount of liquor in his blood. It turned out he'd had nothing to drink for three days so he used up his entire quota in one afternoon.)

· "Drinking is part of my job." (Funny, I've never seen that in a job description!)

· "I have fun when I drink."

· "People who don't drink are self-righteous and I'm not like that."

· "I'm not bothering anyone." (If the family is having problems like those described in chapter 2, the drinking very definitely is bothering someone.)

· "If I switched drinks, I wouldn't get into trouble." (If I've heard it once, I've heard it a million times: "It's the gin that makes me sin. I'm changing to wine." Or, "I'm sure vodka wouldn't give me a hangover.")

I started with rum and Coke, but when I became a woman of the world, I drank martinis before dinner, and liqueurs after. No bourbon and Coke or 7 and 7 for me. (I was not only an alcoholic, but also a phony.) Eventually I decided it was the juniper berries in the gin that made me act crazy. So I switched to Dewar's scotch. I was probably attracted to the high-class types in the Dewar's ads. You've seen them: John Smith, journalist and yachtsman. I thought some of it would rub off on me. Did I expect they'd call me for an endorsement? "Mary Ellen Pinkham, author and alcoholic. Last book read: Can't remember. Can't concentrate. Greatest achievement: Held down jobs while drinking. Quote: My chemical of choice is Dewar's."

Nope, the Dewar's didn't help. I still acted crazy.

· "You're such a nag I can't stay here." (An alcoholic will start a fight with a spouse to defend his drinking. The partner usually falls for this, keeps arguing, thus providing the excuse for the drinker to head out to a bar again.)

The alcoholic will deflect the issue right back at the speaker—every time. If confronted by Sherm, I'd say, "Look who's talking about someone drinking too much!" It's easy to snap back at someone for being too fat, too lazy, or rotten in bed. My defense was also that I'd been under stress. I knew just how to shut Sherm up: "I'm at work every day, supporting this family." I never took into consideration the fact that without Sherm at home taking care of our son, I wouldn't be able to travel around the country promoting my books.

The most snobbish of all defenses is acknowledgment. "I know I have a problem, and I'm going to work on it." How can you badger someone who agrees with you? When I admitted my problem, people left me alone, and strangely, they accepted my statement that I was "working on it." People really do want to believe the best of you. It would have been better if they'd asked me straight out, "What are you doing about it? You may not be drinking now, but what will you do if it happens again?" They never asked those two key questions and I was able to keep them off my back, skipping off to another "drunch." (Naturally, I'd pay the bill. Who would harp on your drinking if he wasn't even picking up the tab? This turned out to be an expensive tactic.)

Alcoholics with physical impairments frequently use their disability as a defense: "If you were sitting in this wheelchair, you'd be drinking too."

Claiming to be under financial pressure is another defense.

So are tears. Turn them on and everyone backs away.

So is guilt: "How can you say such cruel things to me, after all I've done for you?"

And so is anger: "You owe me the shirt on your back! If you don't like it here, just move out."

The defenses range from funny to pathetic, but all of them are beside the point. They're just part of the rationalizing, projection, and denial that are part of the disease.

Other Signs to Consider (The following are not signs of alcoholism, but should be noted if they occur in conjunction with any of the preceding.)

26. Does the person have indefinable fears?

One of the best things that happened to me in treatment was finding out how I felt about my son. It's still really painful for me to admit that when I went into treatment, I wasn't sure if I loved Andrew. I thought I did, but I just didn't trust my feelings. In treatment, I learned that a lot of my craziness came from a symptom alcoholics suffer from in the chronic state—indefinable fears. (Drug abusers become paranoid.) I used to spend a lot of time worrying about kidnaping or fearing some other terrible thing would happen to Andrew, and my fears kept me from getting close to him. I was afraid that if I got close, I couldn't handle losing him. The only reason for these fears was the alcoholism. The minute I began to recover, they were gone, and along with them, my worries about my feelings for Andrew. I don't want anyone to think I didn't love my son. The problem was that all my feelings were in a void, including my feelings for him.

Other people's fears take the form of thinking everyone is looking at them and talking about them. Many alcoholics stop going out of the house and drink only in the safety of their own homes. They worry about things that are unlikely or don't exist.

27. Is the person planning a drastic change?

Many alcoholics attempt to make a fresh start by taking some dramatic action—things will be better if they move to another state, get divorced, marry someone else, quit their job. The sad truth is, of course, that nothing will really change unless the alcoholism is addressed. The same problems will occur with new people, in new places. If you discover that the one you love is considering a major change, that might be a signal that it's time to consider an Intervention. Sober, he can make his own decisions; while he's drinking, the disease is making the decisions for him. Many alcoholics are planning on divorce at the time of an Intervention, only to find in treatment and in sobriety that alcohol was the real problem—and perhaps the cause of dissatisfaction with the job or marriage as well.

28. Is the person deteriorating physically?

Booze really takes its toll on some people. I was one of them. My face (along with the rest of me) would get puffy when I drank and pasty the next day. Luckily, I stopped before my health was completely ruined. "Pretty" or "handsome" isn't the issue: If you keep using, you ruin your health, and an unhealthy body never looks good.

You may be looking at a wife or husband who has no choice but to let herself or himself go. I assure you the same perky, cute gal and the same healthy guy you married is there underneath all the alcoholism. Everything improves once you sober up. It takes hard work, but when you're sober, you're at least willing and able to try to remedy the painful aspects of your life.

So many alcoholics and their spouses have bad sexual relationships. If yours started out good, it certainly will deteriorate as the alcoholism progresses. And the fact is that many alcoholics and their spouses have never—and I mean not one single time—had sexual relations unless they were under the influence of alcohol. They simply can't let go otherwise. I was becoming one of them. Unless I drank, I couldn't even think about sex.

That's another benefit of recovery. I was like a schoolgirl discovering the real feeling and meaning of sex. I'm forty years old, and it was all brand new again—and the same thing can happen for you.

29. Are you concerned about the person's drinking?

Of course you are, or you wouldn't be reading this book. You've probably been concerned about the drinking for a long time. More accurately, you are very likely at the point where you're hitting your head against the wall because of the drinking.

This book is not about detaching yourself from the problem. It is not about how to "adjust" to the drinking alcoholic, or about pretending that the problem will go away. I hate that kind of book, because I know that accommodating to alcoholism is just the same as signing the death certificate for both the alcoholic and you. I've seen people who've gotten the wrong idea about "detaching" at Al-Anon. Years later, they're still hoping and praying the problem will go away by itself. (Yes, and right after that, Santa Claus will pay you a personal visit, Virginia.)

This book is about addressing your concern, helping you recognize the facts about your problem, and helping you realize that *some decisions have to be made*. Now, if you haven't answered the questions above, go back over them and be honest. The fact is, that if you can answer yes to any *one* of them, and particularly if the situation has recurred, you have identified a sign of alcoholism.

If the use of alcohol causes continuing problems in any area of a person's life—family, social life, economic or physical well-being—and if he or she continues to drink, he is in big trouble. If you have answered yes to any *two* questions, you are most probably dealing with an alcoholic drinker and should seek help.

A lot of people bait me: "Mary Ellen, how do you really know if someone is an alcoholic? There's so much information and there are so many contradictory opinions about it." Often they'll repeat the opinion of some "expert" (probably the gal under the next dryer at the beauty parlor) who says that alcoholism is a matter of will power and a personality disorder and, despite the fact that this is absolute nonsense, they're willing to swallow it. Or they're simply too proud to admit their loved one is "one of those"—an alcoholic.

It's time to be humble instead of prideful. Humility means being open to learning more.

I am certain of one thing. The problem will not go away. It will just get worse. But it can be dealt with. One of the reasons you're probably having such trouble working toward a solution is that, like the alcoholic, you're afflicted too. If this comes as a shock, and hurts your pride, let me assure you that I understand—I've been there too. But alcoholism is a *family disease*.

Your Role in the Disease

What follows may me the hardest part of this book for you to deal with. I want to explain the part *you* play in helping a chemically dependent person remain sick.

Throughout my alcoholism, I was surrounded by people who tolerated or even encouraged my behavior and so (indirectly or directly) supported it. *That's what permitted it to go on for so long.* I've discovered that most alcoholics are in the same situation, unless their disease has progressed to the point where they've managed to alienate every caring friend or relative.

Despite their good intentions and concern, well-meaning people—maybe you are one of them—help the chemically dependent person drug himself to death. This probably comes as a real slap in the face. Sorry, but it's a fact.

While alcoholism isn't catching like a cold, it affects the whole family—"family" being anyone connected by birth, marriage, or adoption and including others who share closely in the family's activities and concerns. That's why alcoholism is considered a family disease. There is even a special term for the other members of the dependent's immediate or extended family, who are all considered to be affected by it. The term is "co-dependent."

Everyone who's touched by alcoholism has a different story to tell. Some are living with a destructive alcoholic who mentally and physically abuses his children and spouse. Others are living with a mother who has strangers parading through her bedroom while the children listen from the next room. Some are living with a happy-go-lucky guy who's so lovable it's hard for them to take his drinking seriously. And there are those who live with the guy who drinks at home in front of the TV and just passes out, or with the secret drinker who's a perfect lady in public but a madwoman at home. Some children live with two alcoholic parents or an alcoholic grandmother or uncle, and some families live with an alcoholic like me. But no matter what personality type you live with, *all* members of the family will react to the alcoholism, and as the alcoholic becomes more involved with his drinking, *you* become more involved with *him*. You will eventually experience identifiable and pathological behavior that is as predictable as the pattern of the alcoholism itself.

If the effect on the entire family comes as news to you, I should point out that even the experts weren't quick to catch on. Not until years after alcoholism was acknowledged to be a disease was it also acknowledged to be a family disease. In fact, most of the research has taken place only over the past ten years or so.

More and more is being learned about family members' roles in alcoholism. It has become clear that for the alcoholic's family to lead any kind of a normal life, each family member must be dealt with individually and included both in the process of identifying the problem and in the process of recovery. To change their own behavior, family members need help just as much as the alcoholic does. Otherwise, they remain stuck in the same old patterns, some of which are destructive to themselves and some of which are destructive to the alcoholic.

On certain days, I used to let my anger toward the people I wished would force me to deal with my alcoholism get the best of me. But co-dependents are in as much trouble as an alcoholic. They, too, are sick and very possibly in pain— more pain perhaps than the dependent. After all, when you're using, you can sedate your pain with your drug. While your spouse sits uncomfortably at the party, worrying and wondering what will happen next, you are having a good time. And when you finally get home and begin to think maybe it wasn't such a swell evening after all and, on top of that you're in for a lecture from your spouse, you can use your drug to sedate yourself again. If you use enough of it, you can block out all your discomfort simply by passing out. Meanwhile, your co-dependent has to go through the whole ordeal stark raving sober.

The stages of the family disease

Except on television, there is no such thing as a "normal" family—if by normal you mean problem-free. But problems don't have to drive a family crazy. In a nurturing family, the people like each other (most of the time, anyway), and they support and trust each other. Parents are leaders, not bosses. People talk to each other without shouting down and blaming. You can show anger. You can show fear. Nothing is taboo. You can talk about how other people are affecting you, admit your own mistakes, allow others to make theirs. You can talk about anything from drinking to finances without any consequences; and people actually try to help you find solutions.

A crazy, or dysfunctional, family is a houseful of people who are insecure and in pain and show it by screaming, acting resentful, or giving others the cold shoulder. Lying and deception are a way of life. A child in such a family gets the message from the parents, "Do as I say, not as I do."

Blame is never directed where it's appropriate. Some family members take it upon themselves; others will direct it at one another. Everyone is in pain, but no one deals with anything directly by talking to the key person—the alcoholic. By complaining and blaming, family members delude themselves that they're doing something, but in reality no progress is being made.

When someone in the family becomes chemically dependent, the entire family immediately starts moving toward the dysfunctional end of the scale. Another member may even develop a chemical dependency. Everyone is affected, and everyone is eventually trapped in the same emotional turmoil as the drinker. Because each of you feels you are the cause of the drinking, each of you feels guilty. Everyone feels ashamed and resentful. On top of all that, because talking is taboo, all those feelings are internalized. The family members' opinions of themselves sink lower and lower, and as they do, it's easier for the alcoholic to control the situation.

Remember the stages of alcoholism: Learning, seeking, dependency, and using to feel normal. The co-dependents go through the same four stages.

During the *learning* phase, the alcoholism becomes a growing problem but the family tries to dismiss it as being "normal." At the same time, each member of the family finds a kind of behavior to cope with it. Instead of acting out of instinct, you act defensively, and the behavior you adopt becomes your means of coping thereafter. Children in such an atmosphere develop undersirable patterns of behavior that they will carry into their adult lives. A little girl who learn to keep the peace in the family when dad is on a binge—comforting those who need help (including cracy old dad) rather than experiencing her own feelings of danger and hurt—may grow up to be a person who never really acknowledges her pain and finds ways to sedate it with some other addiction (such as overeating) or with the same chemical dependency.

Alcoholics aren't the only ones who can make a family crazy. People learn to play roles in many types of families. But the chance of developing defensive behavior patterns is greater if you're a member of a family with a chemical dependent.

The *seeking* phase for family members is the one in which you may begin to identify drinking as a real problem. Usually, the first reaction is to find something other than alcohol to pin the blame on. This is called denial.

In this phase, family members will also begin offensive behavior to limit or stop the drinking, in the belief that being more loving, taking on more responsibilities, blaming, acting out, becoming angry, or withdrawing will have some effect on the situation. This is called delusion. Alcoholism is the primary problem and nothing will change until it is dealt with.

What is most important in this stage is that family members begin consciously to take on the defensive roles in which they are most comfortable. In the first phase, you chose them blindly. Now you can put them on like a mask. The family has also begun to act only in response to the unpredictable mood shifts of the alcoholic. When he's up (lively, outgoing, aggressive, ambitious, grandiose, self-confident), you will feel down (lonely, quiet, alienated, depressed, passive, hesitant) and vice versa. On some level you begin to feel you're smothering your true feelings in order to cope, and you become angry, resentful, and emotionally confused. At this point, the disease really begins to affect the co-dependents.

When any attempt is made to confront him, the alcoholic manipulates the family in ways that help the denial and delusion continue. He'll become angry, so you shrink back or think, "Maybe he's right. Maybe I'm making too big a deal of this." Or he'll dump a load of guilt on you. Maybe he'll even cry. Tears, especially a man's tears, are quite powerful in this society. It's hard to stay angry when you're faced with them. Another effective ploy is making promises to stop drinking. And if the other manipulations fail, the alcoholic finds anything and everything to blame his drinking on. He may wind up pitting one family member against another.

All these moves make the family back off. You begin to make excuses for the chemical dependent's behavior, not only to the outside world but also to yourself. This behavior, which is called "enabling," allows the chemically dependent family member to keep on drinking. Enabling is the way in which the "family disease" keeps the dependent sick.

Paralleling the third, or *dependency*, phase in the drinker is the *compulsive* phase in the co-dependent. At that point, you become as locked into your defensive style as the drinker is into his drinking.

Privately, co-dependents blame the alcoholic for the way his disease makes him behave. They also begin to blame themselves for being the cause of the dependency. But the guiltier and more ashamed they become, the more unlikely it is that they will confront the alcoholic. At this point co-dependents have become so out of touch with those feelings of guilt and shame that when they're asked how things are going, typically they will say that everything is fine.

The counselors at Families in Crisis report stories of families who just kept opening their Christmas presents while a drunk father was knocking over the tree or who continued eating their holiday meal though an alcoholic mother was passed out at the table. Everyone just keeps playing the game.

Kids are the most likely to be in touch with the fact that something is wrong, but the adults in the family usually have excuses ready. "Dad has a tough job. He works hard all day." (And that gives him the right to terrorize us.) "Poor Mom. She's so busy taking care of us that she needs a little relaxation." (She gets so relaxed she slides right off the chair onto the floor, and Dad has to carry her up to bed.)

I once asked a childhood friend what he remembered of my father. He said he remembered that my dad drank a lot. And when I asked him how he thought I felt, he said, "You missed your dad. You loved him a lot. You were happy when he came home." The truth was I hated it when he came home, but to the outside world, I gave a different message: "He's a great guy, my dad."

Members of an alcoholic's family can't talk openly inside the family, and they certainly don't talk to outsiders about their problems. Typically, as the disease progressed, I stopped bringing friends home. I never told my best friends what was going on. You stop talking to people because you can't be honest with them. You are living a lie out of embarrassment ("How could my mom do all those terrible things?") or fear (that the alcoholic, or whoever in the family is protecting him, will "put you in your place").

The Families in Crisis counselors have a good opportunity to see how distorted a view families of chemical dependents may have. Working with the families before an Intervention, they form a mental image of the alcoholic or drug user. Often they expect some big bruiser to come through the door. Instead, in walks a very unprepossessing guy. The family has given the alcoholic so much power to manipulate their lives that they've made him into a huge monster.

The last state of alcoholism for the drinker is *using to feel normal*. For the co-dependent it's the stage at which the family's negative life-style feels completely normal to the members. It's often followed by an acute crisis, when everything goes wrong. This is when families break up and suicides occur. (I have been told that an extraordinary number of teenagers who commit suicide have at least one alcoholic parent.) This is the time when co-dependents crack up or turn to chemicals themselves. Or it's when they may finally be fortunate enough to reach out for help.

The signs of the family disease

Many of the signs of alcoholism that the user displays are mirrored in the alcoholic family, which also experiences *preoccupation, rigidity, increase in tolerance, loss of control,* and *defensiveness.*

When there is an alcoholic in the family, other members' *preoccupation* with the disease can take many forms:
· wondering where he is
· hoping the kids will be asleep when he gets home
· hiding the keys to the car
· hoping she's driving safely
· trying to limit social situations to those in which no liquor is served
· driving around town looking for the car in bar parking lots
· calling around town looking for him
· trying to get her to talk to a clergyman or psychologist
· marking bottles or diluting their contents
· hiding or breaking bottles
· handling the family finances so he won't have drinking funds
· wondering how her job is going
· taking pictures of him when he's drunk, to show him how awful he looks
· leaving self-help books around the house
· turning up the volume on public service announcements about alcoholism
· minimizing her drinking
· wondering when his good/bad behavior will start/stop
· changing your appearance to please him
· getting the kids to behave so he won't blow up at them

If you thought as much about your job as you do about an alcoholic family member, you'd probably have a good chance of becoming chairman of the board!

Even the children become preoccupied. They may not talk about it (in an alcoholic family, it's an unwritten rule that you don't), but you'll see them trying to engage alcoholic parents in activities that don't involve drinking. As some kids grow older, they want to be with the alcoholic—so they can keep an eye on him.

Co-dependents become *rigid* and stuck in their own pattern. They may repeatedly try to control the user, try to extract promises that he or she won't drink. They may try to protect the rest of the family from the consequences of the drinking, avoid social functions (not only so they won't be embarrassed but also so they won't risk being confronted about the situation), cover up or make excuses for the drinking. They may repeatedly blame the drinker, resorting to attacks or sarcasm, threats or silence. Or they may hold themselves aloof, becoming a saint, a supermom, or a self-righteous know-it-all. The family may get into a set routine in which a child sides regularly with one parent or the other. Everyone will take on a specific role.

Over the years, you *increase your tolerance* to the problem as well. At the beginning of your marriage, you might have been outraged if your husband stopped at a bar after work and came home a few minutes late. As the disease progresses, you accept shabby behavior as being not only normal but actually praiseworthy. You say to yourself, "Well, she stayed out all night twice this week, but she was home all weekend." If you had some distance on things, you'd see that this way of thinking is totally irrational, but you've adapted to this way of life.

You begin to tolerate unacceptable behavior in other areas. Perhaps you allow the alcoholic to take on fewer and fewer responsibilities at home. Or maybe you've accepted his contributing less and less money to the family—either because he's spending it on liquor or because the alcohol has caused him to have problems on the job. Maybe you're putting up with increasingly abusive behavior, constant anger and insults, or participating in sexual relations when you don't wan't to.

Loss of control for the alcoholic is a result of the addiction. For the co-dependent it's the result of addiction to the alcoholic. For both it results in conflict of values. The co-dependent now acts in ways that are not normal for him or her:

- lying to the alcoholic's boss
- lying to family and friends
- wishing the user were dead
- expressing anger at the alcoholic, then feeling remorseful
- thinking of suicide
- joining him or her in using chemicals
- ignoring the pain and hurt of the children
- abusing the children
- abandoning spiritual beliefs
- having an affair

If you have an alcoholic at home, you could probably add your own personal additions to this list, but you may find that difficult. You've probably become *defensive* about the alcoholic's behavior. You have started buying into the alibis and making excuses for her. Even if you manage to confront her one-on-one, you don't tell her what you're really feeling. Or you let her belittle you or sweet-talk you into silence. Or you can't follow through. You go to bed disgusted saying, "Never again. In the morning, I'm leaving." But morning comes, and you do nothing.

In my family, the unspoken message was: Cover up Dad's drinking and blame the problem on other things. We discussed his behavior plenty, but never the cause of it. Crazy, huh? It was better to consider him a louse than a drunk. Besides, I loved my mother and wanted her to feel okay, and I knew the best thing was not to criticize dad, but rather to find ways to praise him. We had a need to protect our family's image—not just to the outside world but to one another. In our hearts, though, we felt Dad was just a really mean guy who didn't love us.

I'm not the kind of person to sit down and write a *Daddy Dearest*. I don't mean to criticize my dad. With all the material I've laid out about alcoholism being a disease, how could I possibly blame him? Actually, I often have the feeling these days that my dad is watching over me, saying, "Good going, kid. I couldn't do it. You did." I'm sure he'd be proud of me.

I recall the stories about my great-grandfather leaving the kids in the horse-drawn carriage outside the saloon. He was an alcoholic too, but no one understood. No one sat down with us kids and explained what was going on with my dad, either; even then, no one understood.

For centuries people have been living tormented lives because they didn't know what was going on. People today could be much happier if they faced the facts, but so many can't. They keep the same cover-up going.

Nels Schlander tells me he has counseled many families that have come to him because on some level they are aware that something is wrong but can't put their finger on it. Because the spouse may hold down a good job (it could be factory work, it could be the presidency of a major corporation) and feels no negative consequences in that area from the drinking, the family denies that there is an alcohol problem. Home life is a mess, but the spouse and children have learned to live with the abnormal situation. There may be a fifteen-year history of drinking on a daily basis, but when Nels asks the family to come up with one specific example of it, they can't.

You will remember from the last chapter that one of the signs of alcoholism is blackouts. If Nels's examples aren't a form of blackout, I don't know what is. The co-dependents are blocking their painful memories and minimizing their hurts and disappointments. Some people actually manage to forget entire years. I met a recovering alcoholic who doesn't remember all three years of junior high school. He was living with a very abusive, chronic alcoholic father, and the only way he could deal with the situation was to pretend it never happened.

Other people don't forget; they play down the bad stuff. This is a form of what in the alcoholic is called euphoric recall. Looking back, they say, "Oh, it wasn't that bad." In my own family, my dad would disappear, sometimes for months at a time. Then he'd come home and keep a job for three weeks and all of a sudden, we'd be having family meetings and going to church and everyone had to be on time for meals. His past behavior was forgiven, and the illusion was created that since now he was holding down a job and was a regular at the dinner table, we had a "normal" family. We'd go along for a while, and then he'd start drinking again. The promise would be broken.

Just recently, a friend called, desperate for help. She

couldn't take her husband's drinking any longer. I left work and spent the afternoon helping her go over what had to be done step by step. Three days later, we were invited to her house for dinner. I couldn't believe my eyes. She said to her husband, "Darling, I'm going to have a scotch. Would you like yours straight or with water?" My mouth dropped. Clearly she had persuaded herself that things weren't really that bad after all. Have *you* ever expressed concern about someone's drinking to friends and then gone right ahead drinking with him or her? Be honest.

Like the alcoholic, co-dependents will sometimes try some drastic (but halfhearted) new approach, such as threatening separation or divorce if the drinking doesn't stop. But, like the alcoholic's vow to stop drinking, this won't happen. Or the co-dependent will attempt some change of his own— maybe something as small as moving up the family's dinner hour, hoping to cut down the drinking time.

Not only the psychological effects, but also the physical effects of the alcoholic are mirrored in the co-dependents: Ulcers, colitis, headaches, nervous breakdown, and other conditions are common.

Roles the family members play

Simply walking away from the alcoholic family doesn't resolve anything. If you do, you will probably still need help to overcome problems that are a result of peculiar coping habits you pick up from living with an alcoholic. There are four main styles of defensive behavior: Star, Black Sheep, Waif, and Good-time Charlie, and in the next few pages I'll describe them in their most extreme form.

A member of an alcoholic family isn't always doomed to failure. Some, in fact, achieve great success as a result of their lifelong roles as the family Star.

The Star is a super-achiever, is super-responsible, appears to be completely together, is a leader, and knows how to get her way. No wonder she's often a great success. But though she may seem to be the ideal child, underneath a Star is someone who can't acknowledge having problems and who racks up achievements to stay busy and hide suffering. That keeps her isolated and less vulnerable to pain.

The Star is often the oldest child in the family, the embodiment of the wish of the alcoholic—who is often a perfectionist—that, by God, his child will be perfect too. The child gets the message very early that you get a lot of praise and attention if you succeed and that you'll avoid anger if you avoid confrontation (such as telling Dad he drinks too much). The child becomes a perfectionist, too. He learns to follow the rules.

The Star is the one you go to for advice, the one who becomes the parent for everyone in the family. She may be the smart one, too. That way she can intellectualize the family's problems.

The role of the Star is to help maintain the illusion that the family is normal. At school as well as at home, such a child is a big achiever. It's easy for a school counselor to ignore this kind of kid (who needs help just as much as his trouble-making sibling) because his problems are tougher to spot. If the counselor suspects there's a chemical dependency problem in the family, he should try to open a dialogue with this child. Often a Star will appear to be popular, but deep down she's lonely because she never learned to have an open, trusting relationship. Look at her past experience: If you get too close to an alcoholic, you get hurt; if you depend on him to keep promises, you'll be disappointed.

The Star has the same high standards for others as for herself, and when people do fail her (as they will, at least occasionally), she feels betrayed. She knows you can't be open and honest, so she's learned to tell people what they want to hear. Then they'll like her and she can control them. She may be generous, because she's a people pleaser (she may even choose a helping career), but you can be sure she expects something in return—if not financially, then something that builds her self-esteem. Because the Star never achieves intimacy with others, she becomes an unhappy grown-up, a workaholic, a manipulator. It's hard being God.

I was the Star in my family. Good old Mary Ellen. Even though we were in total chaos, I felt I was very special. My mother always told me everything would be okay and one day I'd be Miss America, and I always bought that. I counseled my sisters and brothers, was everyone's protector, and told them how to act. I felt I was the responsible adult, the concerned one, the defender of my brothers and sisters, and the worrier. In high school—this is embarrassing for me to remember—my nickname was Ma.

As an adult, I always wanted my friends to think of me as Number One—very smart and everyone's best friend. I wanted to call the shots. I couldn't stand listening to other people. The other day I recalled how at one point I actually thought that the president of my firm preferred my company to his wife's. After all, I was the one who could give folks what they needed, tell them what they wanted to hear. It came as a rude awakening to discover that he would rather spend time with his wife than working and partying with me.

Yes, I was a Star. And despite all my achievements, I have always had the feeling that everything wasn't real, that it would end tomorrow. Because I needed to manipulate and control everyone, I wound up isolated, a person who never got any straight answers. People have a lot of fear about confronting a Star. They don't realize that underneath she's a pushover, because all she wants to do is please you.

Another family role is the Black Sheep. He helps keep the situation going by taking the focus off the alcoholic. Like the Star, what the Black Sheep gets out of his role is attention, although in his case the attention is negative. Often he's the only one in the family who will confront the alcoholic. He's the fighter. A friend told me that as a youth, he was on the porch with some friends when his dad came home drunk and said, "You think you're tough, don't you? You're not, and you never will be, until you can beat the old man." So he slugged his father and knocked him over the railing.

Black Sheep may be problems in school, nonconformists, rule-breakers. They lie, act defiant, get into trouble, and may reject their families, who usually think the worst of them. The Black Sheep considers himself pretty awful, too, but he doesn't know any alternate way to behave.

These are the kids who pay the biggest price for living in an alcoholic family. Because they crave love, they are very susceptible to peer pressure. They are emotionally dependent on their friends, who initially may be attracted to these kids because they're daring and "macho." But because of their poor social skills and explosive personalities, they have a hard time developing nurturing, intimate, cooperative relationships.

They are the first to leave home. They're the ones who start drinking or using drugs at an early age. They may try to find the loving, lasting relationship they need through precocious sex or by having a child when they're very young.

My brother Johnny, a recovering alcoholic and a former children's counselor, says that when kids are chronically in trouble, the first thing a counselor should do is find out what's going on at home. While a kid may be rebellious by nature, chances are there's something else happening. Since the first rule in an alcoholic's home is never to tell the truth, chances are you won't get the real story from the kid; you must talk to his friends.

Johnny knows the situation well because Black Sheep was his role. When he was in school, my dad's drinking behavior was causing our family many problems. Sometimes Johnny would be up till three or four in the morning. He couldn't do his schoolwork, or he'd fall asleep in class. He was always in trouble. He was using drugs and alcohol. The general opinion was that Johnny Higginbotham was a really rotten student. Still, I know if anyone had come up and said, "Is anything wrong?" he'd have said, "Absolutely not." He'd have defended our dad.

Since I was the Star and was very active in school, I made sure Johnny got into the best clubs. I wanted him to ride on my shirttails. He rebelled against that horribly and (like most people) did what he wanted to. He chose his friends from the wrong side of the tracks, so to speak.

Johnny was kicked out of a lot of high schools. His personal needs weren't met because all the attention went to Dad. Secretly, Johnny felt guilty. "No wonder Dad drinks, when he has a rotten kid like me."

The Waif chooses a third route, one the family is inclined to ignore because she's such a relief. To outsiders, she may simply appear to be peaceful. She stays out of the way, she's passive, quiet, withdrawn. She keeps her distance. She's independent. She stays neutral in the family debates. She may escape into fantasy. She's the one you'll find in her room—watching TV, writing poetry, or staring off into space.

Of all the family members, she's the one most inclined to grow up feeling you have to lie, put your best foot forward, play the game, let people know you're okay or else they won't like you. She's supersensitive to everyone else's feelings and inclined to deny her own, since they won her no attention. She's generally immature and either plays with younger children or has no friends at all. But she never admits to feeling lonely or unprotected, for fear of being beaten up or shouted down. I know one daughter of a violent alcoholic whose family had to leave the house occasionally, and without notice, in the middle of the night. Apparently once she was stuck outdoors in the wintertime without warm clothes, so for the remainder of her young life—no matter what the temperature—she went to bed wearing her socks and a robe.

The Waif may hang out with other kids from alcoholic homes; there, at least, is a place he fits in. If the Waif discovers chemicals, he finds they take the pain away. When drunk, he withdraws further, unlike the Black Sheep, who becomes belligerent and gets into trouble with the law, or the Star, who is a gregarious drinker. The Waif is the secret drinker, the person that no one realizes is alcoholic.

My sister fell into this category. She tried to keep the peace and wound up withdrawing into herself more than the rest of us. In typical Waif fashion, she married an overbearing spouse. As an adult, the Waif is probably pushed around a lot but never complains. He carries around a lot of repressed anger because he feels really used and abused. This is the kind of person who blows his brains out and afterward everyone says, "He was such a great guy, a good child, a wonderful person, never caused anyone any trouble."

A fourth typical role in alcoholic families is Good-Time Charlie, the kid who brings some fun into the family and survives on his charm and humor. He's never taken too seriously, since he's regarded as having a limited understanding of what's going on. Often by the time this child comes along, everyone is in complete denial. If the alcoholic behaves in a frightening way, the child who turns into a Good-Time

Charlie is assured that there's nothing to worry about, that's just how things are. He grows up wondering who is crazy, he or they.

Like the Star, the Good-Time Charlie knows how to get positive attention. He makes the family look good. He turns conversations that might be painful into a joke. He might even laugh at the behavior of the drunk. But underneath he's nervous. He's simply managed to cover up his fear with humor. The alcoholic's shouting and threats bother him, and he's the kind of kid who's accident-prone, spilling milk, knocking over the plants, dropping things. He's often diagnosed as hyperactive and given Ritalin. When he's a little older, he doesn't get things done. He procrastinates. It takes him all day to mow the lawn.

He feels unimportant. He's never taken seriously, he's never learned how to cope with stress, and he needs a lot of attention—a formula that makes him childlike even as an adult. He often seems to be going nowhere. Still, people are attracted to him because he's fun and he has wonderful antennae for sensing the feelings of others. But he can't get into a deep, nurturing relationship because he's lost touch with himself and his true feelings. He might turn to another addiction—such as overeating—or to alcohol. If he drinks, he's a fun drunk.

My feeling is that in many families, the roles switch around. For example, when I tired of being the Star, I let my sister have that role and I became the Black Sheep. I was still also the Good-Time Charlie at times.

When Dad got out of line, my brother remembers that I would go up to him and say, "Okay, big tough guy, just show me how tough you are when I tell you to get out of this house!" For a period in junior high school, my grades dropped, I was very rebellious, and I hung out with the "tough" kids. Any of my old, "tough" friends who might pick up this book should realize I liked them dearly, and still do, but the fact is I didn't hang out with *any* kids who didn't have alcoholic parents themselves. While I broke away from that crowd in high school, I was still always drawn to the kids who had problems at home.

During my junior high school days, if I wasn't getting into

trouble, life was like a Coke without the fizz. Even when my behavior straightened out, I had a need for something to be going on all the time. I think that because of my dad's behavior, I grew up used to a certain level of excitement, used to having all hell break loose all the time. I spent a lot of time in treatment getting over that need.

The important thing about any of these family roles is that they help the other family members survive by masking their feelings and covering their pain. Kids from such families grow up confused and without appropriate role models. You develop a feeling of trust by trusting your parents, but you can't trust your parents when you come from an alcoholic home. You can only guess at what's "normal."

If there are children involved in your situation, knowing that they will pay the consequences should make you even more determined to stop the one you love from drinking. If you don't deal with the chemical dependency, you may even be letting your children in for abuse, since abuse does go hand in hand with alcohol. In extreme cases, the abuse becomes physical and sexual. If that's the situation in your home, *you must get help immediately. Your life may be in danger.*

But emotional abuse is bad enough. If you allow the dependent to continue his behavior without helping him to change, you're acting irresponsibly. The best thing to do is to get some help for your alcoholic and yourself. You can start by being completely honest with the counselors at the treatment center. They've heard it all, and most have lived it firsthand. They are usually dependents or co-dependents themselves.

It may take years for the children of alcoholics to get into real trouble, perhaps even until they're in their thirties, but they won't avoid problems. Statistics prove that. They may function perfectly well in the workplace, but they're usually dysfunctional in relationships. Children of alcoholics don't understand give and take. Their whole lives have been centered around one person. Not only do they not know how to be spouses, but also they don't know how to parent.

A counselor told me she didn't want to be like her mother, who married an alcoholic, so she chose her role models from television. She would grow up to be a wonderful wife and parent like Mary Tyler Moore on "The Dick Van Dyke Show," making meals, taking care of everyone, having a child like little Richie. (What irony. Not only did Mary check into a treatment center, but Dick Van Dyke was also a drinker.)

Children of alcoholics are desperately in need of help. They'll turn to the nonalcoholic parent (if there is one; the number of two-alcoholic families is growing) for comfort, love, and support. If you're that parent, chances are you're caught in the family disease yourself. You don't have those things to give. The kids will eventually catch on. And I believe at that point they'll turn on you, too. They will realize that the nondrinking parent has been the primary enabler.

What is enabling? Who are enablers?

I used the word "enabling" before, when I mentioned that in a chemical dependent's family everyone tends to make excuses or cover up for that person's behavior. In such a family, however, there is usually someone who stands out as the primary enabler. While everyone in the family to some extent enables the alcoholic to keep using, the primary enabler protects both the alcoholic and other family members from the negative effects of the disease. Also, the other members of the household usually look to the primary enabler for cues as to how to treat the alcoholic.

The primary enabler is usually a parent or spouse, but it could be someone else—a child, relative, an employer, a family friend, a minister or doctor. It could be anyone who loves the alcoholic. These people start out with good intentions. They want to protect the one they love. They don't want to acknowledge that a problem exists. They defend the drinking as normal or as what anyone would do at a party or on vacation. Or they explain it's the result of too much stress, or just "a phase," or peer pressure. They consider every act of intoxication as an isolated episode, not as a pattern, and they don't accept that the person is an alcoholic.

The enabling may start in small ways: The alcoholic has drunk too much, so the enabler calls his employer and makes his excuses for him. If he gets sick, she cleans up the mess. If he loses a job or a friend, she'll help blame that on anything but the drinking. He's had a money problem, so the enabler bails him out. The enabler will drive the drunk home and post the bond if he's got a DWI. As a result, the dependent person doesn't suffer any consequences of his use. The laundry is done, the bills are being paid, the job is intact, the family's needs are being met.

I was surrounded by enablers—the president of my company, my mother, my sister, and most of my friends. If I goofed up, my agent or attorney would handle it. If I missed work, one of my co-workers would cover. If I got into trouble, my mom was there to tell me I was okay, and if I did have a few problems, well, if I'd lose some weight, everything would be fine.

But looking back, I'd have to give Sherm top position. If I was hung over, he cared for me. If I threw up, he'd hold my head. No matter what happened, he was there to reassure me. And yet my marriage was crumbling and I blamed him for my problems. At the time I didn't know I was dependent on him. I believed I could get along much better without him, although a little voice inside occasionally reminded me that without him, I'd really have to face the music. Sherm created an increasingly comfortable environment for me. As I told him recently, I'm sure he never would have gotten me help. In the name of love, and because he knew no better, he'd have let me go on until I lost everything, perhaps until I died. I'm surprised that I ever did manage to realize that I was in trouble.

I remember one birthday, after my father had gone off for six months. He called from the Flame Bar and asked to be picked up. My mother asked me to go get him. My father was a large man, very handsome. He came walking out of the bar with a big grin on his face, hopped in the car, and greeted me with a laugh.

"I've been out riding the rodeo," he told me. I knew he could throw the bull, all right. I remember staring at him, thinking how nutty he was. We came home and found my mother sitting in the kitchen drinking coffee. He joined her, and I knew what would happen. She'd sit there with her coffee, and he'd start on the booze, and then there would be the fights. This time I said, "It's him or me, Mom. If he stays, I'm going."

"I just don't know what to do," she said. "We've got to help your dad. He deserves to be happy and to live a really nice life, so we've got to help him again." Of course no one ever confronted him with his irresponsibility in abandoning us as he did. Eventually my father was in intolerable pain: He realized what was happening because of his drinking, so he left. But my mother couldn't do anything for him. She, too, did what she knew how to do—love and protect him. She was one terrific enabler.

The alcoholic rationalizes, and the enabler believes. The alcoholic represses, and the enabler feels crazy. The alcoholic projects, and the enabler believes it's his fault. The alcoholic minimizes, and the enabler "understands" and lends support. The alcoholic is irresponsible, and the enabler protects.

Until I got help, I was Sherm's enabler. I felt guilty, because I believed he drank because the life had gone from our marriage and because I was away so much of the time. Since I hadn't much time for him, what could he do but drink? If I did something Sherm didn't like, I could count on his going on a toot; again, his drinking was my fault. I believed that if I behaved, he would behave, and I allowed him to blame his drinking behavior on me. I know now that he would have been drinking if he'd been married to Mother Teresa. Our life together was like life in an insane asylum. Only the doctors were missing.

Mothers are wonderful enablers because the very fact of being a parent (despite the rumors, you don't have to be Jewish) makes you vulnerable to guilt. At Families in Crisis the staff saw a woman whose daughter was a drug addict. Her mom had all kinds of excuses for her. "Every time she borrows something, it breaks. That's the kind of thing that happens to Bobbie. She's just an unfortunate gal." She blamed her daughter's isolation and alienation on the fact that she was four years younger than her sister. Also, she had a hard time in school. "She was a slow learner." (This gal had been smoking marijuana for eight years, since the age of thirteen, which doesn't tend to make you all that sharp.)

Some of the most effective enablers are the parents of alcoholics. They see only what they want to see in their grown-up baby, and they'll love him right into the grave. I know a mother who sees her alcoholic son as a great salesman even though, because of his drinking, the only job he can hold is in the family business, which the mother runs. She makes excuses for him and sees the people who refuse to enable him as The Enemy. By supporting his habit with a paycheck, she makes herself powerful and maintains the illusion of her own self-worth, which she would find harder to do if she had a son who was unemployed. The son went into treatment after an Intervention, but the mother didn't stick to her guns, and when he began to drink to prove he *wasn't* alcoholic (somehow, that made sense to her), she let him keep his job.

The family is planning an Intervention on the mother, to let her know she is the number one reason her son is still drinking. I looked right into this woman's eyes one day and said, "By keeping him going, you are allowing your son to die. When he does, you will be responsible." She said, "Then he will die, because I will not fire him."

This woman's husband died of alcoholism. Her other children are recovering alcoholics. Still, she refuses to see her role in all of this. You show me the mother of an alcoholic and I will show you a very sick mother. You show me the child of an alcoholic and I will show you a sick child. You show me the husband or wife of an alcoholic, and I will show you a sick spouse.

I have read that the problem of alcoholism is growing rapidly in women under thirty. They're in the workplace, so they've gotten the green flag to drink. It's the thing to do. Most typically their parents are their enablers, but a boyfriend, a co-worker, or a sibling can play the role, too. I know of a young woman whose sister used to lend her money, clean her apartment, type her term papers, substitute at the restaurant where she worked, and lie to their parents, saying that some of the bottles they had found in the room the two girls shared belonged to her.

As time goes on, the primary enabler takes on more and more responsibilities for the alcoholic and gives up personal needs and concerns in order to do the job. Enabling is very hard work. What's the payoff? For one thing, you don't have to confront the situation. For another, you stay in control. And also, you get points for being a martyr. People tell you you're a saint. Unfortunately for them, many enablers don't know any other way of behaving. They went from an alcoholic home to an alcoholic marriage. Like Tarzan, who grew up believing everyone swung from trees, when you grow up in an abnormal situation, you have no idea of what "normal" is.

Eventually, all the primary enabler's feelings are simply responses to the dependent. He gives the alcoholic the power to determine his reactions, feelings, and moods just as the alcoholic gives that power to his alcohol. Nels Schlander told me that once, conducting a workshop for women, he blurted out, "How on earth can you give all your power away?" They had become nonpersons. They'd lost their power to make decisions. They didn't know how to act, just how to react.

The primary enabler's defensive behavior consists of taking on more and more responsibility, giving the impression that he is completely together, and acting self-righteous. This behavior gives him relief, just as alcohol gives relief to the alcoholic.

If you're a primary enabler, you feel a sense of importance but at the same time, on some level, you feel resentful of your burden and of how your own needs are being sacrificed to another person's. You cover your feelings—hurt, rejection, and loneliness—by complaining and blaming, which make you feel you are doing something. But no progress is being made. You keep busy and focus on the dependent, but eventually you become afraid.

You worry about what will happen to the alcoholic and worry about what will happen to you. (Could you support the family and keep the house payments covered if something happened?) Your self-esteem is low. You may feel embarrassed, inadequate, filled with self-doubt. You may even become self-destructive: eating too much or not eating at all, paying no attention to your physical self, perhaps to the point of illness, maybe even beginning to use chemicals along with the dependent. Maybe you accompany him to bars or get hooked on prescription antidepressants.

You feel trapped in the situation and your resentment makes you bitter and cold—eventually, you feel only hopelessness and despair.

Enablers outside the family

Although alcoholism is a family disease, enablers aren't necessarily family members. Unfortunately, they may be the very people that you would turn to for help, such as doctors, psychologists, and ministers. Many doctors can't recognize alcoholism until the patient is in the chronic stage and turning yellow from liver disease. I hear that often if they actually do diagnose an alcoholic earlier, they really don't want to work with him, because they just don't know what to do. Alcoholism is one of our nation's leading health problems, but only a small percentage of medical students takes courses on it. That just blows my mind (and yours, I hope).

I know most doctors do ask their patients if they drink, and how much. The alcoholic says he drinks "socially," or has just a few to relax after work. He's seeing the doctor about a physical symptom of the disease—not about the alcoholism itself. Assuming he's even aware of it, the alcoholic (and his family, too) as a matter of habit conceals the addiction. Alcoholics and their families may visit the doctor repeatedly to complain of depression, high blood pressure, diarrhea, night sweats, headaches, and stomachaches, without the doctor putting two and two together. The doctor isn't a mind-reader. Without input from the family, he can't diagnose the underlying problem.

Often the doctor prescribes tranquilizers or other mood-altering drugs to treat the various complaints. Chances are the alcoholic has a dual addiction. If you're hooked on booze, you're addicted to drugs, whether you've used them or not; and vice versa. (Many an alcoholic finds that the combination of drugs and alcohol, though extremely dangerous, gives him a better time. He doesn't get drunk as quickly. Some alcoholics sniff cocaine so they can drink more without appearing bombed. And people on the wagon may believe it's okay to take what they call "social" drugs—how can they be "social" when they're against the law?—such as pot, coke, etc., and find themselves equally addicted.) As for the others in the family, they're good candidates to become dependents themselves. The last thing they need is mood-altering prescriptions.

Psychiatrists are M.D.s, and they have a license to write prescriptions also. A lot of them medicate their patients instead of dealing with the primary problem. A recovering alcoholic told me she'd seen a dozen psychiatrists and been given all sorts of drugs before the thirteenth said, "You're not nuts. You're an alcoholic. Why don't you go into treatment?" She did, and she quit drinking. She doesn't need shrinks since she stopped acting like a fruit cake.

I believe there are some great counselors—psychiatrists, psychologists, or psychotherapists—but you'll also find a few who are inadequate. An alcoholic is an expert liar, and the therapist won't ever get the real story, since he won't talk to the family and the employer. (I've never been able to figure out how a therapist can get the full picture without talking to the people surrounding the one he's treating.) The time on the couch is usually filled with lies or at least a distorted view of reality.

At St. Mary's Hospital, when relatives of the patient arrive for Family Week, which is a kind of accelerated therapy, you're asked to refrain from alcohol or drug use during the process. The point of it is to get in touch with your feelings—and chemicals block those feelings. Yet I find it's the rare therapist who says, "I can't treat you unless you agree to abstain from alcohol while working with me." They don't, in my opinion, because they'd lose too many patients. Alcoholics act crazy as hell and usually have so many problems they're good for more than an hour a week.

In all fairness, my psychologist, Etta Martin, who practices in Minneapolis, was a major factor in my making the decision to get help. She has a handle on alcoholism and drug addiction. But I never would have seen her in the first place had I not known the heat was on me. One Thursday morning, just before she was leaving on vacation, I made her a promise that while she was gone, I would not drink. Why I made that promise I'll never know, but the next day, Friday, was the day I hit bottom—and I haven't had a drink since. It was Etta, who fortunately was still in town, who helped me make arrangements to check into Hazelden.

A good therapist is a blessing. A bad one only prolongs the agony. A good one recognizes that the only known, proven way to help an alcoholic is treatment followed by AA and aftercare. For me, those have been enough, but many alcoholics find additional one-on-one counseling is terrific. After you get out of treatment, you need all the support you can get. What is dangerous is when a person chooses counseling only, in place of AA. AA should be the number one priority.

Often families of alcoholics reach out for help to the church. Some churches direct these families to Al-Anon (many churches supply space for such meetings, though they are not directly involved), and others counsel hanging in and bearing with the suffering of others. Some go to the extreme of suggesting that the family submit to the authority of the man of the family even if he's an alcoholic. No matter how bad the situation gets, you're supposed to stay with the drinker and pray for his healing. If that's not enabling, I don't know what is. While their hearts might be in the right place, their advice is not very helpful.

Unfortunately, like many other professionals, clergymen often don't have the slightest idea of how to help the families and friends of an alcoholic. If religion had all the answers on alcoholism, there would have been no need for AA to come into being. Most clergymen are uncomfortable with the idea of alcoholism. They believe what they have been taught, that alcoholism is a sin. Branding the alcoholic a sinner has enabled many families and their alcoholics to remain sick until death did them part.

Every single day over the past two years I have read and studied the Bible, and I believe I have at least a little knowledge of what it says. It clearly points out that God creates crises that force you to take a close look at the way you are living. (Those sound like Interventions to me.) And although the Bible asks us to bear with the sufferings of others, it doesn't say you must suffer along with a person who won't do anything to change. As far as being submissive to your husband, I would like to point out that the Bible says husbands are to love their wives as Christ loved the Church. I challenge you to show me an alcoholic (or any spouse, for that matter) who lives up to that responsibility.

The Bible refers to drunkenness as a sin. I believe it is. You can't get much lower than being a drunk and running through the lives of others like a tornado, leaving destruction behind. An alcoholic, though, has a disease. He doesn't have any choice. If your minister or rabbi doesn't believe that, you should know that not all clergymen agree on this issue. Many are recovering alcoholics who finally sobered up with the help of AA. I urge you to talk to a spiritual counselor with a chemical dependency background (you can usually find one through a treatment center).

In every denomination, there are clergymen who don't know how to help. They may try at first and then eventually, like everyone else, throw up their hands in total disappointment and frustration. The families of alcoholics who still attend church (most just send their children) may reach out to their minister about family problems, depression, and feelings of hopelessness. Instead of beating around the bush or playing God, the minister should be up-front and direct them to Al-Anon, with its proven record of success, and to Intervention counselors. Families would get help so much sooner. Instead, they get advice based on the personal beliefs of the speaker.

I wish all religious leaders would truly embrace the idea that God uses all types of people and organizations, not just men of the cloth, to do his work. There is the story of a man who is clinging to the roof of his house during a terrible flood. A boat comes by and offers to pick him up, but he refuses. "God will send me help," he says. A second boat comes by and he refuses that as well. Finally, the waters swell up so high that he is drowned.

On Judgment Day, when he sees God, he says, "Oh, Lord, I waited for you to send help, but I waited in vain." God says, "But I did send help. I sent two boats for you." An enlightened religious leader should help you recognize your boat, in the form of AA or Intervention counseling.

I've heard of a few—very few—miraculous healings. His craving for booze may disappear, but the alcoholic and those around him (including the clergy) many times are deluded into believing he can now drink "socially" because he is "cured." An alcoholic who believes this will wind up right where he left off. The disease is progressive and incurable and nothing—not even the strength of one's religious beliefs can change those facts.

One minister I know of sent a letter asking that he not be invited to parties where liquor would be served. He felt that it was wrong for him to be talking to kids about using when their parents were home abusing. He was trying to put families together while drinking was splitting them apart. Attending drinking parties would put him in the role of an enabler, he felt, and I agree with the stand he took. His role is to be a leader, and he follows his own advice. How many clergymen can say the same thing?

Certain clergymen become uncomfortable when I bring up AA, and it breaks my heart to hear religious organizations knock it. Obviously, they know nothing about AA and the 12 Steps. I attend both regularly, and I can tell you that I have seen as much spirituality in AA as in church, and far more honesty and humility. The Bible teaches you to take care whom you judge, as you, too, will be judged. So before anyone shoots off his mouth about AA, Al-Anon, or Intervention, he would be wise to investigate the facts.

I've seen some good ministers lead their people to treatment and AA and butt out once they've done so. And I've also seen ministers set someone's recovery back five years by looking the other way about drinking or preaching sin. Most of them want to lead a large flock, and they know if they get honest about problem drinking, they may lose members. Or they just don't want to hurt feelings by telling it like it is. Or they too come from an alcoholic family and are themselves caught up in the games co-dependents play.

Many clergymen are alcoholics. One of our clergymen was recently charged with a DWI after crashing his car into a storefront. He made the front pages of the newspaper, and everyone was gossiping. The man has shown signs of alcoholism for years. His face is red and lined with veins, and he's been intoxicated publicly many times. The church could have done an Intervention and helped him avoid a public humiliation, but he *still* hasn't gotten help. Like a classic enabler, the church has considered these episodes to be isolated instances of intoxication and not a pattern of harmful dependency. The clergyman is not recognized as a chemical dependent but as someone who uses alcohol to cope with stress and lets things get a little out of hand now and then.

An employer can be a terrific enabler because he's a powerful person in the alcoholic's life. If despite his drinking, an alcoholic is doing well at work, his boss can reassure him that he's okay. I know one top editor in New York who drinks on the job and everyone knows it. Since she's great at what she does, and no one actually ever sees her drink, the situation continues. I'm sure no one will talk to her about her drinking until she nearly drops dead at her desk.

I was the boss of my firm, but my business advisors became my reality base and enablers. If they acted as if I were doing fine, that was good enough for me, and I stopped worrying about whether the alcohol was a problem. I especially liked it when one of them took me into his confidence and told me that other people might have expressed some concern about my drinking, but that he assured them I was under control.

I read that a longtime employee of a brewing company died and the autopsy showed the cause of death was cirrhosis of the liver. His widow brought a law suit against the brewery, claiming that the policy of free beer on the job killed him. I would like to assure her that the cause of death was not the free beer but her husband's alcoholism and, to a lesser degree, enabling co-workers who made it easy for this guy to drink. Whether or not he worked at a brewery, this man would have been an alcoholic. Plenty of alcoholics manage to drink on the job even when they have to pay for their own booze. The amazing part is that they manage to get their jobs done nevertheless and no one calls them on their drinking. It happens every day.

If you're an employer, ask yourself if you're enabling an employee who may be alcoholic:

· Did you ever question yourself because an assigned task wasn't carried out properly? Or wonder whether, or defend yourself as to whether, your instructions to the person were clear enough?

· Do you pass over him or her in assigning tasks; or do it yourself to make sure it's done and done right?

· Do you fail to trust his word?

· Do you cover up rather than make an issue of job performance? Do you feel sympathetic to family problems that affect the person's performance?

· Are you uncomfortable (embarrassed, sympathetic, angry) at the idea of meeting the person's spouse?

· Do you feel you have to control yourself from blowing up at him or her?

· Are you relieved when this employee goes on vacation?

· Did you ever consider having this employee transferred for a vague reason such as "He just doesn't fit in any more"?

· Do you spend personal time worrying about this employee?

· Is this employee accident-prone?

· Are you uncomfortable giving this person an automatic raise?

· Do you wonder whether the employee's problems are personal and not your affair?

· Do you feel uncomfortable about the person because you are aware of serious financial problems—garnishments, etc.?

· Have you been embarrassed by the person at a company function? Or been reluctant to include the person in a company function?

· Is this person usually the bartender at office parties?

I believe all companies should have an alcoholism policy. It should state that the company recognizes that alcoholism is a disease and that treatment is covered by insurance. It should also state that if anyone himself is in trouble or a co-worker spots the signs of alcoholism in another worker, he can go for help (in confidence).

Because so many people can avoid the consequences of their alcoholism, society itself may be considered a great enabler. There were 23,000 deaths from alcohol-related car crashes in 1984, and estimates are that 65 percent of those killed in single-car accidents were legally drunk. The number one cause of death in young people between the ages of fifteen and twenty-four is drunk driving.

On the day after Christmas, 1985, *20/20* aired a segment called "It Isn't Your Fault"—a show that blamed the server of alcoholic beverages (the restaurant or bar, or the hostess or waiter) for drunk driving accidents.

On the show, a drunk driver, a person hit and injured by the driver, and the restaurant owner who served the driver were brought together. Within minutes the first two ganged up on the third. The driver said it should have been obvious at the restaurant that he was drunk and that the restaurant owner should have cut him off.

Later in the segment, an attorney who had legislated cases against bar owners, a bartender who had attended courses on spotting drunken behavior, and a newscaster were asked to select which people at a bar ordering drinks they believed were legally intoxicated. They failed to do so. If one of the drinkers happened to be an alcoholic, they would have been even less likely to spot him, particularly if he was an early or middle stage drinker. Alcoholics have a huge tolerance and can drink without appearing drunk. They can hide their drunkenness masterfully. But they are still dangerous behind the wheel.

Until the problem drinker is held responsible for his behavior, we are enabling him, but it's the bartenders and servers of booze who are now being held accountable. I'm not actually against this. If insurance rates go up for bars—I think a more accurate description is "filling stations"—then so be it. (If all the alcoholics got help and quit drinking, the bars would close down anyway—60 percent of the drinks are bought by 10 percent of the population.) But I'm not sure this kind of law will do much good.

Public awareness of the effects of alcohol may be raised, and social drinkers may recognize that they shouldn't drive when they've had a few. Hostesses may be a little more conscientious about not pushing liquor on people. Maybe the nonalcoholic will not get into trouble as a result, but the alcoholic is a totally different story.

A New York bar installed a coin machine. When you feed it a quarter and breathe into it, it lets you know if you're sober enough to drive home. The regulars in the bar wouldn't get near that machine with a ten-foot swizzle stick. "I'm not blowing in," said one woman. "All it ever says is DON'T DRIVE." The bartender commented, "Mostly people who don't drink much use it."

Some people are now trying to pin blame on a host who serves a guest too much to drink. Well, you may offer only one drink, but how do you know how much your guest has had *before* he shows up at your place? And how do you know if he's sneaking drinks? Besides, I don't know a host in the world who can stop an alcoholic from drinking. If he closes the bar, the alcoholic will find another one.

Another problem is that many alcoholics start an evening believing they'll have only a couple of drinks so they don't make plans for driving home. Plenty of recovering alcoholics admit they drove when they were drunk. And over 50 percent of those who are stopped are let go (more women, I'm sure, than men) even though they are legally drunk. That's really a shame, since it could be the turning point for many.

Now they've got some $295 device that sits on a car's dashboard. You blow into the mouthpiece for four seconds before turning the key. A green light starts the ignition and a red light stalls the car. I understand the device is popular with fleet owners, drivers who already have a DWI, and parents of teenagers. The money would be better spent getting these people some help. It's a gimmick and only promotes abuse.

I think the road blocks the police are setting up are great. People with a certain blood level of alcohol should have to enter treatment even if the state has to pay for it. It may cost money, but in the long run it will save billions. The 1984 cost to the U.S. economy from alcoholism and alcohol abuse, in terms of health care, lost productivity, crime, and property damage was $120 billion according to the National Council on Alcoholism, up from the 1980 cost (adjusted to reflect 1984 dollars) of $89.5 billion.

I wish the government would spend big bucks on public relations campaigns to combat all the junk coming from the alcohol industry. According to an article by Diane Broughton in the April 1986 issue of *Alcoholism and Addiction* magazine, there is a public service spot played on soft rock stations (whose listeners are teenagers) funded by the American Council on Science and Health. The spot says, "Don't drink and drive. Alcoholism can cause cirrhosis of the liver," but it signs off with the message that total abstinence isn't necessary for good health because tests have shown that moderate drinkers are actually healthier. What isn't said is that anyone who drinks can become an alcoholic. Nor does the spot say what "moderate" drinking means. On investigation, the writer found out that the money boys behind the American Council on Science and Health were representatives of the alcoholic beverages industry.

I wish we could see the number of deaths due to alcohol and drugs on the front pages of every newspaper. I feel the public would eventually get sick and tired enough to do something. If chemical dependency didn't exist, I think there'd probably be a news shortage anyway. Just today, I noticed one story about three basketball players who were charged with rape after a wild party, a top executive charged with embezzling, and a football coach saying that he had to let the cat out of the bag (good for him!) and reveal that twelve of his top players have serious drug problems.

The dependent and the enabler

You'd think that the dependent person would look to the enabler as his helper, but he has tremendously negative feelings about himself and unconsciously winds up projecting them on the enabler—especially when the enabler makes some kind of attempt to confront him.

· "If you cared about me more than you do about the kids and your family, maybe I wouldn't drink."

· "You're giving me so much work, I have to drink at lunch."

· "You can't control the kids, so I drink to relieve the stress."

· "School stinks and you don't have any tolerance for me and my friends, so what's the big deal if I smoke grass?"

· "If you took better care of yourself, maybe I wouldn't turn to the bottle for companionship."

Anger relieves the user's stress temporarily but also creates more pain. And the fact that both people believe that the dependent "hates" the enabler puts the focus on the enabler's behavior and allows the disease to continue.

One of the counselors I spoke to said that when he was drinking, his wife had been reduced to the point where she couldn't even handle something as simple as the grocery shopping. She was a very competent lady, but in those days he believed (and convinced her) that she was the most wicked and messed-up thing on the face of this earth. Though he performed his job well, when it came to family life he was totally irresponsible. On Friday night he'd tell her he wouldn't be around to listen to her complaints. Then he'd spend the weekend getting charged up and come home Sunday night to sleep it off. Throughout their marriage she yelled and screamed, but she never once told him to get any help. Today, she tells him that he didn't love her because he didn't sober up for her, and he can't make her realize that he didn't have a choice. *She* had the choice—to get him some help—but she didn't make it.

Some enabling spouses do leave the alcoholic. Women are less likely to do so, probably because they're worried about coping financially, but I wish I could tell all of them that as the disease progresses your "breadwinner" eventually may not be able to bring home the bread. Women also probably grow more emotionally dependent. They grow "accustomed to his face: His smiles, his frowns, his ups, his downs"—and his breath.

Once he's said good riddance to the alcoholic, an enabling spouse (or child) may believe he will be able to lead a normal, healthy life. But statistics show that unless he too gets help and takes responsibility for his role in the addiction, he may become involved with another alcoholic or addictive relationship and carry these addictive symptoms along with him. Even if he doesn't link up with an alcoholic, he will find someone whose behavior is otherwise abusive.

Of course, you don't believe this. You say to yourself, "The last thing I'm going to do is get involved with another person with a drinking problem." You swear on a stack of Bibles as high as the Empire State Building that it won't happen again. But you'll be attracted to that kind of person unless you get help. Nels Schlander tells me that he often talks to women whom he's helped deal with an ex-husband who's alcoholic. In the course of conversation, he'll ask, "Are you seeing someone?" If they say yes, and he pursues it, the woman will inevitably admit that the new guy drinks. If there's just one person with a drinking problem in a room with one hundred people, an enabler will find him! They have a radar. They think, "This is my kind of guy." They're comfortable with him.

Worse, if the enabler is a woman (either the wife or daughter of an alcoholic), she'll carry those habits into child-rearing and raise a whole new generation with similar problems.

If you recognize yourself here, please let me assure you that up to now you were blameless because you didn't know what was going on. At this point, you should have a clearer picture of the situation. It's now your responsibility to do something. You can't do anything for the alcoholic unless you do something for yourself first. *You must act.* You must begin to tell the alcoholic what you see and how you feel.

Living with an alcoholic, you may not realize that you could be living another kind of life—much different, and much better. You may have convinced yourself that what you have is fine. Particularly if you came from an alcoholic home, you may think your life isn't so bad compared to what you grew up with. Please: Don't compare. The best of a bad lot is *still* not good enough. Besides, no matter how things are now, they'll get worse if the drinking isn't checked.

I was with a friend married to an alcoholic, and I started talking about some of the problems I'm dealing with. She didn't want to hear the details. She just wanted to assure me that everything would be okay. That's how she runs her own life, on blind faith.

Nothing makes me crazier than when I hear people saying of an alcoholic or drug user, "Oh, so-and-so will be okay. He's just going through growing pains," or "He's just having a rough time right now," or "He tells me he'll be better and I believe him."

"What makes you think he'll be okay?" I ask. They tell me

they "just know," and if I ask them how they know, they tell me they "just have a feeling." *My* feeling is that they're completely deluding themselves. The first step toward doing something for the one you love is breaking through your own denial. The way to start that is to get in touch with your feelings.

5/
Exploring Your Feelings

Exploring your own feelings may seem irrelevant to you. After all, you bought this book because you are concerned about someone else. But what you must realize is that your feelings are your most powerful tool to stop the one you love from drinking and are the key to the Intervention process. *Your feelings are all that the alcoholic will listen to.*

Also, exploring your feelings will help you act. It is important for you to be aware of how the chemical dependency is affecting *you*—how often you feel negative emotions, how often you say to yourself: "I am angry." "I am scared." "I am hurt." You may not realize how all of your feelings are tied up with the drinking and how much time you spend thinking and talking about the person you're concerned about.

Acknowledging your feelings

If you are like most people, the counselors at Families in Crisis say, you tend to paint a rosier picture of your home life than what really exists. Usually, in a first meeting, a client is worried that the counselor will think that the dependent is a jerk and that the co-dependent is even more of a jerk for loving him.

So the initial conversation is always rather vague. The counselor has to probe and guess to get the facts. A co-dependent prefers that the counselor do the talking. Not only does he not want to be exposed, but also he wants to be relieved of his fears that his family situation is so unique that the person he is concerned about will not cooperate or the Intervention will not work.

The counselor will suggest that he put his fears aside (the answers will come) and focus instead on his feelings. Even if he is willing, the co-dependent will find that hard to do. Usually the only word he can find to describe his feelings is "angry." He isn't likely to mention feelings of loneliness, grief, hurt, or disappointment at having been "ripped off" emotionally.

Probably, he hasn't even a clue that these are his feelings. Or he may be involved in a conspiracy of silence, and, rather than talk about the problem, he'll be sarcastic or switch the focus just as an alcoholic might. Instead of talking about the drinking, the co-dependent will concentrate on the fact that the alcoholic is looking terrible, has lost his job, or is having an affair.

If this happens in your case, the counselor will help you try to stay on track. He knows that the most effective way to reach the alcoholic is to make him realize how what he does affects other people and how bad his problem has become. (Chances are he hasn't even connected his other problems to his drinking.)

Many people believe that they have addressed the drinking already. They tell the counselor, "I *have* told him how I felt about his drinking a million times." What they've probably done was react angrily. If you're living with an alcoholic, you've probably heard yourself saying these things over and over again: "How can you do this again?" "How can you get drunk when you know we had a party to go to?" "What's wrong with you?" These are questions. They don't explain how the drinking affects you and how you feel as a result.

An alcoholic, because of his disease, is incapable of giving logical answers to these questions. He doesn't *know* why he drank too much. Also at times he knows your anger is justified. He feels ashamed. So either he turns on someone else, or he turns off completely—anything to avoid having the discussion center on drinking.

What's strange is that the co-dependent wants logical explanations of the alcoholic's behavior, but he himself can't be logical. His thinking has been clouded by all his defensive behavior.

Feelings of the parent

When the problem is a child's drug or alcohol abuse, his parents will usually arrive at the counselor's office with all sorts of excuses and explanations. They say that the child has always been misunderstood—by teachers, by employers, by friends. They may even try to pin the blame for the child's behavior on one another. "Why couldn't you have done something? Why did you allow it to get this far?"

They are defensive and full of blame *because they feel guilty*. They're wondering where they went wrong. They're sure that if they had been better parents, this never would have happened.

Many children who abuse drugs and alcohol have family backgrounds of chemical dependency. If the parents are not alcoholics themselves, they look back and think of Aunt Tilly or Grandpa Herb who had a drinking problem and think they passed on "defective" genes. If the mother doesn't drink, she blames herself for raising the kids in a home with an alcoholic father. If a father is recovering from chemical dependency, he knows how his illness affected his child. If the parent is still drinking, he's afraid of being exposed and blamed. All these situations create guilt.

Simply acknowledging the guilt represents a breakthrough, because it stops the blaming. People become more realistic about how much responsibility to assume for the problem and, more important, they stop looking back. They start concentrating on solving the problem. Eventually, everyone will have to acknowledge his pain, and doing so will bring relief. Out of the pain will come solutions.

Feelings of the spouse

Nine out of ten men, compared to one out of ten women, leave an alcoholic spouse. Men are less protective and more frustrated in this situation. Typically, a husband will come to Families in Crisis and say, "She has a wonderful home and family. How could she possibly be doing this?"

A husband will generally consider himself blameless. He'll either put all the blame on his wife or, in cases where she's dependent on pills, point his finger at the doctor. Most of the time, the real story is that the husband has been very protective of the addiction and very effective in helping it to continue.

One man admitted during counseling that he actually preferred his wife when she'd been drinking, since she was a lot more fun to be with. He didn't want her to stop. He just wanted to arrange things so she didn't go beyond the point of being affectionate and sexual. More often, if his wife drinks a man may find another sexual companion.

Since women alcoholics progress in the disease more quickly than men, often a woman is very sick by the time her husband looks for help. He's probably seeking it out of a sense of duty. He really doesn't like his wife any more and he wants out of the marriage, but he wants to make the break with some integrity and in a way that makes him seem decent in the eyes of his children and society. Men don't want to bother sorting through their feelings. They want to get right to the point. They must be persuaded that those feelings are all that will help them reach their wives.

When a wife finally comes in for Intervention counseling for her husband, she's usually doubtful that Intervention will work. Often she's been pressured into coming by a friend or relative. She may be making a final move before going to an attorney's office, but if she hasn't been planning divorce, she's fearful that her marriage will break up. She may be frightened she'll blow the top off the pressure cooker her family is living in. Also, she's afraid that the dependent will be hurt by an honest confrontation. The people at Families in Crisis answer, "He's already hurting. And so are you. Let's talk about it."

They know she's not in touch with her hurt. In fact, she goes out of her way to deal with side issues. For example, when an alcoholic husband is having an affair, the wife will say, "I have to know whether it's the woman who made him drink or the alcohol that got him involved with the woman." She wants to put the focus on the other woman, rather than where it belongs—on the alcoholism. It's easier to hold on to the anger than to probe feelings that are deep below the surface. Even if there is no other woman, if your husband is out drinking, he probably has friends you don't know, he's at parties you're not involved in, and in general you are left out of all the so-called good times. At the very least, you feel lonely, hurt, and rejected because of his alcoholism (unless you're drinking with him). You need help to express and examine those feelings.

When you first allow them to surface, instead of angry, you may feel defensive or despairing. Sometimes the situation appears so hopeless initially that wives just hope their alcoholic husbands will die and leave them the life insurance money. Not only will he be out of the picture, but they'll get more respect as a widow than as the wife of an alcoholic. They fear the husband's dying less than his continuing to live. They're afraid and resentful of the prospect of taking care of an old, sick drunk.

If you're the wife of an alcoholic, you have given up a lot for your husband and are constantly fighting to hold onto whatever is left—affection, respect, money, friends. You have probably started over again with false hopes many times. You are carrying an enormous burden, and eventually you run out of stamina.

But if you're a good co-dependent, you may not be admitting this to anyone. Or else you are talking to everyone, but when they offer help or solutions—or even bring up the topic of drinking without your consent—you put a stop to the conversation or contradict yourself and say that things aren't so bad.

Often not until the Intervention has been instigated does an alcoholic's spouse realize how much pain everyone else is going through. Often, she winds up apologizing to everyone because her husband was the cause of the problems. Actually, she owes them an apology for making the situation worse by putting the clamp on honest communication.

Many wives are very upset by the prospect of an Intervention, even though they may be convinced it's the only hope. From my own experiences, I can tell you that once the door to this solution is opened, you will be amazed at the help you will get, not only from counselors and concerned family, but also from friends. You may have been carrying everything on your shoulders up to this point, but now you can sit back and go along for the ride. It's like lifting a piano. One person can't do it, nor can two. A group *can* handle the piano, and even if you sit on top of it, they'll carry you, too!

Feelings of friends

Friends tend to be far more in touch with their real feelings than family members, since they are less affected by the disease. And unless they are drinking partners, they are far more willing to speak honestly.

Friends are sometimes the ones who suggest to the family that an Intervention is in order. I know a husband and wife who were out to dinner with another couple. The wife had been saying for years that things were tough at home, and on this particular night, when the husband left the table, the friend said, "Your husband is a chronic alcoholic." The wife was blown away. It was as if a veil had been lifted from her eyes.

More typically, friends approach the husband about an alcoholic wife. Friends tend to be more concerned about their female friends, and husbands need more prodding to act.

Friends may be slower to become concerned than family because they are less emotionally involved. Also, you tend to accept your friends as they are and enjoy them even through bad times. On top of that, friends often get a very biased view of what's really going on. An alcoholic tends to do a lot of blaming and enlists friends as allies against his employer and against the spouse.

But in an Intervention, friends are extremely helpful. Even if they haven't initiated it, they will usually participate willingly if they are certain their presence is desired. Once educated about the disease, they are quicker than family members to understand that the alcoholic is dying of an illness and to provide support and help. They can sum up the situation and cut through the baloney a lot faster, since they haven't lived in the denial system for years. They are not afraid to speak honestly. They will get to the bottom line a lot faster—and hold to it more firmly.

If you're considering an Intervention, do it before the alcoholic turns into an s.o.b. who has alienated everyone. However, be assured that once they know the story and how they can be of help, even friends you thought had fallen by the wayside will often show up at an Intervention. You can bring in drinking buddies, too. They can see how someone else is being affected by his drinking even if they can't see it in themselves.

Feelings of the children

An adult child tends to want to protect the nondrinking spouse, the martyr, during the Intervention process. He'll go after his alcoholic dad but he doesn't want to hurt Mommy. She has protected him, or so she thinks, but in reality he has protected her. If he hasn't, he has had to deal with the consequences—dirty looks and the silent treatment, for example. (As a result, the adult child is actually angry at both his parents, but he may not recognize that without help.)

According to Dr. Steven Buckey and Dr. Claudia Black, two California researchers who conducted a two-year study, children of alcoholics often grow up with a nameless, intense guilt because of the blaming their alcoholic parents put them through. A full 75 percent are unable to tell others what they want and need as adults.

But children of alcoholics *may* reverse their feelings and reinterpret the events of the past. If as adults they can understand the disease of alcoholism and apply that understanding to their childhood experiences, they can experience intense relief.

Why you've covered up

The Families in Crisis counselors say that once the families of chemical dependents start to talk about their problems, they often begin to cry. Under their anger and frustration is guilt, and under their guilt is hurt and pain. All these pent-up feelings may come out in the form of tears. They may apologize for crying, but the counselors assure them that tears are in order. At some point during an Intervention, everyone in the room might be crying. You just have to learn to talk through your tears so you can cry and talk at the same time.

When the counselor asks the co-dependents what is happening to them when they cry, often they have no words to express their feelings. If you've lived in an alcoholic family, you've learned to bottle those feelings up. You certainly can't let outsiders know what's going on at home. What would they think? And speaking freely at home meant you risked being brutalized by your alcoholic parent. Or you'd make the other parent, the primary enabler, "feel bad." That parent has been as effective as the alcoholic himself in teaching you to negate your feelings. If you're hurt or sad, that parent feels responsible and tries to placate you. Maybe he buys you a present to make you happy.

Up to a certain age, perhaps your brothers and sisters can be your confidants. But as the family grows more and more dysfunctional, even that intimacy disappears. You learn to cover up your feelings in order to survive. The only place it's safe to cry is alone in your room. Or perhaps you never cry. Or you cry and don't know why.

Maybe you reach the point where you can't be honest even with yourself. On a subconscious level you may be aware that if you did get in touch with your feelings you'd have no other choice than to leave the family, and (if you're a parent) to get the kids out of there along with you.

Healthy families share their feelings and give you the right to experience all of yours. The other day, I mentioned to the spouse of a rip-roaring alcoholic that I felt nervous about a recent financial decision. She jumped on me. "You shouldn't feel that way." Why not? I thought. Why should I cover up?

In a healthy family, everyone has a chance to get some attention. There is give and take. In an alcoholic family, you rarely have the luxury of thinking about your own feelings. The alcoholic rules the roost, and all the attention is focused on him. What kind of mood is he in today? Will he come home drunk or sober? Dad's not feeling well this morning, so everyone should cater to him.

Eventually you spend so much time suppressing so many feelings that even if you are given permission to expose them, you don't know exactly what they are. You consider your unhealthy behavior "normal" because it's the only style you know.

The defenses you've learned

I discovered in treatment that my way of covering up my feelings was by joking. My group finally told me, "Mary Ellen, you've got to knock it off. The minute you get close to the truth or sense that you are about to hear something uncomfortable, out you come with a one-liner." My reaction to hearing this was, "I've given up my drug. Now they're asking me to give up my sense of humor." After some thought, I realized that I did use my humor inappropriately. I joked even when a compliment was directed at me. I was uncomfortable when someone got that close.

Common defensive techniques include denial, blaming, minimizing, moralizing, rationalizing, complying, talking, intellectualizing, withdrawing, and crying. You have to let go of those and let the feelings out. You're entitled to your feelings. They aren't bad or good, moral or immoral. They're what makes you human.

Still, they don't control you. You control them. I hear people say, "I can't help the way I'm feeling," and I tell them that is not true. For example, you may complain that when the person you love has been drinking, he says things that hurt you. Recognize that he *has* said those things because he *was* drinking. But learn how to take the power to hurt you away from him. Work toward being able to say, "I don't like how you're treating me." "I feel terrible and ashamed when you put me down." You have to know how you are feeling before you can make this kind of statement. Once you do, you change your behavior, and ultimately, you change your feelings. Instead of feeling helpless and sad, you will feel strong and capable.

Everyone is responsible for his own feelings—and his own feelings only. You owe it to yourself to get in touch with them.

Finding the words

One way to start is to find words to describe them—words more specific than "angry."

For example, a friend of mine once left her alcoholic husband in charge of their toddlers. While he was drinking with friends, the kids wandered off. After a frantic search, she discovered them several blocks away, on the freeway, trying to walk home. The mother was angry, of course, but her feelings were more complex than that. She felt overwhelmed at having all the parental responsibility. She felt trapped because she couldn't go out without being anxious. She felt disappointed at being married to someone she couldn't rely on.

One of the Families in Crisis counselors recalled going drinking with her alcoholic husband. While he was at a party, he'd be fun and social, but he'd leave the party early and come home to drink alone. She'd be in the room with him, feeling angry—but also lonely and isolated.

When I thought about doing something to help Sherm, I had to go beneath my anger and hurt to other feelings. I realized that while he was drinking, I was living with continual fear. If I went to bed while he was still out, I worried he'd be in an auto accident, or that he'd come home and go to sleep with a lit cigarette and burn the house down. When I thought some more about our relationship, I got in touch with other feelings:

· I felt **frustrated** because I knew life had more to offer from a marriage.

· I felt **guilty** because of my own drinking problem.

· I felt **helpless** because I seemed to be the only one who cared enough to think of an Intervention.

· I felt **indifferent** because I learned that Sherm couldn't hurt me as much if I had that attitude.

· I felt **lonely** because I didn't have a partner in life.

· I felt **obligated** to stick with him because I married him for better or worse and he was the father of our child.

· I felt **misunderstood** by his children and friends, who thought I was the heavy causing Sherm's problems.

· I felt **pious** because I wasn't drinking and he was.

· I felt **overwhelmed** because I carried so many of the responsibilities of our lives (family and financial) on my shoulders.

· I felt **trapped.** I wanted out but I didn't know how to get out.

· I felt **used** by his children, who didn't recognize that the problems in our relationship weren't all my fault.

· I felt **cheated** out of a lovely man-woman relationship.

· I felt **embarrassed** by how Sherm looked when he was drinking.

· I felt **worried** about the future. If the drinking continued, what would happen to Sherm?

· I felt **frightened** at the idea of living with a practicing alcoholic for the rest of my life.

· And I felt **angry** because of all the above.

Today, I have a whole different vocabulary:

· I am **hopeful** about my relationship with Sherm.

· I am **proud** that he went through treatment.

· I am **secure** because he has taken over some responsibility.

· I am **comfortable** when I am home with my family.

· I am **encouraged** when I consider the future.

· I am **pleased** about how good Sherm looks.

· I am **grateful** that I have had another chance in life, another chance to love Sherm and be part of a loving family.

I don't want this to sound sickeningly smug. I am not a saint. There are hours and even days at a time when I feel fearful, when I feel like a hopeless case, and when I'm still angry. But at least these days I know what to do with these feelings: I go to an AA meeting or I sit down and talk with Sherm and let him know how I'm feeling instead of stuffing a sock in my mouth. Now that Sherm's not drinking and not defensive, he's open to hearing what is happening with me, and after we talk I always feel better.

You must start defining your own feelings. Begin by remembering specific incidents, writing down exactly how you felt. For example:

· The night you left the Johnsons' party and insisted on driving, I refused to drive home with you, but you didn't care. You grabbed the car keys and left me standing in the street. I was **afraid.**

· I thought you might kill yourself or someone else. I was **worried.**

· The Johnsons saw your behavior and I had to rely on them for a ride home. I was **embarrassed.**

· The night we had dinner with my parents, you drank a

lot and called me a nag and an ungrateful wife. I was **ashamed.**

Here is a list of descriptive words that might help you out as you try to define your feelings:

abandoned, afraid, alone, ambivalent, anxious, apathetic,
 apprehensive, ashamed, awkward
bored
cheated, contemptuous
defeated, defensive, despondent, disappointed, discontent,
 discouraged, disturbed, down, dull
embarrassed, empty, exasperated
fearful, foolish, forlorn, frustrated
guilty
helpless, hopeless, hurt
impatient, inadequate, indifferent, inferior, insecure, intol-
 erant, irritated
jealous
let down, lonely
miserable, misunderstood
nervous, numb
obligated
pained, provoked, pushed, put out
regretful, rejected, resentful, robbed
sucked in
trapped, tricked
uncomfortable, unhappy, unloved, unsure, unworthy, used
worried

Chances are, the more difficult it is for you to label your feelings, the more advanced the alcoholism. As the chemically dependent person has become sicker, so have you. Starting to write down your feelings is the first step you have taken to getting the one you love to stop drinking. It is the first step toward Intervention.

6/
The Solution: Intervention

You have the power to help the one you love. You probably don't realize that. You assume all the power is in the hands of the alcoholic or drug user. You ask him to stop. You beg him to stop. Although that never seems to work, you hope that somehow he will see the light and "turn himself in." You remain stuck at the point of asking.

I have some very important news for you. Chemically dependent people don't have spontaneous revelations. Hell is likelier to freeze over than an alcoholic or drug user to stop on his own. An alcoholic doesn't *want* to stop drinking. He may want to drink less, perhaps, but he doesn't want to stop completely. Alcohol is his primary relationship, and breaking up (especially when you're still in love) is hard to do.

The day I went into treatment, I was still looking for a way to drink without paying the price of total abstinence. Such thoughts occasionally still run through my mind, but now I put them in the mental trash compactor along with the ones about phoning old boyfriends and asking if they want to run off into the sunset with me.

During my drinking days there were times when I was so guilty and ashamed that I wanted to stop, but all I needed was a week or two of abstinence to forget all about those feelings. All I needed was a happy drinking experience to be convinced I had everything under control again. An alcoholic doesn't get into trouble every time he drinks or he wouldn't stay in the game so long. Most of the time, the payoff is great. That's what keeps us going. We love it.

Nine out of every ten alcoholics will drink themselves to death unless someone or something interferes with the drinking. Most of us don't even know that we need help. Believe it or not, I've talked to Skid Row cases who were convinced that they were fine. We have such a distorted image that half the time we're sure it's everyone else who's in trouble.

The only thing that might cause us to stop is a crisis: Our marriage falling apart. A nudge from a friendly banker. Parents ordering, "Stop or get out." Or an employer's warning that our job is on the line. (Most employers don't bother to warn. They just fire the drunk.)

It might be something more serious: An arrest for a DWI or for carrying drugs. A sentence to the workhouse or jail. A bankruptcy. A doctor saying, "You're a mess. You're going in for treatment and you don't have any choice in the matter."

Some chemical dependency counselors refer to any kind of crisis as either an active or a passive Intervention. The ones described in the paragraphs above would be considered active Interventions. They represent crises so painful or frightening that the alcoholic will do anything to escape them—even agree to go into treatment. In the back of his mind, he doesn't actually plan to stop drinking, but he knows that going into treatment will get everyone off his back.

What we're talking about in this book is a passive Intervention—a move initiated out of love and concern by the people who care about the alcoholic. It involves their getting together to tell the alcoholic the facts about his disease and how it is affecting them. It's the only kind, gentle, and caring way to help a chemically dependent person. It's the only thing that works, the key to stopping someone whose life is in danger.

When I began recovering from my own alcoholism, I read just about every book available on the subject. Today I glanced through yet another one, written by a doctor. In hundreds of pages, it devotes only two paragraphs to Intervention.

I am more and more amazed that the good news hasn't spread—that Interventions are a proven way (and the only way) to help your alcoholic and the rest of the family take a realistic look at what's happening to you all. The immediate goal of the Intervention is to speak openly about the problem; the ultimate goal is to get the alcoholic or drug user to appropriate kinds of help.

As you find out more about Intervention, you may find the solution too easy to be true. But the facts speak for themselves. Many, many families and many, many alcoholics and drug users have recovered as a result of this simple process. Many more could be helped if more people were aware that this solution is available.

How the process evolved

Like many great ideas, the Intervention process came into being accidentally. According to Mary McMahon, who worked with him at his Johnson Institute in Minneapolis, about twenty years ago, a man named Vern Johnson was involved in counseling alcoholics but feeling so discouraged about the effectiveness of what he was doing that he was even considering changing fields.

In those days, Vern would listen to the alcoholic's complaints and murmur, "Um-hm. We understand." This came to be known as the nod-and-grunt method of treatment. The whole time, of course, the alcoholic would deny the facts and blame his problem on everything and everyone around him.

One day, a friend came to speak to Vern about his wife, who was in a psychiatric ward. The friend said, in effect, "I know her problem isn't a mental disorder. She's an alcoholic, but she can't see it. I hate her, I can't stand what she's doing, and I've had it. I'm taking the kids down to the hospital and we're going to tell her exactly what she's done to all of us and what we think of her." They marched in and did just that.

They were very specific. Instead of just saying, "You embarrassed me when you drank," they'd say something like, "Mom, I had friends over to the house and you spilled soup on them and instead of apologizing, you laughed."

To the family's surprise, once they'd told her everything,

the woman began to recover. Having the people she loved finally level with her proved to be a turning point. This experience was the first Intervention. Vern was so impressed with its effect that he began to refine the process and train others to initiate Interventions with loved ones.

Today the term "Intervention" refers to a carefully constructed and orchestrated process in which the family, friends, and perhaps an employer talk to the alcoholic or drug user. Trained counselors prepare the concerned parties, educating them about alcoholism as a disease, guiding them through the whys and hows of the process, helping them to collect their thoughts, giving them reassurance, and preparing them for everything and anything that might happen during the Intervention. The objective is to make the alcoholic agree to have a professional evaluation or enter into treatment.

"Solutions" that don't work

No one can do an Intervention alone, and no one can do an Intervention that isn't thoroughly planned. I know because it failed with me. The year before I landed in treatment, one of my business associates had decided to take the bull (that was me) by the horns. He knew I had a drinking problem. He'd even gone so far as to talk to the key people in my life, so he was on the right track, but he made the mistake of confronting me one-on-one.

At first I tried to dodge him by laughing him off. I accused him of overreacting. But finally I had to respond to the real concern in his face and voice.

"I know I have a problem," I acknowledged. "I guess we'll have to do something about it." He told me he'd made arrangements for me to check into a treatment center. That sounded fine to me. Everything sounded fine until he left the room and I had time to think of all the reasons I couldn't go. Some of them were legitimate, related to my business. But others were the kinds of things you grab onto to postpone any unpleasant task. There was an urgent dental appointment (I was three months overdue already; suddenly the idea of dental work, at least contrasted to giving up drinking, seemed appealing). Somebody needed a fourth for bridge. In the end, I convinced myself that between one thing and another, there was no way I could be tied up by checking into a center. (As a matter of fact, I decided I'd *have* to be tied up if anyone wanted to get me into a center.)

Following our session, my associate had scheduled a meeting with another colleague who was also a close friend. This man had often gone out drinking with me and I knew he thought I was a great old gal when I was at a bar. He saw only the fun Mary Ellen, never the out-of-control, nutty stuff—or so I was convinced.

The minute my associate left the room, I tried to convince my friend that he was taking everything far too seriously. "I may have a bit of a problem," I said. "But let's put it this way. I'm a baby alcoholic."

A baby alcoholic, like a small bomb, is still too big to ignore.

"Eventually, I'll have to face up to this thing," I went on. (In my next lifetime, maybe.) "But I'm okay right now." I'm a convincing speaker. He bought it. I left the meeting feeling impressed with myself and very powerful. This particular man was a very strong influence in my life, someone I considered extremely competent, very much in control. If I'd convinced him I was okay, then I was okay.

At 10:00 P.M., I arrived home. My business associate was on the phone, terribly upset. He told me he was relieved but also enraged. Of course he'd assumed I was out drinking. "How could you? You promised me you were going into treatment." I felt so righteous. "I have been out doing business and behaving myself," I said. "What's wrong with you? You must have lost your mind."

It was easy to persuade myself he had. I needn't take him—or his concerns—too seriously. Within days, I was off to the races again, off on another drinking binge. And guess what? My business associate was at the bar right alongside me.

If you've been living with a chemical dependent for a while, you've probably tried several variations on what therapists call "the home treatment," such as:

· "If you loved me and the kids, you'd do something about your drinking."

· "Can't you use your will power?"
· "Please promise me that you won't drink."
· "Look at this tape/these pictures of your behavior when you were drunk."

All of the above approaches just increase the alcoholic's guilt, so he manages to repress—and forget—whatever he promised and whatever you said. Or he learns more clever ways to hide his drinking.

Maybe you've told him, "I'm getting rid of your bottles and seeing to it you won't have enough money to drink." An alcoholic always finds a way to get his booze.

Or you've warned him, "I'll divorce you/throw you out/cut off your support." Say this often enough without following through, and it loses its potency.

Maybe you or someone else has actually tried talking to him about his drinking. He probably handled you as I did my business associate and friend—convinced you you were overreacting. Alcoholics are masters of deceit and manipulation.

I know one woman whose children reported her to the authorities as an unfit parent. Even that didn't work. The social worker came and discovered that the children were well fed and apparently well taken care of, and she couldn't put the picture together. On top of that, the mother felt so great talking her way out of the situation with the social worker that she immediately headed across the street for a drink.

Another woman was married to a successful attorney who never drank in public. Her son smelled what was in his dad's glass and knew it wasn't Coca-Cola. Her mother-in-law had an idea that the husband was in trouble. But the wife never gathered everyone to fit the pieces of the puzzle together. When she complained, her friends thought she was crazy. They said to her, "You have a marriage problem. He doesn't have a drinking problem."

A doctor or therapist won't usually diagnose alcoholism for the reasons I've mentioned in previous chapters. They may prescribe medicine to make the symptoms go away or concentrate on some small issue of the marriage or the parenting. Or maybe they're just not goal-oriented and think it's okay for therapy to go on . . . and on . . . and on, while the alcoholic and his family get crazier . . . and crazier . . . and crazier. Nothing happens unless the focus becomes the underlying problems, the alcoholism.

Nor may near-fatal consequences of using get a chemical dependent to stop. On TV, I saw Jason Robards (who is now recovering) talking about how he drove while intoxicated and was involved in a serious car accident that ripped open half his face. That didn't stop him from drinking.

One-on-one confrontations, unplanned confrontations, therapy, legal and financial problems, estrangement from loved ones, even the prospect of death may not stop the one you love from drinking. His disease keeps him from stopping. He needs loving friends to create a crisis he can't deal with, loving friends who will help him break through the denial and delusion that are part of the disease.

Why an Intervention is different

Unlike other "solutions," an Intervention is the only way of breaking through denial and delusion effectively. It's hard to deny your alcoholism in the face of so many examples reported by so many people. You can't feel all the love and concern from all the participants without responding. Either you are moved or you become so angry you agree to be evaluated (or even go into treatment) just to show those guys you don't have a problem. It may hurt the family to become honest. It also hurts the drinker to the point that he'll do anything—even go into treatment—to make it stop.

During the Intervention, because everyone is expressing himself so freely for the first time, feelings and information seem to come out of the clear blue sky, things that will utterly surprise the alcoholic and probably all the others as well. You cannot imagine how dramatic an Intervention is until you've been involved. Many alcoholics say that they call on the memory of their Intervention to keep them sober.

What's especially important is that the Intervention has a goal. The alcoholic may have been confronted by his spouse or others in the past, but in those cases he winds up only with feelings of anger, shame, and guilt. An Intervention doesn't leave things up in the air. Once the problems are aired, solutions are proposed.

An Intervention is a relief not only for the alcoholic, but

also for the concerned person in his life. For one thing, if you're worried about someone who is chemically dependent, you may begin to wonder if the whole problem is in *your* mind, particularly in those cases where the alcoholic seems to be skipping through life, loved by everyone. You think, "Why am I having all these inappropriate thoughts about him?"

If you express your concern directly, the alcoholic is so manipulative and evasive that he will just confirm your suspicions that you're the crazy one. If you're his wife, you'll start to believe that his drinking is secondary to some other problem. If you're his friend, he'll persuade you that his wife is such a witch that if you were married to her, you'd be drinking too.

You may become convinced that you're the only one having problems with the behavior of the alcoholic. You may even assume you are the only one he's drinking with. I know people thought that was the case with me. "Mary Ellen's going a little crazy today, but she doesn't do this every day of her life."

Even if you have gone for help, you may have discovered that therapy was as little help to you as to the alcoholic. It may provide you with some relief, but if you don't deal with the real problem and continue to live in the same situation nothing will change. One alcoholic's wife saw a therapist who offered her pills. When she refused them, he said he would have to discharge her. He said her problem was her husband and that talking to her wouldn't change him. The doctor was correct, but if he'd been really helpful, he would have helped the wife to make some changes of her own—to act, not simply to react.

I know parents who are seeing a psychiatrist about their son, who smokes pot daily. They're being told "He's not motivated," which is getting them nowhere. They're feeling ripped off, they feel that the doctor is ignorant. And as usual, no one is addressing the chemical dependency.

During an Intervention, you finally may see the dimensions of the problem. You discover that not only is a person drinking with you, but also with Tom and Joel and possibly Bill as well. When you discuss your concerns with the group, you will be reassured that initiating an Intervention was the right thing and you will develop the conviction to do whatever is necessary. Such discussions will also help relieve the anger you have been living with.

My father was in treatment many times. But never once was the family involved in it. I'm not sure if alcoholism was considered a family disease at that time. I do know that never once did my dad sit down with his children and trained personnel and have the opportunity to hear from us what was going on. I have no doubt that everyone in our family would have turned out a much better person as a result. I have no doubt that my father never realized how low he had sunk. No one had told him, and, being a good alcoholic myself, I know how much help it takes to see things as they really are.

The Intervention is the beginning of treatment for the one you're concerned about and also the beginning of family treatment. The people at Families in Crisis always say that an Intervention is a process, not an isolated event. It's the beginning of the healing process.

What happens in an Intervention?

You may have heard of Interventions, but I'd be willing to bet that whatever you think you know about them is untrue. I've found that the term is often misinterpreted or used incorrectly. Many people are frightened by the idea of an Intervention, which they picture as a free-for-all in which everyone plays Get the Alcoholic. That's not so.

An Intervention is a loving process that brings the alcoholic to realize and accept the need for help through the concern and love of the people who care about him. The first speaker in the Intervention process delivers a message of reassurance. He tells the alcoholic that his family and friends have assembled to speak with him because they think he has a problem and they care about him.

Then, in turn, each family member and friend reads aloud a letter that he has prepared with the aid of the counselor. The letters give specific examples of his behavior while he has been using and, most important, show how the reader has been affected by it. The alcoholic is not blamed or humiliated. The letters are non-judgmental. The counselor has rehearsed the participants to help make sure that drinking remains the issue—that people don't focus on all the crazy things (other than drinking-related) the alcoholic has done, but make it a point to express their love and concern . . . plus lots of hope.

If the letters alone aren't compelling enough, a further means of persuading the alcoholic or drug abuser to go into treatment is to give him the "bottom lines" (also prepared in advance) that are the consequences of his not doing so. A "bottom line" might simply be refusing to be with the person on occasions when he has been drinking. It might be a denial of financial support or refusal of visiting rights. Occasionally a participating employer will explain that unless the alcoholic agrees to get help, he has no choice but to let him go.

It is very difficult for anyone to remain untouched by an Intervention. If you are the subject of an Intervention, you can't help but be affected when people you care about speak about how your disease has made them feel. And, when you hear example after example of occasions of your drinking or drug use, it's hard to maintain the position that you don't have a problem. It's harder still to deny that many people are concerned about you and want you to seek help.

Why are some people prejudiced against Interventions?

I couldn't believe it when a minister actually told me that Intervention was "evil." Naturally, I asked him to tell me why. Most people have a hard time answering that question when they don't know the facts, and he was no exception. "You are arrogant to take control of the situation instead of leaving it with God. Besides, you beat up on people mentally and say things that are cruel." I asked the minister how he knew that God doesn't have a hand in this situation. If you ask me, God is the one who's responsible for AA and the treatment centers.

I asked him if he understood the idea of an Intervention. It appears to me, as I have mentioned before, that God Intervenes in our lives all the time. He constantly creates crises to make us stop and look at ourselves, and He does it with love, too. ("I came to save, not to judge.") He delivers His message with love and understanding, and He points out where we are going wrong in a supportive way. Throughout the Bible, there are examples of His working through other people, and not always the nicest people, either—prostitutes, tax collectors, and plenty of Bad-News Charlies. (Sounds like a potential AA group to me!) The ones God ultimately condemned were the self-righteous know-it-alls.

Love, concern, and the help of others are the characteristics of God's work and also the elements of an Intervention.

Some people who know more than that minister about Interventions also have negative ideas based on outdated information. In the past, Interventions were more confrontational. There wasn't much love expressed. The process wasn't as well thought-out. But today, counselors know that confrontation isn't the answer. An alcoholic can handle confrontation—in fact, he may often thrive on it—but love is more effective. Love is what will really break his resistance.

Other people have negative attitudes toward Interventions because they claim to know of some that failed. I have found that in such cases the people concerned didn't stick with their bottom lines. (For example, the alcoholic will still be living at home although his wife's bottom line was that he must leave unless he got help.) Or else you discover that the Intervention was not professionally run. The concerned parties just got together by themselves and confronted the alcoholic, and inevitably the scheme was a disaster. I heard of one case in Minnesota in which the alcoholic, a man with a history of violent behavior, pulled a gun and shot someone. These are explosive issues, and all it takes is one nut to create a real problem. A counselor would have been able to discern whether the person in question was simply a good old alcoholic or potentially dangerous.

(Incidentally, although it is a common misconception that violence goes hand-in-hand with the disease, I've sat through many AA meetings and rarely do I hear talk of physical abuse. Alcoholics may have tongues as sharp as a two-edged sword but the vast majority aren't into hurting people physically. If you are dealing with the exception to the rule, if you have ever feared for your safety, go with your instinct and get help immediately. You're not being overcautious. Statistics prove that eventually something awful will happen if the threat of violence has been made.)

What is the role of the counselor?

Later on, I'll go into more detail about seeking a counselor, but at this point I'll say only that you must look for someone who has been trained in conducting Interventions and who seems encouraging about doing one. Guiding an Intervention requires a lot of empathy, skill in handling people, and great ability to think on your feet. Not everyone feels up to the job. I have a lot of respect for the counselors I worked with at Families in Crisis. I think all of them are remarkable at their work.

During your first meeting, and based on the information you provide, your counselor should be able to determine whether drinking or drug use is the primary problem, how severe the situation is, and whether or not an Intervention is advisable. He or she will help you determine what kind of care is best suited to the chemically dependent person— such as in-patient or out-patient treatment.

If you decide to proceed, the counselor will advise you how to contact others who may be concerned and suggest who should be included, assuming that all of you need information and education about chemical dependency in order to understand the delusion and denial that are part of the disease. In the course of the education process, everyone will begin to realize that much of the behavior he has been seeing is a predictable part of the disease and not necessarily directed toward him personally. A lot of the myths about the disease will be put to rest.

Next, the counselor will help group members recall and write down the information that will make up the letters they will read during the Intervention. The counselor will orchestrate the process, helping to determine the order of the speakers, rehearsing the reading of the letters, and anticipating any problems. During the Intervention, the counselor will be there to start things off, to answer any surprise questions about the disease or treatment, and to make sure the focus remains on the drinking. Throughout the process, the counselor will help build everyone's confidence and reassure you that you are doing the right thing.

What's the success rate of Intervention?

There are varying reports about the rate of success, but it's always extremely high. One Intervention center I read about reports that eight out of ten Interventions are successful in getting the alcoholic into treatment. Families in Crisis has an ever higher success rate, perhaps because of their vast experience in this area. They report that 95 percent of the alcoholic or drug users on whom they've helped initiate an Intervention have agreed to go to a treatment center for an evaluation. (Arrangements are always made with the center in advance, and generally the alcoholic is driven or flown there directly from the Intervention.)

Suppose our situation is unique, and Intervention won't work?

I don't suppose that your situation is unique. I know for a fact that it *is* unique. There won't be another one exactly like it anywhere in the world, just as there aren't two people exactly alike in the world. But I can also tell you that if you're living in an alcoholic family, you're not quite as unusual as you think. I hope that's becoming clear to you as you read this book. I don't have bugs planted in your house, but I'll bet I've described what's going on there pretty well.

If on the other hand you don't feel that anything you've read applies to you, my reaction is, "Lucky you, you're not living with an alcoholic," or "You poor thing, you're so into denial that you should run (not walk) to the first counselor you can find."

I know all about feeling "unique." All alcoholics are a little grandiose, and I was no exception. I thought Mary Ellen Pinkham was just about the most special and unusual person on earth. What applies to the rest of the world doesn't apply to us alcoholics. And the alcoholic's entire family gets the same idea.

When Sherm was in treatment, I remember going into the

Family Week at the treatment center with his grown kids from his first marriage. We heard some of the other families speak first. During the break, Kim Pinkham turned to me and said, "We're not like these people. Our family has a few problems, sure, but nothing as bad as what we've heard, Mary Ellen." I didn't say anything, but I thought to myself, "You just wait."

Well, a lot of horrible things were brought up—money mistakes, irresponsibility, the works. Andrew was there, and he managed to tell a few tales that put both me and Sherm out of the running for Parent of the Year awards. By the time it was all over, Kim looked at me and said, "Mary Ellen, our family is the worst." Well, we weren't the worst. But we sure weren't any better than anybody else, either.

Your situation, believe me, is not special. It's typical. Your alcoholic is just as pathetic and needy as every other alcoholic, no matter how brave and successful a front he's putting up. If Brooke Shields can do an Intervention on her mom, if the people closest to Betty Ford are successful in doing an Intervention on her, then what's so special about your alcoholic?

You notice I mention only celebrities. That's because the heads of corporations and educators and scientists and doctors and lawyers and clergymen who are alcoholic don't tend to tell their stories to the newspapers so you aren't as aware of them, but, believe me, alcoholics are found in every walk of life. (As a matter of fact, the two highest rates of alcoholism are among clergymen and doctors, and I was in treatment with a sister who was a *real* flying nun.) Even the toughest nuts can be cracked and given some help—and they're better off if you crack them than if you wait until they crack up themselves.

Alcoholics are just human, even if their behavior at times causes you to suspect otherwise. They're sick humans, at that. Don't be afraid to help them.

Can Intervention work on other addictions?

Absolutely. I hope I've made the point that the use of alcohol and the use of sleeping pills, pot, heroin, cocaine, and other addictive substances (including prescription drugs) are all chemical dependencies. Only the drug of choice is different. (You may not need a prescription for alcohol, and it may be legal, but it's still a drug.) If you know the person is using, you don't need to be certain whether his problem is alcohol or another drug before you look for help. If you see behavior changes in the one you're concerned about, and they fall into the pattern I've described (though there are some differences in the behavior of drug addicts and alcoholics, they are relatively minor), then you probably have cause to think about an Intervention.

When is the right time to go for an Intervention?

Treatment can be—and too often is—"too late." The sooner an Intervention is initiated, the better. Today, the prevailing feeling is that the farther the alcoholic is from the bottom, the better the chance that he will be able to achieve sobriety. In the early stages, he is in better shape both physically and mentally. Besides, as the disease progresses, everything worth recovering for will disappear—family, friends, job, health.

I had a lot to lose—a great career, a lovely home, wonderful friends, and a family that cared about me. I'm so grateful I didn't keep going until all I had left was a bottle. Still, I feel that no matter how low he or she sinks, every alcoholic has a chance to recover. I've met people who were living in doorways and who managed to come back. But, to be honest, they were the exception, not the rule.

If after reading through the first portion of this book you are fairly certain that you are seeing a drug or alcohol problem in your loved one, you should immediately get in touch with a trained counselor. (Later in the book I list some specific places you may go to get help, but you should know that if you have any problem finding a counselor, or you simply need reassurance, you can always call Families in Crisis at 612-893-1883.) You don't need to wait until the one you love bottoms out. An Intervention is a way to raise the bottom.

Who should initiate the Intervention?

Any concerned person can take the initiative. It can be a parent, a child, a spouse, subordinate, or employer. In fact, since the prospect of losing a job is pretty devastating, an employer can be especially effective. Usually, the job is the last thing to be affected by alcoholism since it's the source of whatever good feelings the alcoholic has left as well as the source of income.

A friend may initiate an Intervention, too. I was really touched by a Families in Crisis story about four guys who came in and said, "We're concerned about our friend." He was holding down a responsible job as an engineer, was divorced from his wife and was dating a woman who drank along with him. His pals chipped in to see the counselor, and once they decided to do an Intervention, they contacted his employer.

Many people are very uncomfortable about going to an employer because they want to conceal the problem. They don't realize that the drinking may already be causing problems on the job and that the employer might be relieved to know something can be done, which is what happened in this case. The engineer was a valuable employee, but his alcoholism was causing difficulties. His work was uneven and when he went out of town on projects, reports of his alcoholism would be phoned in to headquarters. His boss, who didn't know how to deal with any of this, was ready to let the man go.

Eventually, the friends got the man's two teenaged kids involved in the Intervention also. Not only the kids and friends but also the boss started to cry. He was genuinely fond of his employee, and he too had been suffering because he had felt so helpless.

Suppose no one cares?

The Families in Crisis counselors believe that even one person can act as the bridgehead. If alcohol and drugs are causing the problems in the family, he or she can usually get others involved. They tell amazing stories of family members who have been out of touch for many years rallying around to help in an Intervention.

If there are no suitable family members, then people at work can be contacted. And friends are very helpful. Even someone who has been drinking or using drugs along with the person may be included. This is not group therapy. The focus is on the person who is afflicted with the disease of chemical dependency. If the alcoholic brings up someone else's drinking or drug use, the response is, "We're here to talk about a problem with *you*, and if I have a problem too, maybe we should talk about that later."

How much time must be committed and how is it spent?

The people in Families in Crisis say participants in an Intervention can expect to spend eight to twelve hours on the process. That includes both preparation and the Intervention itself.

In addition to time spent preparing for the Intervention, there is a certain amount of time necessary to make arrangements with the treatment facility and to make sure all the excuses people have for postponing treatment have been dealt with—an absence from a business meeting covered, a doctor's appointment canceled, and so forth. The excuses can be wild. One woman agreed to go into treatment but said she had to go home and clean the refrigerator first. Her husband, who had been coached on how to handle such a problem, assured her he would handle the job.

At Families in Crisis, they prefer that the entire process, from the initial consultation to the Intervention, take no more than three weeks. When they fly out of town to do an Intervention, they can condense the process to as little as three days. They believe that once the family has made the decision to do something, they should be helped to do it as quickly as possible. They also want to reduce the possible discomfort of living in a state of suspense.

In Minnesota and New York, and wherever else you find counselors who are very experienced in leading Interventions, they will probably work within the three-week (maximum) time frame. In other places, the process may take slightly longer, perhaps a month.

The Intervention itself may be surprisingly brief. Families in Crisis was working with one family in which the daughter was so upset and so convinced it wouldn't work that about two minutes before her dad showed up, she rushed into the bathroom, nauseated. By the time she came out, less than ten minutes later, the father was on his way to a treatment center.

What is the goal of the Intervention?

Recently, I read a statement from a big name in the alcoholism field that appalled me. She described Intervention as a process in which those close to the alcoholic confront him, with the goal of forcing him to seek treatment. I don't like the words "confront" and "force." They inspire negative reactions and keep concerned people from investigating the possibility of an Intervention.

Besides, the alcoholic has been "confronted" so many times before that yet another confrontation is old news to him. He'll become angry or tune out. Confrontation is the old way of doing Interventions. Today, the idea is to show the alcoholic, in a loving way, what he is doing and how it affects you. An alcoholic puts up his defenses when he is confronted. But when he is loved, his resistance breaks down.

The goal of an Intervention is to offer hope and a solution, to be honest about what is going on. It is not to "force" anyone to do anything. It is not even to get the problem drinker to admit that he is an alcoholic. (I know people two years into their recovery who can't admit it. It's hard for some people to say "I am an alcoholic." One friend says she agreed to go into treatment because she "can't handle" alcohol. Other people like to refer to themselves as drunks. To each his own. It's what you do that counts.)

The one and only goal of an Intervention is to have the alcoholic agree to be evaluated by a professional or, better yet, to go right into treatment. Often an alcoholic will agree to go as a challenge. "I'll prove to all of you that you're goofy to think there's anything wrong." When the person agrees to go for an evaluation, the letters that have been read to him go along to the treatment center, too. (Either they're forwarded by the Intervention counselor or the family brings them along.) Those letters help make the evaluation much more accurate than it would be if only the alcoholic's appraisal of the situation were taken into account.

If you are concerned enough to do an Intervention, I am sure that in 99 cases out of 100, the treatment center will diagnose chemical addiction. The one you love may still not be willing to call himself an alcoholic, but at least the center will have called a spade a spade. The person you care about is on the way to recognizing the fact that he has a disease that will kill him unless treatment is completed and he follows the advice he is given there.

What happens if an Intervention fails?

There is no such thing as an Intervention that fails. The goal may not be met, but the Intervention has not failed. A beautiful thing has happened. The secret is out. The family has an awareness it never had before. So do friends. Neither they nor the alcoholic can play games any longer.

Anyone who has minimized the alcoholism will now, faced with the evidence, have to acknowledge something is happening. "I never noticed him doing this," they'll say. "I didn't remember that."

Another significant change is that the family will be relieved of its former burden of guilt. Having done the Intervention, they will feel they have done everything they possibly can. They start to take a much more positive attitude on life and now have the tools to effect their own recoveries. Without help, they'll fall back into the same patterns, but I understand that the majority are spurred by the Intervention to join some organization such as Al-Anon, Alateen, or ACOA (Adult Children of Alcoholics).

Over 90 percent of the people whom Families in Crisis see leave on the day of Intervention and go directly into some sort of care. Another small percentage go within a week. As for the other 5 percent or so, even if they don't go for help right away, the problem is never the same. The people involved with the Intervention (unless they're problem users themselves) will not continue to drink or take drugs with him. He will become more isolated.

But the memory of the Intervention will always be with him. Next time there's a crisis—a fight, a job loss, some other loss of control—he'll look back and grab onto the memory of the Intervention and remember that the people who loved him said, "There *is* help." And he'll reach out for it.

7/
How Interventions Work

If you're contemplating an Intervention, I'm sure you'd like to know exactly what to expect. No one can tell you that, since each one is slightly different. What I can assure you is that you're in for quite an experience.

When I believe in something, I tend to get very enthusiastic about it. Friends of mine have said, "Mary Ellen, I'm almost feeling bad I don't know anyone to Intervene on. You make it sound so thrilling." I think it is.

I wouldn't go so far as to say that you're lucky to be involved with someone with a chemical dependency problem, but I can say that it's unlikely you'll ever experience such feelings of intimacy and openness and love as you do in the Intervention process.

Here are some selections from the hundreds of letters that have been written for Interventions in which Families in Crisis has been involved. As you read them, I think you will see why I sincerely believe that although alcoholics may do some terrible things as a result of their disease, they can be terrific people. There is such an outpouring of love in these letters.

The next few examples that follow are from the beginnings of letters. Before going on to the specific incidents, each writer has tried to express the feelings of concern that moved him or her to take part in the Intervention.

Dear Mom: I love you and care deeply about you. I am concerned about your physical health and mental well-being. That is why I am about to share some memories that cause me to believe you are hurting yourself and therefore me as well.

Dear Brother: I'm here because you are more than a brother to me. You are my best friend, mentor, and confidant. Everything I have or ever hope to have is directly related to your influence, but your drinking is driving a deep wedge into our relationship and causing your own family to suffer.

Dear Colleague: I consider you to be my best friend in the firm. I respect your abilities and talents, but I am concerned for you and your family and worry about your health.

Dear Boss: In the past twenty years, I've spent more time with you and your family than I've spent with my own. I've developed a lot of respect for you and what you've accomplished. You not only built up a good strong company, you did it with guts and determination. But I am fearful that you might be endangering your success because of alcohol.

Dear Sister: I feel abandoned. You have always been my role model. Since the day I was born, I have looked up to you. Our parents always compared me to you. I always wanted to be more like you. Now that you've been using drugs, my idol is gone.

Dear Friend: You're one of the nicest people I know. I like you and value your friendship, but I'm concerned about your drinking. Because of it, the fun has gone out of our relationship.

You see how the love is kept in? There is no blame, no anger in those openings. They are meant as reassurance that what follows will be said out of love and concern.

The main part of the letter is then devoted to specific examples of drinking or drug use. It is also specific about the concerned person's reactions to those examples.

Dear Mom: When you showed up at a school event, it was obvious to all of my friends that you had been drinking, and they teased me mercilessly. "She's such a prude, and look at her mom. Who's she trying to kid?" I was angry at them and embarrassed for you.

Dear Dad: I remember arriving for the funeral and knowing right away you'd been drinking. I tried to convince you to come for some food to soak up the alcohol by pretending I was hungry. I wanted to protect and comfort you, but I was confused and saddened by the way you talked so negatively about your whole family.

Dear Colleague: A situation that frequently arises causes us all a lot of stress. You leave work early without saying when you'll be back. When a call comes in, we don't know what to say. It's troublesome when your wife calls, wondering what time you'll be home. I know that you often stop at a bar, and I'm expected to cover for you, but I refuse to lie. I end up feeling confused and embarrassed.

Dear Friend: I ran into you while picking up food to take out. You were at the bar, and as I waited, you bought several drinks for everyone. You were loud. You kept interrupting. You tried to agree with everything people said even when it meant contradicting yourself. It bothered me to see a man like you boot-licking strangers in a bar to get attention. I was embarrassed.

Dear Dad: At the cabin, we'd go out to eat after you'd been drinking all day. While you drove us to the restaurant, you would often argue with Mom and drive fast and carelessly. I was very frightened that we wouldn't make it alive, and I felt helpless. Also, I was confused: Why would you jeopardize our safety?

Dear Brother-in-Law: When you had a sip of a drink, you seemed to fall into a deeper state of drunkenness almost immediately. You were the last to leave but were totally unconcerned how your family got home or when they left. It seemed you just didn't care.

Dear Mom: Mornings, I'd come downstairs to find you with your head and arms on the table. The first time, I thought you were dead. I was so scared even to walk over and touch you. Your speech was slurred and you smelled of alcohol. I tried to help you to bed, but you got very mad. The next time, I just left you lying at the table. The incident happened over and over again. There was always a glass of liquor in your hand. I'd quietly dump it down the sink and hold back the urge to throw the entire glass at the wall.

Dear Wife: I woke up to an awful burning smell. I was terrified, since I thought the house was on fire. The tea kettle was in flames and you were in the kitchen, lying across the table. The second time I worried: When I went off to work, who would stop the fire then?

Dear Daughter: When you began spending more time with your new friends than with Steve, shortly after you said you knew you'd marry him some day, I knew something was wrong. When you broke up with Steve without sharing your feelings, I was sad. You assure me that you weren't drinking, but at that time I didn't look into the possibility of other drug use.

Dear Friend: I called you and you could hardly talk on the phone. You sounded asleep—more than that, confused. Your words came slowly and were slurred. I felt helpless and worried but have learned just to accept your rambling. I knew it would be useless to ask you to join us, so I called Tim and Hank and asked them to check on you, then felt regret that you were this far gone.

Dear Employee: Your behavior with customers has an adverse effect on the other employees and on our reputation. It hurts me that a personal acquaintance would put me and the restaurant in that situation. It disappoints me that you would use drugs while working.

Dear Brother: I hated the times we'd be at Mom's house and everyone would be having fun until it was time to leave. You'd be drunk and you wouldn't want to go. Your wife would be mad and the kids would become tired and cranky. Finally everyone was upset. I felt disappointed and sad that we couldn't have a happy day together like other families.

Dear Dad: One Friday night a friend drove me home from college and helped me into the house with my suitcase. I was nervous about opening the door, because I thought you might be passed out in a drunken stupor. And you were. I felt humiliated.

Dear Husband: We used to have such great hopes for the future. Now the money goes for drinking. I worry about how we will make it all the time. I feel cheated. You hide your bills and take checks out of the back of the book. Because I'm so opposed to your drinking, you have to cheat and lie.

Dear Mom: So many of my friends envy my having such a great mom. I want you to live a long, rich life because I need you, love you, and I like you. But I worry so much. I don't know what to expect when I call. If you're not home I worry that maybe you drank too much and fell down and hit your head.

Dear Dad: When you've been drinking, you mention things three or four times. We went to pick up Grandpa's boat and a couple of days later you mentioned to me twice that Grandpa got a new boat. Then you said something to Bob and five minutes later said it all over again. Then you hit Spot really hard one time when you'd been drinking and she put her paws on the table. I felt like just taking her and leaving the house. It really hurts inside, Dad.

Dear Boss: If you don't stop your drinking, I'm afraid you'll lose everything. It hurts me to see a man work so hard and end up losing it all. I like working for you, I believe in our business, but it seems only a matter of time before I have to look elsewhere for a job. I am losing confidence in you and the future of your family.

Dear Mom: Sometimes you and Dad would come home from a party. In my bed, I could hear you yelling at each other about the drinking. I felt so scared, lonely, and miserable. I kept asking God to let me cry myself to sleep.

Dear Wife: When you were out drinking, and came home late, you'd tell us you had tried to call but the line was busy. I knew none of the kids nor I had used the phone. I was hurt and felt betrayed by your lying.

Finally, I would like to share with you the closing lines of some of these letters—lines that express understanding, reassurance, and love.

Dear Sister: I was at your home and you asked me not to be angry about your past behavior, that it was the result of your grief. I know you weren't responsible for your behavior, and I'm not angry at you. But it wasn't grief that made you so out of control. It was alcohol.

Dear Daughter: You don't hurt me any more. I hurt for you, because I know you are being controlled by alcohol and are totally helpless.

Dear Mom: You're not only killing yourself but hurting the people who love you. Please get some help to become a person not dependent on drinking. I love you, Mom, and I love you a lot more when you're sober.

Dear Dad: I know and love your true spirit, a spirit that finds and brings out the good in others and is capable of enjoying life and its abundance. I hope someday you may share it with my future children, your grand-children. You see, Dad, there are thousands of good memories I have of you too.

Dear Sister: I love you very much. I'll always love you, unconditionally. It's the alcohol I hate, the behavior you display when you drink. I want so much for you to get help.

Dear Daddy: Please, Daddy. Can you stop drinking? I love you. Please go to the hospital. I hope you get better if you go.

Your Right to Intervene

You may be worrying about whether you have the right to Intervene. Please remember that interfering with an addiction is not an infringement of someone's rights. An alcoholic doesn't *choose* to be an alcoholic. He's addicted to booze. When you're an addict, you no longer have freedom of choice.

Alcoholics are held hostage by their disease and deserve the chance to be freed from it. They may refuse the freedom, but it should be offered. Our highways are filled with drunk drivers. Alcohol-related motor accidents are the leading cause of death among Americans aged fifteen to twenty-four. Our hospitals are filled with people suffering the effects of alcoholism and drug abuse, and our jails are filled with others who committed crimes ranging from burglary to murder and rape while under the influence. Sixty-five percent of suicides are chemically related. Together with alcohol-related accidents and homicides, they account for 60,000 deaths annually. Unless we do something, not only our families will suffer, but also society as a whole.

As far as I'm concerned, once you're aware of the consequences of chemical dependency, you don't have a right *not* to Intervene. You're in a life-and-death situation. If you were witness to an auto accident and found someone bleeding to death, would you stand there and let the person die?

Maybe you find this hard to believe. It sounds exaggerated. But time and time again, I hear the people in AA talk about some guy or gal who didn't make it. Or the counselors at Families in Crisis tell me another tragic story. One family, for example, abandoned its efforts when the parents decided they couldn't bring themselves to Intervene on their son. Not long afterward, he died of pancreatitis. In another case, two weeks after a mother delayed the family's scheduled Intervention, her son was killed in a car accident. He was driving while intoxicated. The mother is going to have to live for the rest of her life with the fact that she sabotaged the Intervention.

The ones who survive may see their lives in ruin. They'll go down the tubes without knowing why. You can prevent this from happening. If you offer such a person help in the form of treatment, you give him a wonderful gift. You give him the opportunity to discover, "Hey, I'm not such an s.o.b. I do have some values, after all. The problem is that I have a disease. Now I understand how I've been dishonest with myself. I know what's right and what's wrong. If I can begin to get my behavior in line with my values, things are going to change."

You can't deny your responsibility in dealing with a chemically dependent person. If you know he's in trouble, you must do something about it, even if you simply phone a counselor. As the saying goes, "If you're not part of the solution, you're part of the problem." Indecision is a decision. If you say you love and care about a person, how can you look at yourself in the mirror every morning if you're allowing him to continue hurting himself and the rest of the family?

Why are you hesitant?

Exactly why are you dwelling on your right to Intervene? Could it be just that you are afraid to rock the boat? This is understandable (if not justifiable) when the source of your income—the breadwinner or the boss—is involved. When I was drinking, there were times when my life would be a shambles but I'd go to New York and put together a great deal. I'd come back to the office a hero. "Way to go, kid!" people would say. I wish someone had said, "Good for you.

You put the deal together. Now let's deal with your drinking problem and put this money to work for you."

After I was out of treatment, my brother told me how concerned my associates had become. Because they knew Johnny had been a counselor for the chemically dependent himself, they occasionally would approach him. "John, we have to do something about your sister's drinking. Her behavior has become so inappropriate that we can't trust her." And he'd say, "Fine, guys, but this is how it works. You have to get involved. You have to be willing to say you love her enough to put her in a hospital so she'll get well." The initial reaction usually was, "I can't risk losing my job over this thing. She won't support me anymore if I help her face the music. She'll cut me off." They had good intentions, but they were fearful about the consequences. So they let me drink. In fact, they went out drinking with me.

As I've told you, the one associate who tried to confront me failed because he didn't get people together to form a united front; therefore I could dismiss what he said. The others were as aware of my problems as he was, and I know now that these people, whose salaries I was paying, were talking about me and holding meetings behind my back. I kind of resent the fact that they saw me in action and knew that I was sick and irresponsible, but they didn't deal with it. My brother wondered, "What does Mary Ellen have to do before everyone decides she must be given help? Does she have to be financially wiped out? Burn her house down by smoking in bed? Run over someone? Kill somebody?"

Partly, they had an interest in preserving the status quo. Also, they felt they were protecting me. They didn't really believe I was far enough gone to need treatment. I still looked pretty good. I still had my health. They didn't want to stigmatize me by branding me an alcoholic. Of course their thinking was wrong. You don't have to hit bottom to need treatment. Even if you look good, you can be in trouble. It would have been more humane to say that Mary Ellen is an alcoholic and needs help than to go along with the idea that Mary Ellen is incapable of running her business and should be treated like an imbecile.

But finally, I think they were not sure it was their right to Intervene. I see a similar thing happening with a friend who belongs to a writers' support group. Often the conversation turns to one of the members who has a serious drinking problem. Her friends haven't made a move to do anything. They haven't gotten past the point of talking about her. They don't have any vested interest in keeping her this way, but since they're not sure they have the "right" to do anything, they've chosen simply to sit around gossiping about her and letting her die.

If your spouse is alcoholic

One case where it's not simply your right but your obligation to Intervene is if your kids are growing up with an alcoholic parent. If you do nothing, their chances of being chemically dependent (for which they already probably carry a genetic predisposition) are greatly increased. They are much likelier to abuse chemicals if they grow up in a house seeing chemicals abused. They get the message, "Do as I say, not as I do." An alcoholic parent and spouse is the worst role model in the world.

Kids see when, how, and why adults drink. They are very observant. They discover that when you are drinking, anything goes. If you insult someone, you're forgiven. If you pass out on the floor, people overlook it. If you behaved like this sober, you'd be ostracized. Kids learn it's okay to flout your moral values if you're drunk. They learn that drinking is a primary activity, that alcohol is essential for family and social events. They never learn that intoxication is unhealthy and socially unacceptable, that it's wrong to drink and drive. A kid like this is vulnerable to peer pressure to try alcohol and drugs. No matter what the advertisers say, he won't believe that booze and sports don't mix, because he'll have seen evidence to the contrary.

Beyond this, there are the psychological problems. You hear a lot about teen suicides today. I don't believe wanting to do yourself in is part of the normal growing-up process, but I know that when I was growing up in an alcoholic home, I thought of suicide occasionally, especially during those painful adolescent years in junior high school. I've heard that one reason a lot of children are killing themselves today is because of an alcoholic parent. I don't even know if statistics would back me up, because alcoholism is so under-reported, but it stands to reason that children with loving, healthy parents are unlikely to commit suicide.

You may not realize the pain your child is going through in an alcoholic family. Kids cover it up so as not to burden the family more. They have no one to talk to. They may blame themselves ("If it weren't for me, Mom wouldn't be having all these problems with Dad"). They are trapped, just as the spouse is. They learn to deny everything, to say what people want to hear, to keep the peace. They also have a tremendous amount of shame and false pride about letting anyone else know what's going on. They lay down a road they'll travel for life, and it will be a bumpy one. Adult children of alcoholics have low self-esteem, are isolated and afraid, and always seek approval. They will do anything to hold onto a relationship. Often they marry alcoholics, become alcoholics themselves, or both. They will be affected in every business and personal relationship they will ever have. They are innocent victims.

Despite this, mothers sometimes use their kids as the excuse to put off an Intervention. Families in Crisis worked with one such mother and her four sons, aged fourteen to twenty-four. Even moments before the Intervention, she asked if she was doing the right thing. "I don't know how my sons are going to take it," she said. The boys, who had assured her of their support, finally became angry at her inability to do anything. Two of them already had drinking problems of their own, though I can assure you the last thing either of them wanted was to grow up just like dear old dad. The odds were against them: If one parent is an alcoholic, there's a 65 percent chance the children will be, and if two parents are, the chances go up to 85 percent. The only possible way to lower those odds is to stop the behavior at home.

If you're the spouse of an alcoholic, the kids are probably looking to you to take the first step. If you don't, some day they're going to turn on you and ask why you put up with such behavior. Don't think they'll love you for it. Many kids wind up hating the spouse more than the alcoholic. They get sick of hearing "Forgive Pop," even though he called you every name in the book, or "Forget Mom's behavior," even though once again she humiliated you as well as the rest of the family. The kids hate what the alcoholic parent is doing to the family, but they're even angrier to see the sober one, who has the real power, do nothing.

As a parent, you have no choice but to Intervene. The only time an Intervention isn't the first priority is when there's physical violence. If you explain to any counselor that this is the case, he will help get you out of the house and out of danger first.

In the case of pregnancy

Another instance in which I think it's absolutely criminal not to Intervene is if you know a woman who is drinking while she's pregnant. I drank more than I should have when I was carrying Andrew, but in those days many women were smoking and drinking and nothing was said about it. Personally, I felt guilty. I knew something was wrong if, even though I didn't want to be drinking during pregnancy, I continued to do so. Those nine months were the scariest time of my life. I really believed I would have a deformed child—I didn't think I deserved otherwise—though I could find little specific information about the consequences of what I was doing.

Today, there's no doubt about the connection between alcohol and birth defects. The news is shocking. According to the December 1985 Tufts University Diet and Nutrition Newsletter, Eileen Ouellette, M.D., a pediatric neurologist at Harvard Medical School and an expert on fetal alcohol problems, says a fair amount of research is now showing that "as few as one to two drinks a week may have an adverse effect on an unborn child, particularly in lowering birth weight and increasing the risk of prematurity." Imagine what middle-stage and chronic alcoholism can do.

I think every single doctor should warn every single pregnant woman not to drink and to give her a Fetal Alcohol Syndrome fact sheet when he does. It's devastating. Such babies can suffer from stunted growth (though girls tend to be short, stocky, and overweight at puberty), mental retardation and learning disabilities, central nervous system dysfunction, tremors, irritability, feeling disabilities, speech problems, overreaction to sounds and hyperactivity, facial malformation, small head, long flattened midface, sunken nasal bridge, short receding chin, epicanthic folds, major organ malformation, muscle problems, skeletal and genetic defects, kidney and urinary abnormalities, and heart valve defects. I've heard that some doctors worry that confronting a pregnant alcoholic woman will cost them patients, but it seems to me in light of these consequences, any doctor who tells a pregnant woman she can drink or—let's take it farther than that—doesn't put the fear of God into her about her drinking should be shot.

Even if a child doesn't suffer any gross problems, I understand that if the mother is drinking, the baby may become addicted and go through a mild form of withdrawal after birth without the doctor's even noticing. I've often wondered if these babies whose mothers drink during pregnancy are the ones who end up being instant alcoholics, the kinds of kids who take one drink as a teenager and—whammo!—they're addicted.

Men who want to be fathers pay the consequences for addictive drinking as well. "Men who drink heavily not only are more likely to be impotent but also have lower sperm counts and lower sex-hormone levels," wrote Jane Brody in *The New York Times* on January 15, 1986. "One animal study showed that when males were given alcohol before mating with alcohol-free females, there were fewer live births and the offspring were smaller."

Andrew was underweight, and then he got jaundice, and I was guilty and ashamed of myself for many years even though there's no certainty that his problems were connected with my drinking. Still, I never felt good about myself as a mother. What I had done was always in the back of my mind, and my relationship with him didn't start off well.

Can you imagine how a pregnant alcoholic woman feels— a woman who loves the child she's carrying but who has no idea how to help herself and stop herself from harming it? Can you imagine the guilt she's living with and the justifying she has to do? If you know of anyone who's pregnant and drinking, no matter what the excuse, something is wrong with her. Something has to be done. Why would any pregnant woman be drinking today, with all the advice against it, if she didn't have a problem?

Don't wait to be asked for help

Families in Crisis tells story after story about families so terrified and scared about doing an Intervention on someone they love that they become physically ill. No one knows for sure how someone will react, but more often than you'd guess, the subject comes in and says, "When I was coming here, I felt you were planning to Intervene. I'm so relieved." Some people don't even need to experience the process. They walk in, see everyone gathered, realize what's going on and say, "I'm ready. Just take me."

That's how I would've reacted. Had the people around me realized how sensitive and guilt-ridden and ashamed I was, they would have known that my Intervention would be over before it began. Someone could have told me to march to Hazelden carrying a cross and I'd have done it—willingly. How much pain can you take?

I can't believe that I was lucky enough to realize I had to get help. Most alcoholics will not. If there are no built-in consequences of drinking, an alcoholic will never stop, and most are sheltered from the consequences until it's too late. People who care about chemical dependents tend to protect them. In the name of love, you do things for the alcoholic that he should be doing for himself. The more responsibility you take on, the weaker he becomes, the more he hates himself—and the more time he has for drinking. If he reaches out for help, you may want to comfort him and ease his pain by telling him he's not that bad.

Some alcoholics realize their lives are a mess and they want help. They don't usually say, "Help me stop drinking." Instead, they may say, "Help me not drink so much" or "Help me not get into trouble." Or, more typically, "I know I have a problem, and I'll do something about it. I got myself into this mess and I'll get myself out." But even if the one you love says nothing, don't assume he doesn't want help. He's probably incapable of asking for it. He may not even be able to say aloud that he needs it.

I was in the emergency room not long ago when I noticed a guy so bent over from back pain that his nose was hitting the floor. I realized just from the looks of him that he was a chronic alcoholic, but when I asked what was wrong, he talked only about his back.

I told him I was at the hospital because someone I loved was hurt while drinking. "Booze will get you every time," I said. His ears perked up. He confided that he drank too much but that some day he planned to quit. I told him I had said the same thing many times and that now I was a recovering alcoholic.

He opened up to me and I found out he had started drinking at age ten. His life had been one mistake after another. He was only thirty-four, but he looked sixty. I told him he had a drinking problem and that if he got help, he would probably have no more emergency room visits.

"Some day," he said, "I'll wake up and find this is all a bad dream. Some day I'll be free of this curse." I told him that "some day" could be today if he'd let me help. But oh, no. "I'll help myself. I can do this myself," he said.

I gave him my best shot. I even talked to his mother, who was surprisingly open about her son's drinking, and gave her the number of Families in Crisis and Hazelden. I saw him again on his way out of the emergency room, and I asked what the doctors had recommended. "Painkillers," he said.

"Those pills could kill you," I said. "You must tell the doctors about your drinking."

He looked at me with tears in his eyes. "I can't," he said.

Don't love your alcoholic to death

There were times when I was drinking when my inhibitions were lowered and I admitted to a little bit of self-doubt or concern, but the minute I got back any feeling of power, I'd deny it. I just couldn't overcome my pride enough to come right out and say I needed a hand.

Since I didn't ask, people never reached out. After he failed at convincing me to check myself into treatment, my colleague went back to my other associate to express his continuing concern. The response was, "Mary Ellen is a wonderful gal and she's under a lot of stress. Once we get through the rough stuff that's going on in her business life, she'll be fine."

Meanwhile, my brother Johnny was so concerned that he went to the rest of the family about initiating an Intervention himself. He told them, "Mary Ellen's life is out of control. She's spending money she doesn't have and getting herself into trouble." My mom is one of those people who can really block out the truth, and her first instinct is always to protect me. Her answer was, "Mary Ellen is a great girl. We can't hurt her by doing an Intervention." She loved me too much.

When faced with the prospect of an Intervention, people often minimize the problem. They don't realize the person is dying. Some of the people who were around during my bad times still can't acknowledge how serious the situation was and how different things are for me today. They actually say to me, "Mary Ellen, I don't think you've changed at all." That's because they don't really know what was going on.

I was starting to have more problems in my relationship with my husband. My son was going through a difficult time in school and I wasn't even aware of it. He was getting poor grades and I just told myself, "Oh, he'll be fine." There were so many things going on that weren't being attended to because I was unaware of them. In business, I was going like gangbusters—working hard was the only way I could prove myself—but I made horrible investments. I started giving money away. I started behaving less rationally and doing things I'd never done before, such as drinking and driving.

It's a good thing I didn't get stopped with a DWI. It would have made the papers, and I was feeling so low that would have put me over the edge. I just might have pulled the trigger. A lot of terrible things hadn't yet happened, but so long as I continued to drink they were out there waiting for me. My life hadn't fallen apart by the time I went into treatment, but by my own standards, I had reached rock bottom.

To me, rock bottom is when you become a person you really are not—in my case an irresponsible wife and parent, a careless businessperson. Some people believe that your true personality comes out when you're drinking, but with an alcoholic, that's not so. My friends and family thought they were protecting me by not doing an Intervention, but the truly loving choice would have been to Intervene. I would have been spared a lot of anguish. I'll always carry the memory of reaching bottom with me. Thank God it is behind me now.

My Dad, who died before I was twenty, was not so fortunate. During my second week in treatment, when our relationship was becoming much clearer to me, I wrote a letter to him.

Dear Dad: I'm at Hazelden. It's a treatment center for alcoholics. I'm so ashamed, I could almost die. I never dreamed I would end up like you. An alcoholic. Oh, how I hate that word. It reminds me of you and all the crazy things you did when you were alive.

Let's face it, Dad. You never amounted to much. Either you went from one job to another or you didn't work at all. I tried so hard not to end up like you. To some extent, I managed. Unlike you, I made a success out of my life. I have a beautiful house filled with beautiful things. I drive a nice car. I have a wonderful circle of friends. And you should see Andrew, my son. Your grandson. He's ten years old, and he's terrific. He's athletic, he's fun-loving, he's compassionate. He's a mother's dream.

But in spite of all this, I am like you. Alcohol became one of the most important things in my life. I guess the apple doesn't fall far from the tree.

My first memory of you is when I was about three years old. The sun was shining very brightly. I was wearing a pretty sunbonnet and a frilly dress and was sitting close beside you in the front seat of the car as we drove up to the house. You put your big arms around me to lift me out, and our faces were very close. I remember feeling totally safe and full of love as I looked into your beautiful green eyes.

The next thing I remember: I am lying in bed feeling very frightened. You and Mom are fighting. I want it to stop.

Another image: I am sitting on the edge of the bathtub, chatting and watching you shave to get ready for work. I think you were selling cookware on the road then. "I'll miss you, Daddy," I said. But I wanted you to leave. I didn't like you. You scared me. I was happy you were leaving, but I pretended to be disappointed. Dad, I was only four years old. Already I was starting to deny my real feelings.

It's been that way ever since. I've been denying all my feelings, including my feelings for you. I didn't think I had the right to hate you, but why shouldn't I have? It was tough having you for a father. You embarrassed me so when I was growing up. I never knew what would happen next. Either you were gone or you were drinking. You broke one promise after another. Sometimes, I wished you would die. And when you finally did, I didn't know what I felt. I didn't know whether to cry or be thankful.

You were a very handsome man, Dad. All my girl-friends thought you were a dreamboat. I was so proud of that. Both you and Mom were absolutely beautiful. I remember when you and Mom got all dressed up to go out for the evening. I loved watching Mom put on her makeup. Looking at both of you, I felt there was hope for me!

When you walked out of the door, I felt so good. But when you came home, I was ashamed. You would be drunk and abusive, swearing and saying things about Mom that just weren't true. I'd hide my head under the pillow, praying you would go away.

Until I hit the seventh grade, I was head of my class. Then I began to have a rough time. School work seemed so unimportant. I couldn't concentrate. I worried about what was going on at home, and I was tired from staying up, night after exhausting night, listening to you fight.

When I was in ninth grade, you came to hear me sing with the choir. You were so proud of me, but I was uncomfortable with you. Afterward, we went out and had a Coke together. You took my hand and told me what pretty hands I had. You said that some day, I was going to be a beautiful woman.

I felt self-conscious and wished you would stop. I wanted to believe you, but I couldn't. When I was growing up you had told me so many things that didn't come true. Remember all the new "wonderful" jobs, all the attempts to start over, all the promises that we would be a happy family, do things together, maybe even buy a new house? I was so excited each time, hoping this time would be different. You always broke your word. You disappointed us so often, I gave up hope. I had no choice but to deny my feelings.

Mom denies that anything bad ever happened. You treated her horribly. But when any of us ever tries to talk about what really went on in our house, she changes the subject or rebuts what we say. If we do talk about the past, we have to lie to keep Mom happy. So nobody ever talks about you. Sometimes, it's as if you never existed.

My brother Johnny reminds me more and more of you every day. Remember how you played with us at the lake? You'd throw us in the water and pretend to be a monster. Johnny does that with his kids, too. He walks like you and wears his shoes down just the way you did. But he doesn't like to think much about you, Dad. Just the mention of your name sends him into orbit. He's still angry about how you treated him.

You affected the others, too. My sister Sue looks most like you, Dad. She's sweet and dear. But she's drinking, and it's causing her problems. Tommy never really knew you, but he inherited some of your problems, too.

By the time I was an adult, I'd gotten to the point where I hated to see you. When you'd stop by for birthdays or holidays, I felt so uncomfortable the minute you walked into the room. That apologetic look on your face haunts me to this day. You'd try to make conversation, ask what was happening with me, but I felt it wasn't any of your business. In fact, your attempts to play the father actually made me sick. I had gotten by without you. I resented your asking about my boyfriends and my job.

At one point, I heard that you had remarried, but I couldn't believe that anyone would have you. You looked so down at the heels when I last saw you. You'd always driven a really slick car, but this time, you pulled up in an old, beat-up Chevy with a ladder strapped to the roof. Seeing you that way made me sad.

Months passed. Then I heard that you died. They said

it was from heart failure. Even twenty years ago, I knew better. You died because you drank yourself to death. You destroyed your health like you destroyed so many good things in your life. You loved your booze more than you loved life itself. Dad, I never grieved over your death. The day I got the news felt just like any other day.

Now here I am, Dad, at Hazelden. I remember visiting you here once when I was in junior high school. You didn't complete the treatment program. You left and started drinking again. Your kid is not going to leave. I'm going to stick it out and I'm going to face the facts of life—that I have a drinking problem and I have to learn how to take care of it.

I wondered if I had the right to hate you, Dad. But as I write this letter, I realize that what I feel for you isn't hate. What I feel is hurt and loneliness. It's amazing. I'm a grown woman, but I still have the same pain and anger that I had when I was Andrew's age. Underneath all the hurt and the pain is a little girl who wants to be loved by her father. I really miss you, Dad. I would love to be able to look at you and hold your hand and tell you that I now understand what happened to you and to all of us.

Alcoholism is a family disease. Looking back, I remember hearing that your own father had an alcohol problem. Today I can sympathize with your pain and fears. You went into the world as a walking time bomb, just like me. But you didn't have the knowledge or the tools to handle the situation you inherited. I now realize you would have stopped if you could have, but you couldn't. You were one of the unfortunate ones. The big difference between the two of us is that I recognize that I'm powerless when it comes to alcohol and that my life has become unmanageable as a result of it. I thought I was doing the right thing, but when I look back, I too was starting to leave destruction behind.

My only regret, Dad, is that nobody ever before told me what this disease was all about. I'm sure we would have been spared a lot of pain if all of us—Mom, Johnny, Tommy, Sue, and I—had been involved in a recovery program. At least we would have understood what was happening with you and known how to deal with our own problems, so history wouldn't repeat itself. The greatest gift that could be given to me is to pass on to my son enough knowledge about alcoholism so that in twenty years he does not find himself in the same position as I am now and you were twenty years ago.

I pray that you are finally at peace and resting in the arms of God and that there is some way that God can tell you that I care about you and miss you. I am going to choose to believe that He can. It's important to me, too, that you know that I am going to run the good race—at least I'm sure going to make the attempt. Dad, I'm going to do my best. I'm going to listen to what the people here have to say and do what they tell me to do. I've been running the show for too long. So keep an eye out for me, Dad, until the day we meet again. I love you.

Those of us who are alcoholics today, and those who love alcoholics, are so lucky that we have the ability to do something. Don't hesitate to *use* yours. Without Intervention, I can guarantee that your situation won't get any better. Continue to act just as you have been doing, and the person you're concerned about will continue drinking or drugging. When my dad was alive, we didn't know how to take care of ourselves. We didn't know that, just like him, we were sick, too. We didn't know how to change our behavior so that he would have no option but to make some changes of his own. People change only when they must.

When I left Hazelden, I committed myself to making no radical decisions about my life for a year. I wouldn't switch careers. I wouldn't alter my marital status. The only thing that would be different was that I wouldn't drink. On the drive home, my brother and I discussed how difficult it would be for me to live with Sherm. He was still drinking, and besides, we enabled each other. Even though we both had alcohol problems, we had never drunk together much, particularly during the last five years, when he went his way and I went mine. One of us was always around to take care of Andrew and, in effect, mind the store.

I have admitted that Sherm was my enabler, but that's only half the story. All the time he was enabling me, I was enabling him. Sherm hadn't held a job in years, but when I was on tour, he took over the responsibilities of the household and our son. I convinced myself that he couldn't take a job because of my success. His being out of work was my responsibility.

I carried my suitcase from Hazelden through the front door and the first thing I saw was Sherm stretched out on the couch. "Oh, God," I thought. "I'm home." My husband looked very haggard, very ill. Naturally it occurred to me that while I'd been away he'd had free rein to drink. "Boy," I thought, "he's really been hitting it hard."

I'd promised my brother I wouldn't say anything right away, but I like to get things done up front. Besides, I hadn't paid many consequences for opening my mouth up to Sherm. So I told him where things stood. "Sherm," I said, "I really am going to stay sober. I'm going to work at this program, and I'm not fooling around. It's going to involve a lot of changes in my life, and it's difficult for me to be in a marriage when you're drinking."

Sherm denied that he had a problem even though he drank just about every day. Some days he drank very little and on others he drank to the point of intoxication. He had paid a big price for his drinking but like most alcoholics, he couldn't see that and continued to explain why he was okay. Like most alcoholics, he was quite convincing. Even I, who had lived with him for fifteen years and had learned so much in treatment, started buying his story.

Fortunately, Johnny was there. "Sherm, you're drinking a lot, aren't you?" he asked.

"No. No more than usual."

"Are you getting into any trouble with your drinking?" Johnny persisted.

Sherm said that he wasn't.

"If you get into any trouble will you get help?" Johnny said.

Sherm agreed. "If I get into any trouble, I'll get help."

Johnny looked at me and winked. Later he said to me, "You know why I did that, right?"

"Yes," I said. "You got a commitment from Sherm in front of me that if he got intoxicated or into any kind of trouble as a result of drinking, he'd get help."

Over the next few months, Sherm did a good job of hiding his drinking. He appeared to be functioning normally, and there were no incidents to point to, but he drank steadily and consistently. What amazes me is that even with all my knowledge he managed to deceive me. I did notice that when other people were drinking, he would serve himself a few, but he never drank when he and I were alone. If we went out to dinner, he ordered coffee. I later found out he'd usually made arrangements with the waitress to pour a shot in the cup. He was talking a good story about honesty and commitment to our relationship, but he was living a total lie.

Life went on like this for five months. Then one day Sherm met some friends for lunch. Afterward, he came home drunk. (All alcoholics eventually lose control and get drunk if they continue to deceive themselves that they can drink "normally." Sherm's behavior was classic.) His car swerved down the block. He was so drunk, he could barely steer it into the driveway.

The next morning, I told him, "Sherm, you made your choice yesterday. Five months ago, you said that if you got intoxicated, you'd get help. So here's the deal. I'm asking that either you leave or you get help." His response was to take off for our cabin in the north.

Three days later, the phone rang. "Mary Ellen, I've been thinking," Sherm said. "I've been getting into trouble because I don't have enough to do. So I'm considering taking a Red Cross lifesaving course."

"Sherm," I told him, "I think you should try to save your own life first." And I repeated the deal: He had to get help. Two days later he called to say he'd come up with a new plan. He was just going to be a nicer guy to live with.

The instant he was off the line, I phoned Families in Crisis. I couldn't delay any longer. When Sherm came home, he'd come home to an Intervention. I gathered my group, and we were all prepared. The night he arrived home, I told him I wanted him to come with me the next day to talk to someone about his drinking. He said I was on some kind of bandwagon: Now that I had sobered up, the whole world had to. Still, he knew I meant business, so he agreed to come with me. Underneath, I think he hoped to prove that I was crazy.

The following afternoon, we drove to the offices of Fam-

ilies in Crisis. I had asked only a small group to participate—
my brother, two good friends of Sherm's, and Andrew. I was
the first to speak. I reminded Sherm that when he came into
my life, I had seen him as a knight in shining armor, a handsome guy with a great job who made me proud to be with
him. As the years went by, he had a lot of job disappointments related to his drinking. Eventually he lost his ambi-
tion and, along with it, his identity. He was no longer the
strong man I'd once looked up to.

His friends talked about how they knew his drinking affected his performance at work and how they'd felt obliged
to defend him but that they had to face the facts. They talked
about the social occasions that became uncomfortable,
about seeing an old buddy retreat more and more into himself and his drinking. My brother Johnny recalled bad times
at the lake when he'd seen Sherm sitting on the porch, drinking alone. I talked about my frustration with his lack of
responsibility. Even if there were an important meeting, if
the alcohol called he'd go off and leave everyone else holding
the bag.

At this point, I knew that Andrew was not entirely sure it
was okay to talk freely. He wouldn't really open up until he
went through Family Week. He was used to the family habit
of covering up. Still, when it came his turn to speak, he
amazed me with his ability to say some of the things that
were on his mind. He asked his dad why he slept so much
during the day. "When I come home from school, Dad, a lot
of times you're in bed. When Mom comes home from work,
how come you run up and rinse your mouth out with mouthwash? One time I sipped your coffee and there was alcohol in
it. And Dad, one of my friends said the other day you looked
like you were drunk and that really embarrassed me.

"And," he continued, "remember when we went out with
J.J. and you kept saying, 'Let's just have one more drink,
and then I'll go home,' and you kept giving me quarters
to play the video game? You kept having 'just one more,'
Dad, and then you'd start talking to your friends again.
When we finally left, Dad, J.J. and I were in the back seat
and did you know we were very frightened? You were
swerving."

He came out with stuff that amazed me. For example, I

never in a million years suspected Sherm was driving while intoxicated with kids in the car, nor had Andrew felt free to tell me that before.

Sherm sat there stoically through it all. I thought I noticed a tear in his eye, especially when Andrew spoke, but Sherm is a tough guy, a war hero type. He was our John Wayne, a man who wouldn't let on if he were moved. The Families in Crisis counselors tell me that they see this kind of behavior often.

It occurred to me how strange it was that Sherm's friends, who had always given him points for being a two-fisted drinker, "a man who could hold his liquor," were the very people who were now Intervening on him.

The Intervention didn't take us very long, not more than ten minutes. The time went by much more swiftly than I anticipated. Sherm finally said, "Okay, what do I do now?" I knew that he would do just about anything to get everyone off his back. He wasn't going because he thought he had a problem; at that point, he really didn't "get it." (He wouldn't "get it," as it turned out, until the third week of treatment.) I didn't care. My only goal was to get him into treatment.

We went home after the Intervention with the understanding that he would check in the next day. Frankly, I don't recommend going home; I think you should get the person into treatment immediately, and Sherm knew it. I had given him my bottom line: Get help or you'll be out on the street—legally. I'd made threats about separation and even divorce before, but Sherm had been able to talk me out of them. He always knew how to put a temporary patch over the wound. Now, since I'd sobered up, I would stick with my word and he knew it.

The Intervention had strengthened my conviction that I had good reasons to be concerned. Since Sherm was a more silent drinker, everyone's attention always focused on me and my problem, but hearing my brother and Sherm's friends speak made me realize that even in my own alcoholic delusion, I had been correct in thinking that Sherm had big-time problems with alcohol himself.

But I was somewhat off base regarding Andrew. I knew how close he was to his father, and I didn't think he saw a lot of bad in his dad, but when my son started talking, I knew I was wrong in trying to "protect" him. My little boy understood what was going on, and he was with me in trying to help his father. For Andrew's sake as well as Sherm's, I had to be firm.

I didn't have any more fears about whether I had made the right choice. Intervening on Sherm wasn't my right, it was my obligation. And if you want to stop the one you love, it's yours as well.

9/
Overcoming
Your Reservations

After Sherm's Intervention and successful treatment, I felt things in my family were starting to become normal. Wrong.

I couldn't help but notice that my sister Sue was displaying one alcoholic symptom after another. Like Sherm, she drank differently than I did. While I'd go off once a week and drink to the point of intoxication, Sue would drink steadily and consistently. She'd have a drink at the cabin, one at the beach, maybe a couple in the boat, then one before dinner. She never appeared to be drunk, but I realized that the drinking was consuming Sue.

Sue was hurting. She began to make bad calls in business. I observed that her son was having some problems in school that I was sure were related to her drinking. She was surrounded by enablers and drinking buddies, and I had no choice but to do something. It would be only a matter of time until she crashed, and I wanted to spare her that pain. Besides, I wanted my sister back, and I knew that wouldn't happen until the drinking was arrested.

I felt we had to move fast. My brother and I knew she would be next at the treatment center and we told her so, but she continued to make the same old excuses. "Yes, okay, but—" She'd go after the summer. She'd go after the trade show.

One night up at the lake, Sue went out with some friends for dinner. They came back pretty high. Next morning, she and her son J.J. were in my car. J.J. knew I was in recovery, he knew Andrew and I had discussed my drinking, and for the first time, the night before, he had managed to talk with us about my drinking and his mother's.

"Hey, Mom," he said now from the back seat. "Last night you told me you would be gone only three hours and you stayed away six and came home drunk and Mom, that really hurts me."

I could see my sister stiffen. I could see the pain in her face. I knew how she felt and what she was thinking. She wasn't a full-blown drunk, after all. She still managed to run her own business and keep a nice home for her family.

I said to my nephew, "That was honest, J.J." Sue just said, "J.J., we'll talk about this later," but the heat was on. About three weeks later, my brother, Sherm, and I did the Intervention. It didn't take long. We gave our data about the long lunches, the business errors, and so forth. The last speaker was her little boy. "Mom, won't you go and get help?" Sue was in treatment within 48 hours.

All of us—Johnny, me, and now Sue—have gone over to the other team, the sober team. For families to recover together is not uncommon. I was at an AA meeting in northern Minnesota, where we have our cabin. One of the women said, "About five years ago, we were all drinking. We didn't have cookouts then. We had blowouts! One time my brother nearly fell into the fire. Now we're all sober."

I thought that was funny and strange. Imagine an entire family so out of it! And then I realized how inappropriate some of our own behavior had been. Our family has always gone on vacations together, and as the drinking progressed, more and more activities centered around it. We had many more parties, many more nights spent around the table drinking and talking.

When we're together now, our entire experience is different. The adults don't stay inside drinking while the kids are out playing, nor do they drag along a cooler full of drinks. We're all much more active: We're with the kids and the boats, we're out hiking and walking. We've got a family entertainment center going instead of a cocktail lounge.

I'm telling you all this not only to convince you how much better life can be but also to share with you the fact that as important as I felt it was to Intervene on Sue, it was a little uncomfortable. When I began to zero in on her alcoholism, she badmouthed me. "Who does she think she is?" was her attitude. Like Sherm had been, she was irritated by the suspicion that now that I was sober, I had to change the rest of the world. In reaction, I put off the Intervention, but fortunately, J.J. helped bring the situation to a head.

It worked out great (as the Families in Crisis counselors told me it would). Guess who is Sue's best friend today? Like me, though, you may have some reservations. I'm sure I know exactly what they are.

"I feel sneaky going behind her back"

That's not unusual. Many people feel that way, especially when they're told not to inform the subject of the Intervention just what will take place. The point is not to be deliberately deceitful. But the counselor knows that an alcoholic is in a state of emotional turmoil. That's part of the disease. He may misinterpret the purpose of the Intervention or he may assume certain things about an Intervention that are not so. There is no need to increase his anxiety. Maybe you'll feel less guilty about being sneaky if you remember that an alcoholic is sneaky about his drinking, too.

Keep your eye on the goal. Families in Crisis was planning an Intervention on the head of an insurance firm. Three days before it was scheduled, his wife spilled the beans. He denied he had a problem and threatened to retaliate if anyone proceeded, so the Intervention never happened. Shortly after, he was hospitalized for an alcohol-related disease.

It is possible for an Intervention to take place even if someone is forewarned, but you lose the impact that comes when the person walks into the room and sees the significant people in his life gathered together. Don't worry that the shock will be too much for him. As I've pointed out, most of the people Intervened on know immediately what's up and most of them want to be stopped.

An alcoholic I met was legally committed to treatment. Three people came to get him. "I was terrified," he said. "They had a piece of paper saying I was an inebriate and I didn't even know what that meant. I'd never had anything to do with the law, never even a DWI. But I remember having two separate reactions. Part of me was thinking, 'Oh, my God, what are they doing to me?' and the other part was thinking, 'Maybe I can finally get some help.'"

I think most people have mixed feelings. While you may be relieved to have the problem out in the open, you may also wish to keep it concealed, because you're ashamed. While you may welcome help, you may still want to meet the challenge, to "fight it" by yourself. Most practicing alcoholics really believe they can do it on their own. Plenty of others, though, will say, "I'm ready. Just take me."

One family I know was absolutely terrified even to contemplate their alcoholic's reaction to the Intervention. When he came into the room, he glanced around, immediately realized what was going on, then hesitated only a moment. He said nothing, just walked around and gave each and every person there a hug and a kiss.

"Everyone will find out about the using"

When the people at Families in Crisis tell families to ask others for help, they're usually reluctant to do so. "We can't tell the neighbors." "We can't tell the children." They don't want to let the secret out.

They've all known for years, I'm sure. And if they don't, just remember that this is not a moral issue. All you have to do is tell people, "I'm worried about so-and-so. I think he has a disease—the disease of alcoholism." Being sick is nothing to be ashamed of. Ignoring a sickness is.

"I won't be able to get enough people"

You don't need to fill a football stadium. You can do an Intervention with as few as three people. But I think you will be surprised at how much help you can get if you try.

Yes, you will have to make a certain amount of effort. And you will have certain disappointments. A lot of families worry about whether the people they and the alcoholic know are truly friends or merely acquaintances, and in some cases your concern is justified. My sister and her best drinking buddy had often talked about stopping. Now that Sue's sobered up, the friend isn't around as much as she used to be. She still drinks, and she doesn't want to hear about Sue's sobriety. In recovery, you often discover that a lot of the people you'd been hanging around with don't want much to do with you. You are a threat to them. You're not drinking with them any longer. I'm annoyed by how many "good friends" dump recovering alcoholics and quickly find another "good friend" to drink with.

Go about the job of assembling the Intervention group like a sleuth or a reporter. Recall past relationships. Often an alcoholic has alienated many of his former close friends. Healthy people may have begun to stay away from him. You will have to track them down.

When such a person is asked to help, at first he or she may be reluctant, saying, "We've drifted apart. We aren't close any more." Often these people do care but are so frightened and baffled by the disease they are afraid to come forward.

It's not enough to phone someone and say "I'm concerned, come and help." You must meet with the person. You should be prepared to go into some detail. "These are some instances that have caused me concern. Can you remember others?" Try to remind him or her how he once cared for the person you're concerned about. If he is hesitant, ask him to come to just one session before ruling out participating. You'll be more successful than you imagine. You'll be amazed at how many people will eventually come forth and say, "Hey, I'll help. I might not have that much information, but I'll be there to support you."

Many families decide, on the counselor's advice, to reach out to employers and co-workers (who can be invaluable) despite an initial reluctance. They say, "We can't get those people involved because he doesn't like them. They just don't get along." Of course they don't get along. The alcoholic is full of problems that he's inflicting on the people he works with. Either he's not pulling his share of the work or he has personality problems that won't win him any congeniality contests.

Ed is a friend of mine, aged about fifty, who recovered as the result of an Intervention. If he hadn't landed in treatment, he might be dead today. What I especially like about his story is that there was no family involved.

Ed was a political worker. His life was such a mess that he'd actually embezzled money from the office. Looking at him today, you'd never believe he was capable of sinking that low. He's very suave and intelligent, a wonderful conversationalist and a snappy dresser. Perhaps outwardly he never did turn into the person he'd become inside.

He was lucky that the people who worked with him realized that his behavior was the result of sickness. They got together to Intervene on him. They even chipped in the money to get Ed into treatment. What an act of love! Some of the group were Ed's friends, but others were only acquaintances. This just goes to show what people can do if they care enough.

The story has a happy ending: When Ed finally went to court for embezzlement, all charges against him dropped. The judge took into consideration that he was in treatment and in a recovery program.

Ed's story certainly makes a case for initiating an Intervention: "I decided that night would be my last night on earth. I had already attempted suicide twelve times before. I discovered that you can't drown yourself after I tried it in Lake Calhoun. Another time I tried injecting myself but, thank God, I wasn't a junkie so I didn't know how. I spent two days in bed with a whole package of syringes trying to inject air into my veins and ended up with massive hematomas on both arms—great big air bubbles that puffed up on the hands and the feet. I had to wear long-sleeved shirts for a week. I also tried a wide assortment of drugs. Two nights before I'd mixed two ounces of metallic arsenic with a glass of booze, but I'd thrown up. I decided to use milk this time, plus four ounces of arsenic.

"Of course, I wouldn't acknowledge that drinking was the underlying problem. That seemed too easy an out. I felt I was a bad guy. I'd embezzled money because the drinking had put me in financial trouble, and I considered myself just a low-down crook. I guess I suspected something about the alcoholism because a friend of mine who went into treatment asked me to come up for Family Week since his relatives were unavailable. I gave him 2300 reasons why I couldn't. The fact is I didn't want to get that close to an alcoholic treatment center. I was damn sure that the first thing they would say to me was, 'We're delighted you're here to help Jeff, but *you've* got a problem.'

"The night I'd planned my latest attempt, I was in bed reading. (That shows you how warped you become. You're going to end it all, but first you're going to finish your book.) My bedroom is at the back of the house and I can't hear the doorbell, but I heard someone shouting. I got up, put on my robe, and went down the back stairs to the kitchen. There were four people at the back door, there was one person halfway up an extension ladder to the second floor bedroom window, and when I got into the living room I found five more people who'd managed to get in through the front door. Several others showed up after checking with neighbors to see if I had gone out for the evening.

"There were thirteen in all, including a counselor. We sat down in the living room and they proceeded to tell me I had a problem. What was hilarious was that half of the group consisted of my drinking buddies. One couple was in recovery. I didn't even know him, but he put the picture together and he and his wife were the ones who got it going.

"For two hours, they explained to me why it would be better—they never used the word 'should,' by the way, just suggested 'it would be better'—if I went into treatment. They cited all kinds of examples of my alcoholic behavior, from being verbally abusive on up. I remember arguing about one anecdote, telling them there was a logical reason for my behavior, though I was bombed at the time.

"Later, I found out that they had been more scared than I. I wasn't frightened at all. I didn't really care. I listened for two hours and finally agreed to go into treatment. They had been reasonably sure I would go because they had already reserved the bed at Hazelden for 10:00 A.M. Sunday morning. We discussed whether I should leave with them right away. I assured them that I wouldn't do anything dumb but that I had to prepare for going away.

"Actually, I didn't even know what or where Hazelden was or how long I would be there. The only reason I agreed to go was because on the kitchen counter stood the good-night potion. Of course, if I had been halfway sane, I would have realized my gut was in such turmoil that nothing would stay down.

"When they left at 11:30, I went right into the kitchen and drank the poison. I went to bed and sure enough, within an hour I got violently ill. I lay there in a limp sweat until Saturday morning, when a few of them picked me up and took care of me.

"I didn't have any insurance or cash—nothing; but somehow, they managed to pay for the entire treatment. To this day, I don't even know where the money came from. I just know that somehow they got it. I feel awed by and eternally grateful to these people. They saved my life, and of course they hadn't even realized about the suicide attempt. I finally did write and tell them the whole story once I got into the program and realized how sick I was."

After you read this story, you understand why Families in Crisis recommends that, except if the person has walked out, you should never leave anyone alone after an Intervention. If he has agreed to go to treatment, he should go immediately, just in case he is depressed enough to decide to end it all. Remember, an alcoholic will lie through his teeth—like Ed, who promised "not to do anything dumb" while planning suicide.

"I don't think anyone cares"

If you think you're the only person who cares, that's all the more reason to get help for someone. Besides, if you haven't asked, how do you know how the other people in the alcoholic's life actually feel? When was the last time you sat down with any of them and talked honestly about this problem?

I have a close friend who is married to someone whom I

believe to be a chronic alcoholic. She doesn't feel that an Intervention would be appropriate because she doesn't feel that there is anyone who cares about her husband. I care. I have been with him when he was using. I would be able to prepare a letter. I can't convince her that I'm not the only one who would help. It's frightening to watch her because I know that deep down she wants to do something. She just wants someone to push her over the edge. I'm working on it.

She thinks if there were other family members involved she'd have an easier time, but of course that's not necessarily so. Families in Crisis recently told me about a first meeting they had with a family preparing to Intervene on a father. It had been difficult to get them there. Two of the children said they hated the man. The counselor took each one aside and spoke to each individually.

One daughter said, "I have had three miscarriages. I have had so much stress in my life. I can't wreck my life by doing this." I'm amazed to think she can't "wreck her life" by being honest. The counselor had to work with her to help her see that blaming her father for her miscarriages and divorces was a result of her own co-dependent behavior.

By the end of that session, each child realized that what he thought was hatred really hid an underlying emotion. By the second meeting, the mood in the room had changed dramatically. A family friend who participated in the Intervention thought he'd be attending a Salem witch trial. "Instead," he said, "I can see all the love in this room."

Members of an alcoholic's family have denied their feelings for so long that they have completely lost touch with them. When someone you love hurts you, your response is anger. The point is that you wouldn't be vulnerable to the hurt unless you loved the person in the first place.

"When I'm told that a lot of people don't like this s.o.b. and none of them may help, that's usually a clue that we've got tons of people coming. When I hear that there are a lot of people who don't care, that's usually a sign there are a lot of people who do care," Nels Schlander says. "You can't hate someone you don't feel strongly about to begin with. Usually, people look forward to the chance to break through the frustration and helplessness that's making them so mad."

"She won't even listen to what we have to say"

This is another typical worry, and from what I've seen and what the counselors at Families in Crisis tell me, it very seldom happens. During the preparation for the Intervention, the counselor helps you prepare for the possibility that the person may walk out. One mechanical way to help avoid this is to arrange the chairs so that the one Intervened on will be seated as far as possible from the door. That makes leaving somewhat awkward. But it is always possible that he will leave nevertheless.

If that happens, the procedure is to retrench, follow through with your bottom lines and prepare for another Intervention. You can be certain that a crisis will occur in that person's life, perhaps as soon as the next day. When it does, the group will be ready to act.

"He's too powerful to cope with"

One counselor in training asked Vern Johnson how to deal with a powerful person. He said, "I know it's hard. But the world needs risk takers." I'd go in and Intervene on the President if he needed help. (That's not as farfetched as it sounds. When you learn about the incidence of alcoholism in the U.S., you realize that the chances are pretty good that one of our past or future leaders had or will have a problem.)

One experienced counselor told me, "Nobody intimidates me anymore. If he's got a drinking problem, so far as I'm concerned, he's just another drunk." That wasn't a putdown. What the counselor meant was that such people are victims. They need help.

Unfortunately, plenty of the wealthy go untreated because no one has the guts to go in and be open and honest. They're all scared. I heard of a family that canceled an Intervention because one daughter and her fiancé were afraid the parents wouldn't pay for the wedding if the mom's alcoholism was brought into the open. Two other daughters were worried they'd be cut out of the will.

In treatment, I met a beautiful, aristocratic woman whose in-laws had taken charge of her estate because of her drinking. She thought the purpose of the Intervention was to get her money, but after a month of treatment, she saw the light. I admire the people who had her declared incompetent. It must have been frightening. But they did it. Instead of letting her run around wasting her money, those loving people kept her financial security intact. Bravo for them.

I wish some of the people around me had stepped in on me and my "investments." If someone had tied up my money, I would have been forced to look at what I was doing. I wouldn't have listened to anyone who tried to tell me I was generally an incapable person (I really believed I was doing the right thing), but perhaps I would have listened if someone had said, "You are incapable of handling your money, so we are going to do it for you."

Some of my employees were very aware of how my business was suffering because of my drinking (for one thing, I was horrible at delegating authority), but it was hard for them to Intervene. If the drinker is the boss, people are intimidated. Besides, I believe most of my employees liked me and didn't want to "hurt" me, and all they needed was to have a few people to pooh-pooh them and they back off. It's human nature to think you're the one with flawed thinking when no one else agrees with you.

In some cases, people love it when the boss is nuts, since that allows everyone else around him or her to be nutty too. But remember: What you're doing is trying to save a life. There are secretaries who have been involved in Interventions on their employers out of love and concern. So don't back off from doing an Intervention on a person who has the power. You might be surprised to see what an effect the group has.

The Families in Crisis counselors helped Intervene on a partner in a big CPA firm, a very take-charge guy. He walked in, saw the group assembled, and realized right away what was going on. He said, "Forget it," and walked out.

Right away the family panicked. "How could we do this?" they began to ask themselves. They had been worried that he was too powerful to deal with. Then one of them voiced the fears of all. "He's going to commit suicide." K. D. and Nels assured them what he would probably do was get drunk.

"How do you know?" they demanded.

"Because that's how he deals with his feelings of anger," K. D. and Nels explained. "We are as sure as we can be of anything that he'll just head for a bar. And then he's going to try and work on you individually, one by one. But if you're prepared—and you are—and if you stick together and hold to your bottom lines, he'll be in treatment in 48 hours."

It turned out that when he left the Intervention, he'd gone off and put away a quart of liquor. But the counselors were wrong on one point. He was in treatment in 26 hours, not 48.

What family members don't realize is that they have a lot of power when they're united as a group, focused on the single issue of the alcoholism.

"He may wind up hating me"

You're dealing with some pretty heavy stuff here. You're opening up some wounds. So, chances are you may see some anger.

During the preparation, you may even find that some of the anger is directed at you. When I started the Intervention process with Sherm, I discovered that his family felt I was the bad guy. After all, I was the one who left him home alone all the time while I was out on the road. They had all kinds of excuses for his behavior. I never realized that Sherm was playing the martyr about staying home and being over-worked taking care of the family and the house. He never actually uttered a word of complaint, but he was clever about getting people to read between the lines and feel sorry for him. They were convinced I was the ogre.

Until we started putting together the data during Family Week, I wouldn't have believed Sherm could ever make me look bad to anyone. Of course, his family drew their own conclusions from seeing me in action, lashing out at Sherm (who took it in silence) and being much more public about my drinking. They blamed me for his problems. My family and friends blamed him for my behavior. That kept us both crazy for years—but we both had halos around our heads.

The person you're Intervening on may become angry, too.

Well, so what? If he's a good alcoholic, he's been angry before, and what normally happens? All is forgiven and life goes on. The same will happen here. Look at what you risk by avoiding his anger. Do you want your kids to know their father as a drunk? That's more harmful than having no daddy at all. Remember, the anger is not really directed at you. What you're seeing is the person's anger at himself or anger he's using as a shield.

Hostility is just part of the package that comes with the disease. If the Intervention is properly prepared, and if you don't let the anger get to you, everything will go smoothly. That's why you put your feelings in writing after thinking about them at a calm time.

Most likely the alcoholic will not get angry. If you must face one of the few who does, keep in mind that you are only telling the truth, explaining your feelings and stating how the drinking affects you. You don't have to feel guilty about that. You should be proud of what you're doing. Chances are, after a successful recovery, that person will come back and thank you.

After his Intervention, my friend G. did just that. G. is a nationally-known artist. He and I were involved in a business deal together. To be perfectly honest, it failed. Today, we both know why.

When his Intervention was planned, the counselor had wanted a lot of participants, since she felt G. would need a great deal of persuasion. Here is G's version of what actually happened:

"Mike, who's been a good friend of mine for thirty-five years, ever since we were kids, called me on a Monday night. I thought that was a little unusual. I'm not a night person and all my friends know that. I did my drinking in the afternoon. I crammed it all into a couple of hours and then, being a househusband, I'd go about my normal duties. Looking back, my pattern seems crazy. I'd get sloshed, then go and pick up my daughter from school.

"My friend told me he had a problem that only I could solve, and he wanted my advice and counsel. Naturally, I was flattered. He didn't go into details, just made arrangements to meet at his house in the morning. I mentioned the call to my wife, who said only, 'That's interesting,' and I offered to drive her to work in the morning because I'd be heading that way. She refused. She said she had to be at work early and would take the bus. I dropped her at the stop, got our daughter off to school, and arrived at Mike's at 9:00 A.M.

"We went upstairs to the living room. There was my wife, another good friend, my twenty-year-old daughter, and a woman I didn't recognize who turned out to be the counselor. I sensed immediately what was happening. I knew just what was coming down. I greeted everyone and asked for a cup of coffee. Then I sat down on the couch next to my wife. There was a deathly silence for what felt like 24 hours but was probably only a couple of minutes. I said, 'What's happening?'

"Each person there proceeded to read a letter about me and my drinking, my personality, my attitudes, my productivity, and how these affected them. I found out later that it was very difficult for everyone. But after they read their letters, I didn't deny a thing. If I had, I later learned, they had other bottom lines ready. They didn't have to produce them. I was ready. I was totally ready to accept. I was at the point where I had already stopped drinking hard liquor, but I knew how bad my drinking had become. It wasn't uncommon for me to sit at a bar with a drink, stare into the mirror across from me, and cry.

"Still, even though I knew I had a problem, I didn't realize how much I had hurt my family. I really felt for my daughter. She couldn't find a lot of negative things to say. She didn't want to say anything that would hurt me. It took a lot of courage for her to be involved.

"I found out later that the counselor had wanted about 35,000 people present, but Mike reassured her that he knew me and that when the Intervention came down I'd accept it and go. Mike knew this because several years before, he and another good friend and I had done an amateur Intervention. We had just met with some guy over lunch and started to talk to him about his drinking. At the time I knew my own drinking was out of hand, too. I thought I had enough willpower to quit on my own, and for eleven months I didn't drink.

"When I started again, I switched from Jack Daniels to beer plus a little wine, thinking they weren't as bad as the other stuff. (In treatment, I learned that no matter what you're pouring down your throat, if it's alcoholic it affects your brain the same way.)

"I had come to Mike's at 9:00 and they were checking me into St. John's for treatment by 10:00. My treatment went smoothly. Me, the tough guy the counselor thought needed a crowd at the Intervention—I became the ideal patient in treatment."

"An Intervention and treatment might jeopardize his job"

Chances are if you put the whole thing off, he'll be fired from his job anyway. At least while he's employed, he's covered for treatment under hospitalization. Both your counselor and the treatment center can help you decide whether contacting the employer is appropriate, and if necessary, they can do an excellent job of explaining the disease of alcoholism to the employer and holding things together.

One woman who had been persuaded to get the boss involved was very reluctant initially: "My husband was a salesman, and on our bill every month we had hundreds of long-distance phone calls back to his home office. But I was so paranoid that I thought he'd notice one call on a date when he was out of town and realize I had made it. This was insane, since he never looked at the bill, but I phoned from my mom's house, just in case.

"I called the main office and explained that I wanted help with an Intervention. The guy asked for my number and said someone would call back. I waited with my fists clenched. The person who called said, 'We are a national organization, and we have gone through six months of training here to teach our people about chemical dependency. Our personnel office has been waiting for someone to call so we can use all these services. We will do anything. We will go anywhere you ask us to.' The national sales manager and the district manager came to the Intervention."

The counselor knew this company had a modern attitude about chemical dependency, and that's why she advised the wife to contact the employer. I think more and more companies are getting "with it." They should. If they suspect an employee is sick with an illness, and if they know the family is concerned about the employee's chemical use, it's their responsibility to be involved. Some employers take the attitude that if an employee can't do the job, they will just get someone else. They regard alcoholism as a disability and (although technically it's not cause for a dismissal) focus on other performance issues and find an excuse for firing. Others feel they have no right to pry into someone's personal life. But more and more companies are becoming enlightened.

A gal who works for a large New York corporation told me that not only did her manager acknowledge her alcoholism problem, but also the company paid for her treatment, for her parents' airfares to the treatment center for Family Week, and for additional treatment when she ran into some trouble during her recovery.

"This may not work on our adolescent"

Most of the Interventions on adolescents are for the abuse of alcohol in combination with some other chemical and yes, they do work. An Intervention helps lay the cards on the table with adolescents. They already know that Dad is mad at them and that Mom is frustrated, but they need to know how scared the family is and what they're concerned about.

Adolescents are expert manipulators. One child Families in Crisis came across would steal from the rest of the family—rob Mom's pearls or raid Dad's wallet. Instead of getting the child help, the parents simply began locking up everything. The kid was running the household, which is often the case in these situations.

The parents don't want to hurt their child, but they tend to be very much locked into the paradox of addiction. What feels like helping is probably hurting, and what feels like hurting is helping.

After they've listened to some parents' stories, the Families in Crisis counselors suggest that the parents do what they've already been doing, but just carry it a bit farther. Hand over the car keys. Put the checkbook in the kid's name. Have the child set the curfew for his parents.

When the parents consider the absurdity of such suggestions, they realize how crazy the situation has become. Somewhere along the line there has been a reversal of roles and the person with the problem is in control. This is what happens in every family with a chemical dependent.

What makes these cases even worse is that parents have enormous guilt when something goes wrong with their child. The child plays right along with this, of course. Someone who has a problem with alcohol or drugs is only too happy to put the blame somewhere else. My AA friend Ralph's mother is still convinced that his drug use stems from the fact that she sent him to military school in the seventh grade.

When the kid is in trouble, he'll often play Mom and Dad against each other. Sometimes what appears to be a marital problem is the result of a child with a chemical problem. On the other hand, when an adolescent is into drinking or drugs, it's very likely one of the parents is as well. The child's behavior is then ignored: The other parent plays dumb because to look into the kid's problems means taking a good look at the spouse's behavior as well.

I am amazed at how parents fail to recognize how much influence they have over their children. A friend of mine mentioned that she knew of a teenager who was a lovely boy but was having problems with drug addiction. She told me that the boy had been sent to live with his father while he straightened out but that it hadn't helped a great deal because his father used recreational drugs. I commented on how insane it was for parents to drink or take drugs in front of a child and expect him not to be a user himself. "Aren't you judgmental!" she cried. Of course, I said; having judgment is the sign of an adult.

Her feeling was that drinking in front of a child wouldn't turn him into an alcoholic, so why should taking drugs in front of a child turn him into a dope addict? In either case, of course, you're condoning the use of a harmful substance, and in the case of the drug use, you're also putting across the message that it's okay to do something illegal. Parents who do this obviously have no idea how much power they have over their children, and of course they have an enormous influence. In fact, one reason the success rate on adolescent Interventions is as high as with adult Interventions is because once they've regained control, parents do have so much influence over their children.

While I don't believe that Interventions are necessary with children, I do believe they have the right to know that the family loves and cares about them. Sitting down and telling your child about your concerns and how his or her behavior is affecting you is a way to demonstrate that. Many kids are shipped off to treatment centers because their folks exercised authority without showing any love.

"Both my parents are alcoholic"

Families in Crisis calls these situations "double-headers." The children work with the counselors to do a simultaneous Intervention and prepare letters for both, reading first one letter and then another. Neither gets off the hook—one parent doesn't become the good guy and the other the bad guy—and the parents can't point fingers ("You're worse than I am") or take the blame ("I'm worse than you are"). It takes more work and more preparation to do a double Intervention, but they're very effective.

If the spouse can help in a healthy way, it may be possible to Intervene with one member of an alcoholic couple. One case where this was not possible involved the father, in a shaky recovery, who didn't want Mom sober because he was planning to drink again when he retired. By contrast, Families in Crisis had another case in which the husband was extremely useful. A son gave his parents airline tickets to Minneapolis, where he told them there would be a family meeting including a daughter who was coming from Chicago. This daughter had chronic emotional problems so they thought they were coming to deal with those, but what was planned was an Intervention on the mother. Once the data was presented, she turned to her husband for advice about whether to go into treatment and he told her she should. The family had planned that if she was willing to go, they'd ask the father to accompany her. He agreed to go along.

In the experience of Families in Crisis, women resist going for treatment more than men. They had at least one case of a double Intervention in which the father went but the mother would not. "I remember sitting in the room and watching her kids unhook from her, one at a time," the counselor recalls. It was a major turning point. They stopped allowing her to blame the father for her behavior. She freed them from feeling they had to take care of her. She had made her decision.

"I'm worried about the cost"

In the first place, as I'll point out later, much if not all of counseling (including family visits prior to the alcoholic's getting help) and treatment may be covered by insurance. Besides, when you're on your deathbed, money isn't the object. Get the person you love healthy again and you'll find that money becomes less of a problem anyway. Maybe he'll do better at the job. Certainly he won't be squandering his income on booze. I wonder if you're aware of how much the disease is costing you already. "Who buys the liquor?" the counselor asked a woman who outearned her alcoholic husband.

"He does," she said. "No," said the counselor, "you do." "But he's buying his own," she said.

"How does he get that money?" the counselor repeated. "If you weren't working, where would that money come from?"

Aside from the money saved on the liquor itself, once the person you care about is in therapy, less money will be going for other things caused by the alcoholism—things like legal bills, therapy, car accidents that happened while under the influence, medical bills for related illnesses. I'm even saving on my dry cleaning bills—less spills these days. That may seem like small change, but every penny counts, since I'm still paying megabucks for the business mistakes I made in my drinking days. Alcoholics try to make decisions quickly, because they have other things to do (like go out and drink). I remember being shocked when someone had told me that the bad judgments you make because of alcohol and drug addiction come back to haunt you, but it turned out he was right.

And though I'm talking about financial "costs," here, I'd hate to tally up the losses of work and play time that my alcoholism caused me.

"What's the point?"

I know people who are secretly convinced that the alcoholic or drug user can't handle life without his crutch. They believe the person is just drinking to relieve stress, and no matter what you tell them about it being a disease, incurable and progressive, a shield goes up before their eyes.

Some people say, "My dad is seventy-five. Just let him drink. What else does he have to look forward to?" The family simply turns its back on such a person. They figure, "He's going to die anyway." But while he's living, he's miserable. The rest of the family is miserable. He's a burden to them.

People will sometimes say about fellows at the Veterans Hospital who were injured or in shell shock, "Why not let them have their booze and their pot?" I tell them, "If you feel that way, you don't know anything about alcoholism."

K. D. Dillon says that one of the worst mistakes she made as a counselor was in dealing with a quadriplegic who drank and smoked pot. The only part of his body he could move was his mouth, and his life looked so miserable that she thought, "Why not let him get high once in a while? If I were in that position, I'd want to escape reality, too." She talked to him and asked why he wanted to remain in treatment.

"I have an illness," he said. "I want to get better. I want dignity, like everyone else."

"Can't he just go right into AA?"

I've talked to some of the old-timers who got sober the hard way—right off the street and into AA. All of them had reached rock bottom, and nothing was left but the helping hand of AA. These guys were and are a great bunch. They are the ones who made it possible for people like me to sober up. They nursed each other back to life without the aid of professionals. Because they did it that way, they naturally have a tendency to feel that everyone else should too.

I feel it's fair to ask them this, though: Why not choose the treatment route? Once anesthesia was developed, who would go through an operation biting on a bullet? Some things do change for the better. Besides, to me, a 28-day treatment is the equivalent of two years of AA meetings.

Don't get me wrong. The old-timers have a lot of love. They're all for anyone getting sober, no matter how. While at one point AA felt you had to hit bottom before you could accept help, I believe they were the first to take the position this isn't necessary.

"I'm worried about what will happen to her in treatment"

I'll discuss treatment in more detail later in the book, but I can assure you no one is going to lock up your alcoholic and throw away the key. There will be no pajamas, no straitjacket, none of that stuff.

Families worry that in the treatment center the alcoholic will be beaten up or that people will be mean to him. They're still protecting him. No matter how rotten he's been, they don't want him to feel any more pain.

As far as I'm concerned, treatment is one of the best things that can happen to a person. Imagine a whole month in which you have nothing to do but learn about yourself. You can devote all your energy to it. Someone provides clean linen and takes care of your meals. I believe everyone in the world would be very fortunate to be able to spend a month in treatment learning what makes him tick.

"He's had one or more treatments already"

Sometimes treatment doesn't work the first time. If the one you love has been in treatment before and is starting to drink again, the reasons are clear. He didn't listen to the advice given him. He didn't attend AA. He didn't read the literature. He didn't stay away from the places and people that caused him problems before. He didn't do what he was supposed to do. (And what about you? Did you follow through? Did you go to Al-Anon? Did you own up to his drinking problem?)

A person may need a second treatment to "get it," to understand his disease. Second treatments are not uncommon, and usually this time around the patient will listen. It will have dawned on him that if he didn't have an alcohol problem, why is he back in treatment?

Don't be concerned that the first treatment was "wasted." His experience will help him realize that if he doesn't start listening and following through, he can plan on making treatment a way of life.

If you know someone who has just gotten out of treatment and has started to drink again, it is very important to move in and do an Intervention. He needs help desperately, since he has begun to lose hope. If someone has been out of treatment many years, an Intervention is equally appropriate, particularly if he remained sober for only a short period after the first treatment.

"I'm worried about the changes that will occur"

Counselors will tell me that the minute they explain how the family disease works and how it's affected everyone, you can look around the room and see everyone's eyes get bigger and bigger as they imagine how, once the person has gone into treatment, everyone will live happily ever after. Later, they think about—and worry about—some of the consequences of the person's changing.

Spouses worry that once the partner can stand on his own two feet, the marriage will break up. Wives know there are other people chasing him (many alcoholics are charming and popular) and worry that the guy is hanging around only because he's helpless. Or they decide that he's faithful because he's had no other opportunities, opportunities that sobriety would present. Don't kid yourself. There are many opportunities for glamor (or what passes for it) in the life of an alcoholic. When he's out there using, he's subject to a lot of temptations. There are a lot of bright lights and a lot of pretty people out there, and he's had plenty of chances to stray already. If you allow the using to go on, the likelihood is that you'll lose him anyway. If your marriage is worth holding onto, it'll get better once the family gets help.

Once someone has been in treatment and has been in the program on the outside for a while, he will begin to reclaim his responsibilities—and rights—in the family. This may cause some initial problems. He'll start controlling the checkbook again. He'll have to be included in decisions where he was once ignored. I think of the women whose husbands went to Vietnam and who became the head of the household. It was hard for them, too, when their men came home.

The family will have to change along with a recovering alcoholic, or his chance for relapse goes up to 80 percent. You need help in making those changes, and a good treatment program will have some aftercare for the family as well as for the chemically dependent person.

Yes, there will be changes. But, believe me, all of them will make your life better.

"The timing isn't good"

I wish I could corner each of you reading this book and personally convince you that doing the Intervention will change your life. Stop whatever you're doing and get on with it! It's the most important thing you can do. Forget the winter vacation. Forget the kid's upcoming exams. It's more important that your family be mentally healthy than suntanned—or even that the kids pass a particular exam.

I've heard so many tragic stories like the ones I have already mentioned—the family delayed and their loved one died of pancreatitis, another was in a car accident caused by drunk driving. Just the other day, Families in

Crisis told me about a son who hesitated because he was convinced that his mom was too far gone to get help. Finally, they brought in a friend of the mother's. Initially, she too had about ten million reasons why Intervention wouldn't work. When the counselors finished talking with her, she was ready to pay for anyone and everyone (including the gardener) to be flown from all over to do an Intervention.

Preparations were in the works when the son called to say his mother had died suddenly of a stroke. They might not have put it on the death certificate, but that woman died of alcohol abuse.

Get help. It's there for people like you. At least start talking about Intervention. There is so much false pride and so much shame about chemical dependency. Forget about your shame for now. That's what's getting you into trouble. It's not what people think of you that counts. It's what you think of yourself. Call for help. Yell for help. And guess what—you'll get it.

"It's just too drastic a measure"

You do have a choice other than Intervention. You can continue to do just as you've been doing, but I assure you the disease will run its course and the alcoholic will die of it. At the funeral, you'll be wondering, "Did I do everything I could to help?" On top of that, you'll be passing on a legacy of suffering to your children and their children. Alcoholism, as I can't say too many times, is a family disease. Unless it's Intervened on, it will continue long after you've gone.

All I'm telling you to do is to be honest. If this seems overwhelming, remember that once you've gone for help, you will no longer be making all your decisions alone.

"Maybe there are some people who just can't be helped"

I don't believe there is anyone who can't be helped.

10/
If You're Not Quite Ready

I've already given you lots of reasons to get on with your Intervention. I can give you a million more. But you might not yet feel ready. Even so, while you're working toward making the decision, you *can* work on improving the overall quality of your life.

What can you do for yourself?

For starters, try finding small ways to be good to yourself. The Families in Crisis counselors often ask people with whom they are working, "What is some little thing you'd really enjoy doing?" The answer might be, "I'd love to go shopping on a Saturday afternoon. But my husband's around, and I can't do that." The counselors urge them to try and find a way to make such an outing possible. Can you think of a small, attainable pleasure you have been denying yourself? Maybe you can make it happen.

Also, do what you can to improve your physical condition. If you've let yourself go, start getting some exercise. It doesn't have to be anything major. You may simply start walking fifteen minutes a day. But do it on a regular basis and work up to an hour a day. It'll improve your attitude more than you can imagine.

Begin to keep a record, too, about the person you're concerned about. Jot down examples of his or her behavior and your feelings about the person. Buy a notebook and divide it into columns: What I saw or heard. What I think. What I feel. What I want. What I did/am doing/will do. I am sure you will be amazed by what you wrote when you read it back to yourself. It may help you make your decision to Intervene. Some of it will be the basis for the letter you prepare.

An organization that can help you

The real key to helping yourself is joining Al-Anon. Every day, all over the U.S. and around the world, hundreds and hundreds of these meetings are taking place. Some of the meeting rooms are unappealing and dark. Others are cheerful and bright. Some of the people who come into these rooms are young, and others show on their faces how much life they have seen. Some arrive on foot, others are chauffeured to the door in their Rolls-Royces. What they all have in common are the fears, doubts, and pains that come from living with an alcoholic as well as the desire to better their lives.

Al-Anon is the last stop for thousands of people who have tried everything else. They have no resources left. They have become as addicted to their drinker as he is to his booze. The minute they come to Al-Anon, they're on the road to recovering. They will make a fresh start. They will stop merely existing and begin to start living again.

You may have convinced yourself that Al-Anon isn't the answer for you. Earlier, I cited the rationalizations: I'm a nonjoiner. I'm not ready to take my problem public. I'm not sure the problem is alcohol. By now you should be aware that every one of these excuses is just another example of family denial. Let go of them.

Everyone around you is probably tired of listening to your problems. I think of my friend's mother, who was married to an alcoholic. She spent her life complaining to everyone. She was told to go to Al-Anon, but before she did, the marriage ended in divorce. Then she married again. The new husband is a successful attorney. His bank account is bottomless. So are his cocktail glasses. The man doesn't know a lot about joyful living. Money can't buy happiness—even for an alcoholic.

And what's the wife doing these days? Still complaining and blaming. Rather than go to Al-Anon, she calls her three kids (and anyone else who won't hang up on her) to complain. They spend useless hours worrying and trying to help. She used to be fun, but now she's the world's greatest martyr. Her children have become great enablers. Their role is to tell Mom she's great and he's a jerk. Their innocent involvement will unfortunately affect all their future relationships. Once an enabler, always an enabler—until something or someone Intervenes.

None of her complaints will ever be backed up with action. I used to play her game. I used to threaten Sherm with divorce regularly. He paid no attention to any of my threats. The truth is I never once even got as far as contacting a divorce lawyer, and he was on to me. I was just trying to control him, but what I actually did was give him another excuse to hit the bottle. "My wife wants a divorce, so I want a drink." Stop the empty threats. If you want a divorce, get one, but before you remarry, ask yourself some questions about your situation. Might you be creating it? If the real issue is the alcoholism, go to Al-Anon.

At the meetings, you'll discover people who have been in worse shape than you've ever dreamed of—and also people who are probably pretty much like you. You'll find yourself hearing stories that sound so familiar:

· "He lost his job yesterday and then went out and drank up our last ten dollars."

· "Business is failing because of his drinking, but he refuses to admit it."

· "I know he loves me more than the booze. Why does he keep going back to it? Worse, why do I keep going back to him? Am I crazy?"

· "I hate the creep. If he lays a hand on me once more, I'll leave. I really will."

· "I don't care about anything anymore. That's how low I feel."

· "All I do is sit home and cry, wondering what will happen to my family."

You'll hear the good news, too:
· "It's gotten so much better since I joined this fellowship. I owe my sanity to this organization."
· "The kids are doing better in school and I enjoy them so much more."
· "I don't blame myself for his drinking anymore."
· "I can face the world again and it really isn't such a bad place after all."

What you'll get out of Al-Anon

You will have the opportunity to share your personal experiences with people who are all in the same boat. (Just like the crew in Noah's Ark. And remember, all of them made it.)

You will have the opportunity for help at any time. No appointment, no waiting—and free coffee. If you smoke, that's okay too. And if you don't, there are nonsmoking groups that meet alone or, in some cases, in a split meeting with smoking groups.

You will have the chance to work at your own pace and on the areas you're most concerned about.

You will get encouragement from others who, unlike your spouse or mom, won't offer you unsolicited advice (that's a switch!) but will wait until you ask.

You will be assured that you won't be thrown out if you goof and fall back into your old patterns. (If that were the case, there'd be no membership.)

You will enjoy the fellowship of wonderful people who will give you love with no strings attached and make you feel that you're okay just being yourself. I have even made some great business contacts in meetings. I trust these people.

You will have a chance to find role models, people who really have a handle on life. At least you will see and hear how responsible people behave. You don't see many such examples on the street or on TV, but you do at Al-Anon. The old-timers welcome your presence to give them new insight and help them see how far they've come. (Incidentally, it isn't always the ones who seem most together who are most helpful. Some of the newest members have helped me. Anyone's opinion may prove to be valuable.)

Best of all, you will have opened the door to unlimited opportunity to go on learning who you are and why you got that way.

No one has any ax to grind or mission to promote. AA and Al-Anon have no leadership and are not allied with any denomination, political entity, organization, or institution. They are self-supporting and they keep on working and helping. I don't think most PTAs have so noble a spirit.

Try Al-Anon. You've been living your life your own way, and things haven't turned out so well, so why not try something else? Don't be a fool and dismiss something until you know what it's about. As Bob, one of AA's founders, has said, "Take the cotton out of your ears and put it in your mouth."

A word about the 12 Steps

In Al-Anon, you work with the same 12 Steps that are part of the AA program. I know that one reason people never make it to AA or Al-Anon is that the last thing most alcoholics and their families want to hear about is God. Don't be put off by the "God" stuff. I assure you, this isn't a religion. What's called a "higher power" is just something, or someone, bigger than yourself. It so happens that for me, God is the higher power. But there are others for whom the higher power is just the group itself. It doesn't matter. Everyone finds his own way. The 12 Steps are simply tools for living.

A friend says one of the best things that ever happened to her was when her husband was in treatment at a center that had no family program. His counselor realized what kind of pain she was in, so he arranged for her to stay as a patient in the chemical dependency unit for a week. Although she herself was not chemically dependent, there was simply no other help available for her. She took AA's first step—admitting you are powerless and that your life has become unmanageable because of alcohol—and from that point on, there was never any way she could deny her part in her husband's problem.

The 12 Steps may sound a little hokey to you. They did to me at one time, too. But they open many wonderful doors that you might have thought were shut forever. Different types of 12 Steps groups are forming everywhere—Over-eaters Anonymous, Gamblers Anonymous, Debtors Anonymous. People don't lose control of their lives to alcohol only.

The program works. It has staying power, unlike the latest diet or self-help book that promises you everything and then disappears from the scene. There's not a professional in the field of mental health who can find fault with the 12 Steps program. If you find one, check his rates—and his alcohol blood level!

I've been going to AA for two years now, and I've met people who've been going for twenty years and more. When the conversation is centered around the 12 Steps, we never run out of things to say. We never outgrow them or graduate to higher and "better" things.

Which group is for you?

You may find some groups more helpful than others, so you might want to spend some time looking around for one in which you feel really comfortable. One friend says that she's been to meetings that left her feeling worse when she left than when she went in. But she realized that if she had bad food in one restaurant, she wouldn't stop going to restaurants. So now she looks for meetings where people seem to have a strong mutual desire for help and a mutual sense of the direction in which to progress.

My feelings about Al-Anon meetings are the same as my feelings about AA meetings. You don't drink with everybody, and you won't want to be sober with everybody. Shop around a little. You'd do that if you were buying clothing, wouldn't you?

But you don't have to keep looking until you find a place where you agree with or like every person in the room. Nor should you feel that your personal growth depends on a particular group—in other words, if they do things right, you will be okay and if they don't do things right, you won't. You can go to the worst meeting around and as long as you know what you are looking for, you take away pieces of that meeting that are useful to you and meet your goals. You can make it into what you need it to be.

Also bear in mind that you might not be such a terrific judge of what's a good group or a bad group, especially at the beginning. I wasn't thrilled with my first AA meeting either. I felt self-conscious, as if I didn't belong. After showing up a few times, I became a part of the gang. I always dreamed of having friends like the ones I made in meeting—people who believed that I was okay just being myself. You will find this kind of person in Al-Anon.

I have never made judgments about the kind of people who were at the meetings I attended. I never paid any attention to what walk of life they came from. I know that I have more in common with every one of them than with any group I happen to meet in a boardroom.

If you do decide to go, you should be prepared to give Al-Anon the same commitment an alcoholic would give to AA. Don't go just once—go a couple of times, or more, to any group you find. Commit yourself to going to eight or more meetings a month. That won't kill you. (But living with the alcoholic might.)

A lot of people make the mistake of attending one or two meetings, then quit. They expected a miracle right away, and they wind up feeling frustrated and disappointed. Well, maybe a miracle does happen for some people, but for most of us, nothing happens without time and patience. Let's face it: The effects of the drinking are profound. The wounds are not going to heal overnight.

Don't compare your situation to the ones you hear about. Just listen, and learn. And when you're ready, share. In time, I know, you will see and feel the change. Going to the meetings and having frequent contact with the other members can bring about wonderful changes in your life. When things get rough, don't quit. Double up on meetings. Where else can you find this kind of help without paying a dime? You'll learn all the following:

· How to rebuild your life and self-respect. (If you never had any, you'll learn how to achieve it.)

· How to find lectures, books, and films that are valuable

learning tools and that motivate you to want to change more.

· How to change your behavior and your feelings.

· How to be honest.

· How to accept help and give help, without feeling you'll pay a price.

· How to live in a world plagued by alcohol and drugs.

· How to love and be loved.

· How to restore your entire person—body, mind, and spirit.

· How to have peace of mind by recognizing your own shortcomings.

· How to have a healthy relationship.

· How to continue to grow after sobriety. There will still be problems. That's life. But the problems disappear once you learn how to make decisions.

A note of caution

Having mentioned all the positive things about meetings, I now want to express my reservations. Don't come away with the wrong message. If you go to a meeting, you might hear the word "detach." You're supposed to "detach" from the problem. To me, the best way to detach is just to walk out. What they mean is to separate the alcoholic behavior from the person. They definitely do not mean refusing to acknowledge the problem. If you're a typical member of an alcoholic family, you're probably already doing a good deal of denying.

I'm not sure that "detaching" is possible in all situations. Can you detach from a raging alcoholic? Do you detach to the point where you do nothing? There comes a time when you must take a stand. And you must have a goal. Setting the goal is the purpose of Intervention.

Another thing to watch out for are the armchair counselors you may run into. They're violating the principles of Al-Anon. While psychologists and doctors might be at a meeting, they're simply members of the group; the opinions they volunteer have no more weight than those of a truck driver. Al-Anon is a self-help group, not a therapy group. Members tell you what has worked for them, and you can share your own experience and reach out for strength and hope. No one says, "If you don't do it this way, get out." If people counsel you in Al-Anon it is very unfair. You'll be left hanging. Therapists know that if you take people apart, you'd better be able to put them back together again.

No one should be telling you whether or not to Intervene. You may find some negative attitudes toward Intervention, but in 1966 the Reverend Yvelin Gardner, then Deputy Director of the National Council of Alcoholism, directed this quote to Al-Anon: "Intervention can be helpful. Intervention is family therapy. Moving in, when it's properly planned and properly timed, can be effective. The spouse doesn't have to sit back and wait, wringing her hands, and asking, 'How long, oh Lord, how long?' There comes a time when the family can and must, in fact, take a stand, and honestly tell the alcoholic what he's doing to himself, and what he's doing to the family."

You shouldn't look to Al-Anon for guidance in starting an Intervention or for advice about whether to initiate one at all. Nor is it a substitute for an Intervention. Members can only tell you what's worked for them. What you will get from Al-Anon is the knowledge and support to make a decision for yourself and the realization that you must take care of yourself. If you get that message, you have taken away the greatest gift that Al-Anon can give you.

Other sources of help

You might also consider joining one of the Adult Children of Alcoholics groups that are springing up around the country. If you're married to an alcoholic, there's a pretty good chance you were raised in an alcoholic home, and these meetings will be right up your alley. I have found a great deal of help and support through this organization.

If you want further information about any of these groups, or want more material about alcoholism, here are the addresses of some organizations. (Be sure to check your Yellow Pages for local information, too. For example, AA is listed in virtually town.)

Al-Anon Family Group Headquarters
Alateen

P.O. Box 182
Madison Square Station
New York, NY 10159
(212) 683-1771

Alcoholics Anonymous
General Service Office
P.O. Box 459
Grand Central Station
New York, NY 10153
(212) 686-1100

American Council on Alcohol Problems
2980 Patricia Drive
Des Moines, IA 50322
(515) 276-7752

Association of Halfway House Alcoholism Programs of
North America
786 East 7th Street
St. Paul, MN 55106
(612) 771-0933

Children of Alcoholics Foundation
200 Park Avenue
New York, NY 10017
(212) 980-5394

National Association of Children of Alcoholics
31706 Coast Highway
Suite 201
S. Laguna, CA 92677
(714) 499-3889

National Clearinghouse for Alcohol Information
P.O. Box 2345
Rockville, MD 20857
(301) 468-2600

National Council on Alcoholism, Inc.
12 West 21 St., 7th floor
New York, NY 10010
(212) 206-6770

National Institute on Alcohol Abuse and Alcoholism
Parklawn Building, 5600 Fishers Lane
Rockville, MD 20857
(301) 443-3885

I hope that your efforts will bring you to the point where you are ready to stop the one you love from drinking. When you are, your first step is to find professional help.

11/
Locating Help

Once you've decided to initiate an Intervention, your first major step is to find a counselor.

The need for professional help

I've said it before and I'll say it again: You must use a *professional* counselor. In addition, whomever you choose should be knowledgeable about chemical dependency. If you believe that the person you love has a problem with alcohol or drugs, my advice is to forget all the other places you might have gone to or are thinking of going to for help—the psychiatrist, the marriage counselor, the doctor or clergyman. However well-intentioned, most such professionals have tried to treat chemical dependency without results; and in many cases, their services are costly.

I am amazed at how many people who are perfectly willing to pay for other kinds of services balk at the idea of using and/or paying for a chemical dependency counselor. I tell them to turn their thinking around. The right counselor will be worth every cent you pay. (And if you find someone who claims he'll do an Intervention for free, he's probably worth exactly what he's charging.) As a matter of fact, your visits may be covered by insurance. In New York State, for example, every hospital insurance contract by law covers sixty outpatient visits for treatment for alcoholism including twenty visits by the family; and five of the visits can be made by the family before the alcoholic enters treatment. (See the section on financing treatment later in this chapter.)

It may take you some time to find the right counselor and still more time to plan the process and make sure everyone is certain of his or her role before the Intervention actually takes place. If you are impatient, just remember how long you've waited already. Wait a little longer and get it done right.

What you can do immediately is start collecting your data, but no matter how articulate and confident you may be, don't delude yourself into thinking you can do the Intervention without professional help. You need help to break through the denial. After all, you have lived in your particular family system for years. If you bear in mind that Interventions are more accurately referred to as "family Interventions," you will realize that the whole system is being Intervened on. As your counselor will repeatedly tell you, this is a process, not an event. While your major focus may be on the particular day when you sit down and have a talk with the member of your family you're concerned about, the family as a whole is also being dealt with. You can't imagine what an impact this process will have on each person involved.

Families in Crisis tells me that every family they work with is awed by what happens to the entire group as a result of the Intervention. They are astonished at how united everyone becomes. The family usually tells the counselors, "You people were wonderful," and the counselors always respond, "We're not the ones to be congratulated. You were the ones who did the job."

An Intervention is a very thrilling experience, one of the few times in your life when your emotions run at such a high pitch and when the tension you feel is followed by such a positive release.

But if you do it on your own you risk failure. It won't be done properly, or it may not even be done at all. Two family members out of four might agree that there's cause for concern, and the other two will protest that the person you're talking about is the greatest guy in the world. That may be true, but they have to separate the fact that he's a swell person from his alcohol problem. What often happens in the case of an amateur Intervention is that the sickest person takes over. I can easily imagine some overly zealous, powerful person saying, "Okay, I'm going to take care of this thing myself," then making a major blunder. It is not appropriate to feel that you're "going to take care of this thing." What you should be feeling is apprehension, fear, and concern.

The counselor keeps things in perspective and has the expertise to handle difficult situations. Some friends of an alcoholic who's a very creative man were talking to the counselors at Families in Crisis about doing an Intervention. His personality was so tied in to his drinking that when they began to talk about him they painted a picture of a regular Ernest Hemingway. What would he be like without his booze? they wondered. They debated about whether they should take it away from him. Finally, the counselor told them, "I don't want any more opinions. Just write down on a piece of paper what this guy does when he is drinking."

When they saw the evidence in black and white they said, "My God, he's killing himself." But they had almost managed to persuade themselves that without his alcohol, he'd be nobody. With it, of course, he'd be dead.

There are groups such as Lawyers Concerned for Lawyers and Doctors Concerned for Doctors that sometimes initiate Interventions. In most cases, they do a wonderful job, but I have heard of a case or two in which they were not properly run. One involved a good friend of mine, a doctor from Wisconsin. Some of his colleagues, members of such a group, got together to Intervene on him but they didn't consult a professional nor did they involve his family.

He did go into treatment and he's still sober, but he's carrying with him a tremendous amount of resentment toward all his former friends. Some of his unresolved anger is due to the fact that no professional was there to keep the anger out of the Intervention itself, and part is due to the fact that his wife was never included in the proceedings nor even told that an Intervention was being planned.

In addition to keeping the conversations objective and focused and making sure that everyone who should be involved is included, the counselor knows how to keep the

Intervention from going on too long. The goal is not for everyone to ventilate his anger but to help the person agree to be evaluated or go into a treatment center. This can happen within two minutes. Once it does, there is no reason to continue. In salesman's lingo, you've "closed the sale." Don't keep going until you talk the customer out of it.

The very presence of the counselor also helps the alcoholic and the people around him stay in control. (They tend to be on slightly better behavior in front of a stranger.) If things threaten to get out of hand, he or she knows what to do. Also, if there are questions the family can't answer, the counselor will be there to answer them.

How do you select a counselor?

Where do you find a counselor? How do you know if the counselor you have found is good? Part of my purpose in writing this book is to provide some guidelines. The field of chemical dependency is becoming big business. There's a lot of money to be made, and like any other profession, this one has its share of charlatans. If an Intervention isn't done properly, the potential for harm is enormous. However, it was impossible for me to check out everyone who advertises himself as an Intervention counselor. There are many of them, and the field is growing rapidly—there are new counselors entering it every day.

Because I am so convinced that an Intervention is the only way to stop the one you love from drinking, I am also concerned about the possibility that you may run into a professional who puts down Intervention. A friend of mine called a crisis hotline that promised help for drug users. She was told flatly that Interventions didn't work and the organization wouldn't refer her to anyone who could help her with an Intervention. Meanwhile, the organization that sponsors this hotline listed Families in Crisis in its directory!

I know of other hotlines that refer you directly to treatment centers that tell you to make a reservation. When you say, "But my husband won't go," they answer, "Well, then, call us when he's ready." I can't imagine anything worse.

If you get enough courage to call and say, "I need help," and someone gives you the feeling that the situation is hopeless, please, please don't be discouraged and give up. Help is available, and you should get to it as quickly as possible.

Rather than recommend individual counselors, I suggest that you locate an Intervention counselor through the National Council on Alcoholism, your state alcohol or drug agency, or a treatment center. You'll find a partial list of excellent centers in the Appendix of this book. Treatment centers don't move around, but Intervention teams do, and had I attempted to list counselors individually, my list would have been out of date before this book was published.

You could also get a personal recommendation from someone who has been involved in an Intervention. Or you could check with the human resources department (what used to be called the personnel department) at your company or your spouse's. Companies now have EAPs (Employee Assistance Programs) as a company benefit. Some of them even cover up to five visits to a counselor, on a confidential basis; and if the problem is alcoholism, the counselor will refer you to appropriate help. Check to see what is covered under your (or your spouse's) plan. At any point in your search you can write to Families in Crisis at 6101 Green Valley Drive, Bloomington, MN 55437, or phone them at (612) 893-1883. They do out-of-state Interventions or can refer you to a local source.

What to look for in a counselor

When you first contact a counselor by phone, you can expect that he will ask some questions about your concerns. From that brief interview, he should be able to make some assessment of the situation. If he believes that you need help, he will set up an appointment and may ask that you bring another concerned family member or friend if possible.

There are several qualities you should be looking for when you meet with him to help you decide if he's the right counselor for you. Of course, there are "different strokes for different folks," but there are some things all good counselors have in common.

First, he should make you feel really comfortable with him. Go with your instincts. All people have facades, and people in the helping professions are often particularly expert at creating their own. If something about the person seems not right to you, look elsewhere.

Something as superficial as dress may disturb you, but the fact is that a good counselor is sensitive enough to understand the protocol of every situation. Nels Schlander points out that if he's meeting with or Intervening on a chairman of the board, he'll be there in a three-piece suit; but if he's trying to reach an adolescent with a drug problem, he'll probably seem less threatening in jeans.

A good counselor will welcome your questions, both about himself and about the process. It's a good sign if a counselor volunteers information on how he became involved in Interventions. Many counselors were Intervened on themselves or were involved in a successful Intervention and realized what good work can be done in this way.

You can ask how long the counselor has been doing this work and what his track record is. If he's honest, he will tell you he has had some Interventions that simply didn't work out. Be on your guard if someone tells you he's been successful 100 percent of the time. The people at Families in Crisis have come pretty close to that, but they do have their failures.

If the counselor says, "Fine, we'll do an Intervention. Bring him in tomorrow," he's also not the guy you want. You want someone who is planning to spend from six to ten hours on preparation before the Intervention. Beware, too, of a take-charge guy who says, "I can handle any alcoholic. Let me at him." This is the family's Intervention, not the counselor's.

This is a serious disease. Do it right so you don't have to do it over.

Once you've gotten past the preliminaries at the initial meeting, the counselor will review the situation further, explain something about the disease, and find out who else is concerned about the alcoholic. He will help you decide who to contact and how to do it, and he will set a date for a meeting to which they will be invited. At that second meeting, the education process continues and the foundation is laid for the preparation of the letters.

Although you are focusing on the alcoholic, your preparation for the Intervention should also include some time to explore your own feelings. If there isn't a lot of planning, if the family isn't educated, if the process isn't structured and filled with a lot of love, forget it. The Intervention should be handled the way it has been laid out in this book. If not, run for the hills.

I have heard of counselors who haven't kept out the anger and who have actually gone on the attack. Families in Crisis heard about one such case when they were working with an Intervention group that included a past participant. As they proceeded, she kept saying, "This isn't at all like the other Intervention I was at."

She explained that at the other so-called Intervention, the spouse was forbidden to speak. Then, during the setup for the Intervention, the counselor requested two special chairs—one higher than any of the others and one lower. He explained that he would be sitting in the highest chair and that the person being Intervened on would sit in the lowest, to "intimidate him."

When the alcoholic showed up, all prior instructions went out the window. The counselor grabbed the fellow by the arm and told everyone to wait in the living room. He took the alcoholic into the kitchen, told him, "Buddy, you and I are going to a treatment center right now," and hustled him out the door.

Other than identifying himself and starting things off, the counselor should *not* participate in the Intervention. It is the family's Intervention, and the job of the counselor is to teach you how to do it in a respectful way.

The more I work with K. D., Nels, and Mary, the more impressed I am by how good a good counselor can be. And the more I am concerned that you find the right one.

What happens in treatment

Treatment for chemical dependency deals with all three aspects of the illness—physical, psychological, and spiritual. Your counselor will help you decide what kind of treatment is appropriate—in-patient, out-patient, or other community-based facilities. The treatment process teaches the user to handle everyday life problems without depending on his chemicals.

My own preference is for in-patient treatment, to get the alcoholic out of his regular environment. It might be more expensive, but insurance may cover it. Don't let the money stop you. It's a lifesaver. Some centers provide even financial assistance. Go for it if it's at all posible. Take up a collection if you have to. If family and friends share the costs, they won't seem so overwhelming. What a wonderful way of expressing your love to the one you're Intervening on.

By taking someone out of his daily life and putting him in a treatment center, you give him the opportunity to deal with his problems in a controlled atmosphere, where he has time to reflect and learn. The goal of treatment is to break the patient's denial about his disease so that by the time he leaves he'll have a full understanding of his addiction and how it has affected him and the ones he loves. The process usually takes about a month (and a month in treatment, I believe, is the equivalent of two years in AA), though sometimes the patient is asked to stay longer.

If he's in a good center, he'll be working with professionals in the field of psychiatry and psychology as well as lay people who have many years of sobriety beneath their belts. Besides, he'll get three big square meals a day, physical exercise, nursing care, and a lot of companionship. I think treatment is a wonderful experience.

Finding the right treatment center

When it comes to choosing a treatment center, I believe you have three main concerns. Look for a place that believes chemical dependency is a disease. Look for a place that feels it's a family disease and that in order for the problem to be resolved, the whole family has to get better. And finally, look for a place that follows the 12 Steps program. The treatment centers listed in the Appendix meet all three requirements.

Treatment centers have been opening up for only fifteen years or so. For the first decade, not much was heard about them because there was even more of a stigma connected to drug and alcoholic addiction then. In the past few years, people have been coming out of the closet and talking about how they got help. All this publicity gave a lot of people the idea that there was money to be made, so there was something of a gold rush in the field. A lot of strange people came up with even stranger cures. In one place, they give the alcoholic enough booze to make him sick. That's supposed to stop him. God knows what else they're coming up with. I don't want to knock these people one by one, but in my opinion, all of these so-called cures belong in the category of witch doctoring. If you have any knowledge of the disease, you know it can't be cured. It can only be arrested.

And I can tell you for certain that any place that doesn't follow the 12 Steps plan can't help someone have a happy recovery. The person may stop drinking or taking drugs temporarily, but he still hasn't the tools to live a happy, drug-free life. The 12 Steps offer that, and only AA has such a track record of success.

You should personally check out any treatment center in which you're interested. A friend of mine mentioned that when he got out of treatment and visited his family, not one of them had asked what happened to him there. He believed it was because they were afraid he'd gone through a painful experience—shock treatments, cold water showers, and so forth. Call up. Make an appointment and go there in person to take a look. I'm sure you'll feel better when you discover there are no bars on the windows.

In addition, for your own reassurance and for the sake of the patient, research the place. You would do it for someone who had cancer. You'd find out about the reputation of the facility and who was on the staff. Do it in this case too. Also, make sure there are chemical dependency counselors on staff along with the psychologists.

Whether the alcoholic is in an out-patient or in-patient facility, the family should be asked to participate. Everyone will explore the role he has played in the disease and begin to find ways to operate differently. Some of the in-patient centers I have listed will treat the family on an out-patient basis and some will have a special one-week in-patient plan.

If it's any good, the treatment center will also provide aftercare. No one gets sick in a month, and no one gets well in a month. Recovery is an ongoing process. To follow up treatment, attending AA is necessary. Some people will want additional counseling, but I personally didn't need it. However, during the first year of sobriety, some need all the support and help they can get. They should do whatever is necessary to stay sober.

Financing the treatment

I know that one of your concerns is cost. This is an expensive disease, but think of the cost if the alcoholic continues to drink—from the price of the booze itself to the money lost as a result of bad decisions or job stagnation.

Anyway, if you are covered by an insurance plan, many of your costs may be paid. In June 1968, the AMA Board of Trustees approved a joint statement with the American Bar Association setting forth principles concerning alcoholism. The first said that alcoholism should be regarded as an illness and on medical and hospital care insurance contracts should be subject to benefits comparable to those that apply to any other chronic illness. As a result, insurance may cover from 80 to 100 percent of the treatment costs. In addition, many employers will continue to provide a paycheck while someone is in treatment.

The coverage for drug addiction varies from state to state and carrier to carrier, and not all coverage for alcoholism is the same. In New York state, legislation has insured that every hospital insurance contract pays 100 percent coverage if you are treated in member facilities (which are not necessarily hospitals) and 80 percent if you are in other facilities. But some insurance carriers will pay only if the patient is being treated in a hospital, so it is very important that you examine your policy. (Although Hazelden is not hospital-based, my insurance did pay 100 percent. As far as I'm concerned, you don't need to be treated in a hospital unless you're seriously ill, and personally, I preferred a nonhospital setting. I didn't see anyone dressed in white all day long, and that was fine with me. But these things don't matter. If you're following the 12 Steps program, you could sober up in a garage if you had to.)

If your company or your spouse's offers an EAP (Employee Assistance Program), you can meet with a counselor who will probably help direct you to an Intervention counselor and figure out your coverage. If you have to investigate on your own, call the employer's human resources office. You don't even have to give out the name of the person you're concerned about. Just ask the telephone operator at the company for the name of the director of human resources. Then phone and ask, "What is your policy on someone receiving help for alcoholism or chemical dependency? What kind of coverage do you offer?"

You can call the insurance company and ask general questions, too. "What is your coverage on chemical dependency or alcoholism?" You should mention both alcoholism and chemical dependency. Or phone the treatment center staff to discuss what your policy covers. I think you will discover that they will be more than willing to help you with this.

Some specific recommendations

In the Appendix is a list of treatment centers across the U.S. All of them are AA based, offer a family program, and provide some form of aftercare. Through any of them you should be able to locate an Intervention counselor.

The ones that Families in Crisis and I recommend personally are indicated by an asterisk. Other centers on the list have been recommended by others. *In every case, make your own personal inspection.* Also remember that this is only a partial list. I am sure there are many other excellent facilities.

When you look at the list, you will notice that costs do vary and at first glance the figures may be deceptive. Minnesota centers on the whole seem to be cheaper, perhaps because in my home state they do a booming business and are always filled to capacity. (Minnesota has been a pioneer in treating chemical dependency. We may freeze in winter, but Minnesotans' hearts are warm. My community has scores of caring people who are helping hundreds sober up each month.)

Bear in mind that some statements of costs include the family program, medical care, and aftercare. Some do not. The major portion of each cost is for primary treatment, which in some cases includes a couple of years of aftercare. (That is a way of making you think you're getting more for your money, but I should point that my two years of aftercare cost me only $160.) Price is not always a measure of excellence. Hazelden is comparatively very cheap, yet I can vouch for the fact that it gives the finest of care.

A final word about locating a counselor and/or a treatment center. If you are having no success at finding what you want or need, again I urge you to contact the offices of Families in Crisis, 6101 Green Valley Drive, Bloomington, MN 55437, telephone (612) 893-1883. Any of the counselors there will assist you.

12/
Assembling the Group

Once you choose the counselor and have a treatment center selected, you begin to prepare for the Intervention.

Everything that I describe here will be reconfirmed with your counselor. I've chosen to answer the questions that are most typical just to give you a better idea of what's ahead, to help you judge if the counselor you're working with is on the right track.

How do I approach the people who should be involved?

Don't say, "I think Joe has a problem." That just encourages further denial. "Yes," they say, "but . . ." And then they start making excuses for him.

Be specific. Say, "I think Joe has a drinking or drug problem, and this is why. Every Friday he comes home from work drunk. That's been going on for four years. And did you know that every Saturday he just sits around the house with a glass in his hand?" And so forth.

Again, I want to remind you that it's no big deal to talk about his using. If he has a problem, everyone knows, but they are doing as good a job of denying it as the drinker. They'll be relieved to have it finally brought out into the open and to discover their own assumptions that so-and-so has a drinking problem are not crazy. Open the discussion, and then listen. Talk to your family. Talk to your friends.

Families in Crisis told me about an Intervention in which the critical person turned out to be a son-in-law. After everyone had spoken to the woman they were concerned about, he was the one she turned to. "What do you think?" she asked. "Go for it," he replied, and she said, "Okay." You never know who'll be key in reaching the goal. That's why it's important to include everyone.

How many people should be involved?

Families in Crisis has had as many as twenty-eight people involved in a single Intervention, though a group of that size is not necessary and most of the time is probably not even appropriate. Usually, they ask for a minimum of three people, but they told me of one case that involved a fellow who was desperately ill. His drinking had progressed to the point where he'd lost everything—money, friends, family. Only his brother still seemed to care about him. The brother mentioned a sister who hadn't spoken to the alcoholic in more than twenty years.

"Just call and say 'Your brother is dying. You must show up.'" the counselor said. The brother made the call reluctantly. Sure enough, at first the woman said, "I have nothing to say." But her brother did as the counselor had suggested, and finally she agreed to come. She had no data. She hadn't prepared a letter. She just looked at her brother and said, "My God, have you gone downhill in twenty years," and that's all it took. The guy went into treatment and today he's recovering.

Must I go outside the family?

The family—and the spouse in particular—often has the least power to influence someone to get help. He tunes them out. (Families in Crisis says that during the Intervention, the most powerful person in the alcoholic's life is the last to speak, and the spouse virtually never winds up in that spot.

To me, the fact that the people he loves most have the least influence over him is just another sign of how sick he is.)

In addition, when people outside the family are present, the alcoholic is less likely to act out. He doesn't want to be a jerk in front of his boss, his doctor, his priest, or his friends. He might act like an idiot when he's been drinking, but you know from experience he behaves better when he's sober.

Outsiders can also be effective (especially outsiders whom the alcoholic regards as being important) because most alcoholics are real people pleasers.

One of my friends is a functioning alcoholic. He holds down a job, but he doesn't have a driver's license. He lost it long ago because of repeated DWIs. His personal life is crumbling, but he keeps up appearances. Finally, he had a heart attack, and while he was in the hospital, his wife decided to hold an Intervention. She wanted only family involved, because she regarded this as a family problem. But after they had spoken with the alcoholic, he remained unconvinced that he needed treatment. Once they were gone, he phoned a friend.

"By the way," he mentioned at some point in the conversation. "My wife and kids were over here telling me I have a problem with alcohol. You know me well. What would you do?"

"Who pays the bills?" said the friend.

"I do."

"Then tell them to go to hell."

The wife made a serious miscalculation in deciding to keep the problems within the family. Reach out and involve your friends. The more facts that are presented, the easier it will be to break through denial.

In one case I know of, I would have brought in the garbage collector. This particular alcoholic managed to cover up most of his symptoms at least to people outside of the family, but he'd sneak quite a collection of empty bottles into the trash can early each morning. I'd like to see a bartender show up at an Intervention some time.

If you're Intervening on an adolescent, you might go to the school counselor for help. And it's most important that you get former friends there—the ones who have fallen by the wayside. One sign that a kid is using drugs or alcohol is that he has acquired a whole new group of friends.

Should the employer be included?

You might want to investigate the company's policy about alcoholism by phoning the human resources department, as I suggested before. Without identifying yourself, ask some questions about the company's policy toward chemical dependency—alcoholism and/or drug abuse.

Your counselor will help you judge whether to include the employer. An unenlightened manager may react negatively to learning that someone is an alcoholic, but if he is involved in the Intervention he will become a very useful ally. It's better to get his support and sympathy before he winds up firing the guy without waiting for an explanation. Furthermore, many laws prevent your being fired while you're in treatment for alcoholism. (Check the state laws in your area.) Neither I nor anyone in Families in Crisis knows of anyone who was fired for such a reason.

On occasion an employer has called Families in Crisis after the family has asked him to be involved and said, "I don't have any issue with the guy. I don't have any data." And the counselor has said, "Please just come and be supportive to the family. Explain that the guy won't lose his job and that you'll allow him to go to treatment." What usually happens is that after the employer sits in the room and hears what the family and friends are saying, he realizes, "My God. I had no idea the problem was this grave." Of course that's the point of an Intervention: Putting all the pieces together to get the whole picture.

A boss is powerful enough to be the key to the Intervention. He can nail the guy. He can say, "I would like to keep you with us, my friend. But you're in serious trouble and if you don't get help, I'll have to let you go." Co-workers can also be helpful. So can secretaries. They know exactly what's going on. They're the ones who cover for the guy when he's off at his long lunches and track him down at his "business meetings" in a saloon.

What about a minister?

If he does have some influence over the one you love, of course invite him, but don't ask a minister to participate in the Intervention just because you think you ought to have one there. The last thing an alcoholic wants to hear at an Intervention is a sermon reminding him how he's let down everyone including God. Some ministers come in and try to run the Intervention with a holier-than-thou attitude that can be very destructive.

But the ones who are useful come in to Families in Crisis with an attitude of genuine concern. They say, "How can I participate? How do you want me to be part of the Intervention?" Many times people who've fallen by the wayside in other areas of their lives fall by the wayside spiritually, too. The spouse keeps going to church and the minister notices that Dorothy is showing up, but without Sam. She may eventually go to the minister for help for family problems without mentioning the drinking, but a sensitive minister will realize what's going on. At the Intervention, he could be very useful to help point out what's happening to other members of the family because of the drinking.

What about including a doctor?

Again, the attitude of the person is what really counts. If you have a family physician who is aware of the problem and feels helpless along with the family, he can be very useful. He can either participate in person or simply write a letter saying he is worried and concerned and wants his patient well.

Often a doctor will give a prescription without realizing his alcoholic patient is going home and taking the pills along with another prescription and perhaps a shot of Jack Daniels to wash the whole thing down. If the family gets him involved, the doctor can be very helpful in presenting the medical side of the picture.

What about including people who drink along with him?

You should have no hesitation about inviting them. Even alcoholics can see in other people what they cannot see in themselves, so they may turn out to be very valuable during the process.

However, some of these drinking buddies may be reluctant to show up. They think they're going to be put on the carpet. I knew I couldn't call on certain of Sherm's drinking cronies for his Intervention because I knew their attitude was "Mary Ellen's quit drinking and now everyone else has to." My answer would have been, "Absolutely! How else, boys? Do you think I can live with this guy after all I've found out about alcoholism and have him out acting like a nut with you guys on Friday nights?" But they wanted to protect their right to drink. I notice that no social drinker feels the need to defend his drinking. Defending it is a symptom of alcoholism.

Other friends who drink want to be involved but feel guilty. They feel like traitors and hypocrites. "How can I say anything to him about his chemical use when I use chemicals too?" Tell them, "Please come to one meeting before you decide whether or not to participate. None of us is completely clean. We're not gathering to talk about your use. Joe needs your help. He thinks the world of you and you can help him see that he is in trouble. The Intervention will be directed toward him. It will not be turned around and thrown back at you. During the Intervention, if he says, 'You drink, too,' you just say, 'That may be true, and we can talk about that sometime later. But now we're here to talk about your drinking.'"

The counselor will ask everyone involved in the Intervention not to use alcohol or drugs during the preparation. They explain that the point is to allow your feelings to come to the surface, and you can't be in touch with your feelings if you're under the influence of chemicals. Everyone usually agrees to this condition. If someone can't abstain for seven to ten days, the counselor usually suggests they take a look at their own use.

"It amazes me," says Nels Schlander. "They must think I'm out checking up on them, because sometimes they'll come in and say, 'I screwed up,' and I'm not sure what they're talking about.

"I assume that by 'screwing up' the person means he's let the cat out of the bag about the Intervention, but he'll say 'No, that's not it. What I mean is, I drank.'" The counselors say that after the first session, they can always tell who else in the room might have a problem, and they have found that every Intervention seems to have a ripple effect. It starts others thinking about their own use. One son wrote his letter about all the times he drank with his father and at the end of the Intervention, he said, "Dad, I need to come in and get evaluation with you."

Suppose I think someone will sabotage the Intervention?

Don't get such a person involved, for Heaven's sake. Why ask for trouble if you can avoid it? (And don't be afraid to ask everyone involved to demonstrate their concern for the person involved by keeping the Intervention a secret from him.) During preparation your counselor will evaluate members of the group to figure out whether anyone within in it is a classic enabler, someone who feels that the person being Intervened on can do no wrong. If so, he will ask that person not to be part of the Intervention.

Be reassured, though: There have been attempts to sabotage Interventions by telling the alcoholic in advance, and although it is better if someone is not forewarned, they have been successful nevertheless.

Suppose someone will be very angry or judgmental?

The counselor will explain that everyone must prepare and read his or her letter before the actual Intervention and must be willing to take criticism from the others. If the person indicates that he cannot or that he will be unable to stick to the points in the letter during the Intervention, the counselor will ask him not to be involved.

Families in Crisis was working with a group that included the brother of a man being Intervened on. The two men had been in business together and the brother was extremely angry because he had lost a lot of money as a result of the other's drinking. He couldn't get past his anger. He saw the Intervention as an opportunity to get at his brother. Finally, the counselor asked the man not to participate.

The man made amends to his brother, paid him back the money he lost, and is enjoying a wonderful sobriety. His brother is still angry. I guess his sober sibling has become too responsible to suit him. Unless he gets help to sort out his problems, he'll remain miserable. Again this proves the point that alcoholism is a family disease.

The counselor will also help avoid the tendency to take the focus off the main person and direct it onto others. I think of my mother's reaction when I told her I was going into treatment and invited her to join in the Family Week. I was hoping her response would be, "Mary Ellen, that is such a relief. I wasn't able to help you years ago, but I would love to participate in helping you now." Instead, she put the blame on herself. "Oh, Mary Ellen," she said. "I tried my best for you." That really brought me down. We've talked since about this, and I know today she would handle it differently. She tried her best for each of her children and the children of her friends too. But as a loving mother of an alcoholic child, she didn't realize that what she considered her "best" wasn't what worked. She loved me to death.

Suppose someone important can't be at the Intervention?

If he can't be there in person, Families in Crisis has occasionally had someone who was key to the situation phone in at a prearranged time. If someone just can't handle being part of an Intervention, they will ask him to prepare a letter that another person can read.

Should the children be involved?

The Intervention is a healing process. At last people are talking about things honestly. You put the kid through the drinking. Why can't you put him through the healing? He deserves to be there.

Sometimes the counselor will ask, "Do you have any children?" and the answer will be, "Yes, but they don't know anything about it." Don't kid yourself that the children don't know what's going on. They are the eyes and ears of the family. If you want any information, talk to the youngest child. Once he gets permission to start talking, he'll spill the beans.

One family Intervening on a twenty-six-year-old son claimed to have no firsthand evidence of his drinking. "All we know is that he gets DWIs and has trouble on the job." Finally the eleven-year-old brother said, "Mom, what are you talking about? Remember how he was drinking at Christmas?" The brother elaborated on that episode and went on to give several other examples. The parents were embarrassed by their own denial.

Some people say, "I don't want to involve my child because it's going to embarrass my spouse to have the child hear the whole story. I don't want to expose the child." He's been exposed already. Or they say, "It will be too painful for her to participate." It's too painful if she doesn't.

You want to protect children from the fact of the drinking, but they know about it without being told. An adult can at least express his pain by talking about it to friends. Kids have learned to keep it all inside, but that doesn't mean they aren't suffering.

A woman told me she'd brought her four-year-old with her to treatment because she didn't have a babysitter. Although he was too young to participate, he started the whole group off. He sat down and said, "My Mom used to get real sad because my dad wouldn't quit drinking and she had to buy her own house. It was real sad when we had to move into our own house because I still love my dad. The only time I get real sad is when my mom's sad and I don't know how to make her happy. But my mom's getting better now." His mother was astonished at what her son had observed.

When I was in recovery, Andrew said to me, "Mom, I like you better when you're not all dressed up," and I realized that if I was all dressed up he recognized that was probably a sign I'd be going out drinking. He also told me, "You were never mean to me when you drank, but Mom, you were all over me, hugging me and kissing me. You loved me too much." I was so full of guilt about my drinking that I tried to express my love by grabbing on to him.

Before my sister's Intervention, we were up at our house by a lake. Both of us were out—my sister with several of her friends and I with another group—and there were babysitters taking care of the kids. When my group came in, the kids checked us out pretty thoroughly, and then one of them said, "You haven't been drinking." The only reason they had never actually said that out loud before to me is that I used to come home drunk. But Andrew had been telling them about my recovery and that had opened it up for all the kids to talk about drinking. I was so glad to see them letting out their feelings. I encouraged it, and they started being very candid.

A lot of attention was focused on my sister Sue, and her son J.J. started acting uncomfortable. Finally, I said, "J.J., come here," and I sat him on my lap and said, "J.J., your mom's drinking isn't your fault." I told the kids, "It would be good for us to talk about this." So the kids started sharing, like a normal conversation. There was no fear; now there was even some humor involved. And it was the next morning when J.J. talked to his mom in my car about her drinking.

Families in Crisis includes children from the age of five in an Intervention, but children under thirteen aren't brought in until the last meeting prior to the Intervention itself. If they go through the whole process, they may get too caught up in the adult fears and enabling.

The Families in Crisis counselors tell me that these young children become wide-eyed at the Interventions. They can't believe their relatives can speak so honestly. They hear other people talking and get permission to talk themselves. That must be an immense relief.

Usually a child is the last to speak. He or she need not have prepared anything. The counselor just asks, "What do you want to say to your parent?" and the message comes out very clear. The kid says simply, "I love you, and please won't you get help?"

Andrew was very aware of my recovery, of course, and so he was gung-ho about his dad's Intervention. He had written a letter because I assured him it would help. As far as I was concerned, no one else held a candle to Andrew at Sherm's Intervention. There was no judgment in his voice, no anger. It was all love.

Ever since, Andrew has always felt free to talk to me or Sherm about any problems with alcohol. He'll mention a problem with a friend's parent and know I understand. "Isn't it terrible we can't help Mr. So-and-So?" What a great opportunity this gives me to talk to him about peer pressure and drug addiction and about his own potential for using.

If we hadn't stopped drinking, Andrew would have been a sitting duck for a chemical dependency problem. Now at least we've got the tools to help him make wise choices. The minute the using goes into the closet is the minute the problem starts. My dad may have had his flaws, but he used to tell us something that I always remember. "If you lie to me, I can't help you, but if you tell me the truth there's no problem in the world I can't help you with." I've found that to be so true. If I'm up front and address a problem, people will help. When you start blaming everyone else, they tell you you're on your own.

Should we leave the older folks out of it?

People tend to protect not only the children but also the older people. Their attitude is that Grandma is seventy years old and she can't handle this. Grandma knows what's going on, too, I assure you. I remember a friend telling me that her sister got pregnant in high school. Their grandmother, a very religious woman who'd led an exemplary life, never discussed it with anybody but just got out her sewing machine and started making maternity clothes for this gal. The girl's mother walked around denying what was happening, but the grandmother dealt with reality. Older people are not so fragile or out of touch as we think.

If there is a chemical dependency problem, you can bet that Grandma knows about it and she's sitting there wondering what the heck is going to happen to her child. Chances are she's been concerned about him for quite a while, but she's been hoping that everything would go away. She should be given the opportunity to do something for her loved one. Also, remember that a parent has a lot of clout and can be tremendously effective at an Intervention.

I know a family that tried to get older parents involved. They were very reluctant because they were afraid their son would be angry and because they felt a lot of guilt. The father's behavior hadn't been so terrific when the son was growing up, and now they had an alcoholic on their hands. Their daughter-in-law finally said, "This is for your son, who is in a lot of trouble. There will be nothing said about you, no blaming.

"I can divorce this man. He won't be my husband anymore, but he'll always be your son. Here's the literature. Look it over and let me know."

Three hours later, they phoned. "We'll do it." They realized they had no other choice.

Once they are educated even a little about alcoholism and its consequences, anyone you approach about participating in an Intervention will realize that he, too, has no choice. The only humane thing to do is get involved.

Preparing the Letters

There are several reasons why you should write down what you plan to say in the Intervention.

One is that you will probably be under some stress. Either you'll become so emotional and/or frightened that you say things you didn't mean. Or else you will be so overcome you'll forget part or all of what you wanted to say.

Another is that Intervention not only helps the alcoholic break through his denial but it helps the family to break through theirs as well. Collecting the data gives you a clearer picture of the situation. When you see it in black and white, you have to take a good look at it.

Sometimes families evade the truth so much they cannot bring themselves to use the word "drunk." They'll say, "Mary Ellen, you came to the party and you hogged the conversation to the point of being obnoxious, and I felt angry," but never "You were drunk." It's a word the families (and alcoholics) avoid like the plague. They use words like "intoxicated," "sloshed," "ploughed," "tipsy," "blasted," "stoned," "wasted," "high," "feeling good." Of course, "You were drinking" could mean a guy was nursing half a beer during the evening when in fact he probably put away a case. Another phrase the family may use is "the problem." The counselors will pin them down. "What problem?"

"That he was drinking too much."

"Was he drunk?"

"Well . . . yes."

"Then put that down. Write down that he was drunk."

Family members also have blackouts and deny that incidents have happened. The letters help produce corroborating evidence.

When you put your information together with someone else's, you may understand the reason for some of the odd behavior you've seen. I know a gal who saw a flying saucer. Now, since she was drinking a soft drink at the time of the sighting, people were inclined to think that maybe she really did have a close encounter. The family later discovered from friends who were involved in the Intervention that the only close encounter she had on that particular evening was with some cocaine.

Finally, these letters will be used by the treatment center in making an evaluation. They speed up the process and help make it more accurate than an assessment based on material supplied by the alcoholic himself. You should understand enough about denial at this point to imagine a situation in which the spouse puts the heat on his wife to go for help. She says okay and off she goes to the psychologist or counselor. "You know, doc, this husband of mine is on my tail. I have a drink once or twice a week, but he's the kind of person who's holier than thou. I can't even have a glass of wine after dinner without him raising his eyebrows."

"Gee, that doesn't sound like a drinking problem to me," says the therapist. "Maybe you just need a marriage counselor."

In an evaluation, self-reporting is not allowed. It is based on material from at least two or three other people who are significant in that person's life. A patient who comes in for an evaluation must sign a release so that the counselor can contact friends or family to get an idea of how others view his drinking. If the patient asks what that entails, the counselor will mention specific persons he means to contact.

If as each name is brought up a patient says, "No, don't call her," and "Forget him," and "That one's a bad idea too," he will be told that the evaluation is incomplete and the data inconclusive. The counselor can't give any diagnosis or suggestions. But if an Intervention occurs, the letters can provide the basis for a complete evaluation.

Dos and don'ts in writing the letter

You saw some examples of letters in chapter 6, and if you followed the suggestions in chapter 4, you may already have begun to gather your material.

Remember, the letters are not supposed to be literary masterpieces. They are a way of telling the person about whom you are concerned specific reasons for your concern. They should be written from the heart. They are supposed to be nonjudgmental, but that is not the same as unemotional. Honest feelings are not criticism. The dependent person has to hear and learn how he is hurting the people around him.

The idea is to give data about using, not data about behavior. In other words, you don't say, "Mary Ellen, at that party Friday night you acted like a jerk. If you ever come to another party, no one will have anything to do with you." That's a judgment of character rather than a specific example of use. Say, "Mary Ellen, at the party Friday night when you were drinking you were very sarcastic and boisterous. I felt really embarrassed. I was angry at you and sad."

If possible, describe what you actually saw. "You were in the bathroom Wednesday. Your hands were shaking. You looked terrible and I saw you take five Valiums." If secondhand information is used, it should be a quote. "Your boss called and said you were drinking at lunch Thursday. Then you were three hours late getting back to the office. He says this has happened four times in the last two weeks." But be aware that it's more likely the alcoholic will dispute a secondhand story than a firsthand observation.

Try to tie your example directly into the person's use of alcohol (or drugs). Don't say "You were driving recklessly" if you were in the car but you weren't at the party or wherever the person drank. The idea is to show the person that each incident derives directly from chemical use.

Avoid opinions and generalizations ("You shouldn't drink so much"), which serve only to raise the person's defenses.

Don't moralize ("You should know better").

Don't be long-winded and boring. Long explanations will only be confusing. Be specific, and be brief.

Don't be surprised by evidence of blackouts. The alcoholic may not remember events. Be ready with specific information about behavior.

Don't ask questions. Don't say, "Remember the Fourth of July?" This is not a dialogue or a conversation—this is a fact-presenting session. These are things about which the group has information to share, *not to discuss*.

Stick to the issue. Talk about the drinking, not about the person's mother.

Feel free to go back as far into the past as necessary. You'll notice the progression of the disease.

Be as specific as you can about times, dates, and places. I was used to hearing, "Mary Ellen, you drink too much, you get loud, you get mean," so I could have ignored those generalizations. But I would have been wiped out if someone had given specific examples. After I was sober, someone mentioned that once when I was walking out of a party I staggered in front of everyone. That humiliated me.

Here are some examples of specific data:

· "In May, we went to The Willows for dinner with friends. You drank a whole bottle of wine by yourself and yelled loudly at the waiter. I was embarrassed."

· "Last summer, you promised you'd take me fishing and you never did. You went drinking that day instead. It really hurts me when you break promises. You seem more interested in drinking than you are in me."

· "Since you went away to college, we thought you were living your own life. But when you called us at 2:00 A.M. with slurred speech and asked us for money, it scared me. I've been really worried about you since then."

· "We've been friends for a long time, but I can't rely on you anymore. Last September, I bought tickets to the ball game and you never showed. Then I found out you were drinking. I was disappointed and annoyed."

· "You used to like to come watch the high school softball games with me. Last weekend, I asked you to come out with us but you said you'd rather watch TV. When I came home there were two empty six-packs in the garbage and you were asleep in the chair. I ate dinner alone. I felt sad about never having your company anymore."

When you're having difficulty collecting data

Your counselor will help you remember if you are having trouble recalling specific incidents. If there's an alcohol problem, I'm sure there were incidents, but part of the family's denial is not being able to remember them. In one extreme case, a woman told me that her husband had been chemically dependent since he was sixteen and she had lived for him for fourteen years. She had been subjected to verbal and physical abuse and lived with all kinds of bad behavior, but it took her ten months to come up with eight examples of his drinking.

You don't have to see someone with a glass to give an example of drinking. You can simply observe appearances. "I came home at 5:00 P.M. and you hadn't gotten dressed and your eyes were bloodshot."

Take a look at the expense accounts of the person, plus credit card records of his entertainment expenses. They'll help you get a picture of the problem, too.

If the person is on prescription medicine, go to the druggist and get the list of what he's taking. (Is he taking medicine that advises "Do not take in conjunction with alcohol" and continuing to drink? That's another sign of a problem.) Or simply check the bottles to see how many doctors he's seeing, each of whom is prescribing something else. You may very well be amazed. One man who had really had it with his wife was too angry to show up at the Intervention. To the kids, aunts, and uncles in the group he sent along all the medical bills and the drug prescriptions together with a cover note: "This is all I have to say."

Often mothers and fathers see only odd behavior. They see the symptoms, but they don't have specific examples of drug or alcohol use. Old friends can be helpful in collecting such examples.

One way to jog your memory is to sit down for a while and

try to look back over the past few years. Have you seen a change in the alcoholic's behavior? Is he less motivated than he used to be? Is his personality different?

Sometimes adult children of alcoholics don't know what they are looking for because they are so used to the alcoholic behavior that they don't know what's "normal." If you feel like that, ask yourself to recall a friend in high school whose house you just loved to visit, or a TV family you wished you were part of. Compare your household to those examples. I've asked people to do this and then watched the tears pour out.

Editing the letters

During the dress rehearsal, everyone will read his letter aloud and you will have the chance to see if the data is repetitive. If five people were at a party with the person, they may not all have to describe his behavior, but a couple may do so. People at the same event have different feelings and may observe different behavior. One group reported that the person they were concerned about was supposed to help a friend move, but when they picked him up, he wasn't ready. Someone noticed the empty bottles in his apartment, and another person saw that there were joints in all his ashtrays.

What to leave unsaid

An Intervention is not the occasion to bring up every problem in your life—just drinking behavior that you have observed and to which the alcoholic can relate. In your mind, you may believe everything that's going on is because of drinking and the poor judgment that results. You may be right; but at this point, the alcoholic won't be able to make those connections. You shouldn't bring up things like embezzled money or extramarital affairs. Those matters will be dealt with in the treatment process.

Incest and physical violence are matters that are outside the scope of Intervention, too. For years, alcoholics have gotten away with being physically abusive ("I'm a drunk, so I can do this") but this issue and that of incest must be addressed when the alcoholic is sober. The counselors at Families in Crisis say that only some of their alcoholics are physically abusive (emotional abuse is a far greater problem), and note that some people will be violent even when they're sober. They have never learned to control themselves and will need individual counseling later to handle this problem. I suspect in many cases the violence will disappear when the drinking stops, but a person has to get sober to deal with his dysfunctional behavior.

Talking about your sex life might be treading on an area that's too sensitive unless you can do it delicately. "I remember when we used to make love and it was very beautiful. Now, we never do." Or "I grieve because the intimacy we once shared is no longer there due to your drinking."

On the other hand, adultery might be brought up just to point out how the alcoholic has violated his moral system. Among the people who have a lot of trouble letting go of their anger are wives whose husbands are unfaithful. As a counselor has pointed out, if you don't approve of an alcoholic spouse's drinking you probably don't approve of him either. Why wouldn't he find someone else to get drunk with and go to bed with? The affair is just a symptom of the illness, and if you can look at it that way, you can get on with the Intervention.

One of the counselors said she used to overhear a group of alcoholics discussing their wives and their girlfriends and which one they loved. Finally she said, "How do you know whom you love? All you know is that you love your alcohol." If the "other woman" realized that her presence in the alcoholic's life was just symptomatic of his illness, do you think she would be happy with him?

Keeping the anger out

Anger often is a cover-up for another feeling, like hurt, loneliness, or fear, and it is also a great means of control. It can have a positive effect, too. It was probably the one thing that motivated you to Intervene in the first place. Even if your primary motivation was despair, certainly anger was high up on the list.

Remember the Peter Finch character in *Network* who said, "I'm mad as hell and I'm not going to take it anymore"? That's exactly how I felt about Sherm for years. But I never did anything about that anger until I got out of treatment myself and really began to think I wasn't getting a fair shake. I was sober, and he was still drinking.

My anger turned to rage. Then my counselor helped me use my anger to express myself and assert myself. Instead of asking, "Do you know how hard you are to live with?" he taught me to express the same feeling by saying, "I feel hurt when you do that," or "I'm so hurt by your rejection but I only know how to respond to it with anger." I felt a sense of accomplishment when I could express myself this way although I noticed friends were more willing to listen to me ventilate my anger about Sherm than to listen to me say how sad his rejection of me made me feel. I suppose friends can cope with your anger and frustration more than your sadness and confusion.

When you prepare for an Intervention, the first thing the counselor will ask is that you try to separate the behavior from the person. It's typical, for example, for an addict to express anger to such a degree that when the lid blows he doesn't care who's around—he'll wipe out anyone. Such behavior is the result of drinking or drug use, not an indication of someone's underlying character. Once you accept this, you can begin to move forward.

In the Intervention, the counselor will normally sit next to the person he thinks will have the most difficult time controlling his anger. He may just use gentle pressure on the hand to check that person if things begin going out of control. But he'll try to eliminate the anger by working on the letters beforehand and paying careful attention to how they are phrased.

The idea is to avoid a negative approach. Don't say, "How could you?" or "You know better." The person you're Intervening on already feels defensive and ashamed. Pushed beyond that, he'll defend himself with anger. He's comfortable that way. Anger is his turf. He'll feel safe with his anger wrapped around him. I knew if anyone called me on the carpet during Family Week I'd turn them off with my anger.

"So you think *I* drank a lot? Well, who was paying for *your* drinks?" Anger gets you off the track. You close down communications.

Anger can actually send someone back to the bottle. One man who participated in a Families in Crisis Intervention group had six years of sobriety behind him. He started to cry as the group read their data. "God," he said. "I wish someone had done this for me instead of the way they did it." He had been confronted by family and friends who did nothing but tell him what was wrong with him. He disappeared for two years and lost a wife and child.

Never use the word "should" in an Intervention. Don't say, "You should go into treatment," but rather, "It would be better for you to go into treatment." You wouldn't like someone else "shoulding" you. When he or she hears that, the alcoholic goes on red alert: You're putting your values on him. You're attacking someone whose self-esteem is so low he's like a cornered animal who's going to turn and fight.

Don't say "always," as in "You're always drunk." (That's impossible.) And don't say "never." Those are the words that get us all into trouble.

Phrases that you ought to use are "I care for you," even "I know you can do it." You'll be more effective if you start with something positive. Say, "I enjoy being with you when you're sober. At those times, I'm so happy to be your wife. But when you're drinking, I get scared you'll insult me and I hide." Love and caring are hard for the alcoholic to handle. They are what finally will break down his defenses, and they introduce the Intervention. The first person to speak says, "We are all here because we love you and we care about you." Your love is the hook to catch the person you love.

Keeping the love in

I asked people to tell me what "love" meant to them. Someone described it as a warm feeling around the heart, another equated it with sex, and a third said it's a feeling that makes you feel good all over. To me, it's not a word on a greeting card but a pretty heavy-duty emotion. Love is caring enough about someone else to step outside of yourself and do what's right for that person, regardless of the price that has to be paid. It's a feeling a mother has about her children.

Can you do that? Can you help a person who is incapable of helping himself (and not expect a bouquet of roses)? You love the person you're concerned about or you wouldn't have picked up this book. It's worth the risk to go beyond your fears, your anger, your self-doubt and hurt to be there, to tell him you love him, to tell him that you believe he needs help and why, to tell him that no matter what has happened, you're there to help in any way you can. Love is the one thing that you can give away and get back in even greater amounts.

A large family, many of whom had been in therapy, did an Intervention with Families in Crisis. Two of the sisters who were very close said they decided to Intervene in order to talk candidly with their father about the sadness everyone had experienced so he could share in their future lives. They saw the Intervention as a clear way to say, "Dad, we love you," even though terrible things had passed between them.

Sometimes, when there's a lot of anger, the counselors ask the people who are participating in the Intervention to go back and find a point in that relationship at which you did feel something positive. "Frank, we were such good friends five years ago. We had such marvelous times together." Or "I remember thinking you were such a kind person, but because of your drinking you have become mean and obnoxious. I miss the part of you I don't see anymore." With a husband or a wife, the counselor will say, "What initially attracted you? What did you fall in love with?"

You may have to go back decades. My own father died before we could ever work out our problems, but I know that if he were alive, I would not hesitate to do an Intervention on him today. Despite the anger I came to feel toward him as an adult, I could go back thirty years and say, "Dad, when I was a little girl, I felt safe around you."

A mother who hated what her son had become was asked to tell the counselor about her boy. She was a poet, and said she would be more comfortable writing a poem. She wrote about her feelings when she was pregnant with her child, when he was born, and when he was christened. That was probably one of the most direct expressions of love the man had ever had from his mom.

When you're compiling your letters, you have to come up with facts and feelings. Don't just come up with the bad ones. Look for the good ones. Look under the mountain of bad feelings that have accumulated, toss aside all the garbage, and you will probably see something special. Look for reasons to be thankful this person is part of your life.

Although statistics are on your side, I can't guarantee that Intervention will work. Your chances are great if you are willing to get at and let out the love. That love will help you take the risks and conquer whatever you're afraid of. Love works, people. It always has, and it always will.

14/
Anticipating the Reaction

Though the one thing you can't know in advance of the Intervention is exactly how the one you love will react, everything can and should be planned for.

The need for a dress rehearsal

I'm a great one for spontaneity, but not in the case of Interventions. And while practice may not make you absolutely perfect, it can certainly make you better. You definitely should have a dress rehearsal, and anyone who feels that practicing is kid stuff will be overruled by the counselor.

One of the things to work out in dress rehearsal is the order in which everyone will speak. Usually a person whom the alcoholic respects speaks first, so often this role goes to an employer. Or, if the Intervention is being held in someone's home, the host may be first. It often happens that if the person being Intervened on is a man, a man will open the meeting and vice versa. A young child generally goes last, as his message will probably be the most touching.

Prior to the Intervention, and possibly during the dress rehearsal, you come to a consensus of opinion about your response if the person being Intervened on wants to make a deal. "I'll quit drinking, and I'll start going to AA." You may want to bargain. Maybe you'll agree to consider out-patient treatment instead of in-patient treatment. However, never accept promises to quit that aren't attached to specific methods. Everyone thinks he can quit if he wants to and, of course, he can't. There must be a plan of treatment or some other therapy acceptable to the group. Otherwise the Intervention ends without the situation being resolved.

If you're having second thoughts

I believe that on the whole alcoholics are supersensitive. The person you're concerned about may have antennas so accurate that he senses something is in the air and seemingly out of the blue announces his plans to "reform."

Without realizing it, a family may send subtle signals once they've made their decision to Intervene. Their altered patterns of behavior give the alcoholic a clue to what's going on. Just before I checked myself into treatment, my brother and the others around me were considering an Intervention. When I look back, I realize that once they focused on my drinking, my business associates changed their own habits. Some ordered soda or coffee instead of having a drink with me. Families in Crisis counselors tell everyone to behave normally during the pre-Intervention period. They say that if you usually drink with the person you're concerned about, continue to do so. But I think you probably can't help being affected, even subconsciously.

When a family comes to Families in Crisis to report that all of a sudden, the person they're concerned about has stopped drinking, they are usually thrown into chaos. Once again, they wonder, "Are we doing the right thing?" Or because things have improved, they'll try to pin the family's problems on themselves. They look at what's happened in the past few days and forget the record of the last fifteen years. This is all part of the family blackout.

In such a case, the counselors suggest you read your letters again. You'll know you're doing the right thing. Or would you prefer to wait until your alcoholic comes home drunk and trips over and shatters the glass cocktail table, or makes a fool of himself at a party, or calls you from the police station needing bond money for a DWI?

If the alcoholic has stopped drinking, even temporarily, that will help the Intervention. It's almost impossible to Intervene on someone who is under the influence of alcohol or drugs, so you try to schedule an Intervention at a time when he's unlikely to be using. If the use is so habitual that the person rarely has a sober moment, you may have to go ahead with the Intervention anyway, but your chance of success is reduced.

If by some chance, the alcoholic finds out about the Intervention, just go ahead with your plans. Occasionally, an Intervention will be sabotaged. Families in Crisis reports instances in which someone said, "Dick, your family is going to do an Intervention. I think they're railroading you." When the family finds out, they're sure the Intervention has been ruined, but the counselor always tells them to proceed as planned. I think no matter how much of a struggle he puts up, the person with a using problem does want help.

Getting the alcoholic there

To get the person to show up at the Intervention, you don't play games. You don't tell him you're invited somewhere to dinner and spring this on him. I know I would be pretty angry if I were set up this way. On the other hand, it's unlikely you'll be able to say, "Today we are going to talk to someone about your drinking." (I did it with Sherm, but I had made up my mind that if he didn't go, I'd ask him legally to leave.) The most appropriate thing to say is that you're going to have a family conference that affects you and every member of the family. Explain that you've been getting some help for yourself and you would like him to come along. (Lots of times he will be only too happy to come because he's *convinced* you're crazy or you wouldn't be so concerned about his drinking.) Or have someone he cares about call and ask him to come help with a problem.

According to a 1985 story in *People* magazine, TV actress Heather Thomas's family sent news that her father was in the hospital, and when she rushed to meet him at his bedside, she discovered he was fine. The illness was just a ploy to get her to meet with family and friends, who I assume did an Intervention, and she checked into a hospital to treat her drug addiction. I wouldn't advise this kind of a ruse. It could backfire and you might have to deal with an enormous amount of resentment.

Conditions for the Intervention

Families in Crisis makes it a written rule that not only the person being Intervened on but also all members of the group will use no drugs or alcohol during the Intervention. (Cigarettes are forbidden to the others, but if the one being Intervened on smokes, an ashtray should be in place for him so he has no excuse to get up.) What prompted the no-use rule were some early Interventions at which everyone was fortified by a few drinks before the process began. One subtle hostess graciously summoned her maid to serve iced-tea—to the others. Her own glass was filled with scotch on the rocks. Even nonalcoholic drinks are taboo ever since the Intervention at which someone spilled a cup of coffee and the person being Intervened on got up to clean the mess. She walked into the kitchen, got paper towels and a sponge, and took her sweet time mopping up.

For a variety of reasons, you don't do the Intervention in the alcoholic's home. For one thing, being at home allows the alcoholic more freedom to go out of control. One woman on whom an Intervention was scheduled was at home when the counselor and her husband drove up. Since she had an inkling of what was going on, she ran out of the house and jumped into her car but couldn't back out because her husband's car was parked behind her. She just sat in her locked car with the radio turned on full blast. The counselor spent twenty minutes coaxing her out.

One woman owned the apartment she shared with her boyfriend. When everyone arrived for an Intervention on him early one morning, he locked himself in the bedroom. She was so annoyed that she called the police, but they refused to get him out since the guy had been living there with her permission. Everyone wound up reading their letters through the locked door. (In case you're wondering—yes, he went into treatment.)

Obviously, the main objection to doing an Intervention in the home is that a person can simply order you to leave. If you're in his home, he may tell everyone to get out of "his" house. That may touch off a quarrel between the husband and wife ("Well, it's my house, too") and you wind up with a situation comedy instead of an Intervention. If you're elsewhere and he refuses to listen, *he's* the one who leaves; the group can remain together to talk and plan the next step. Finally, when he's at home, the person being Intervened on can actually serve himself a drink.

So the Intervention is always done in neutral territory such as the office or the home of a friend or relative. You can rent a hotel room, too. Families in Crisis has prepared an Intervention that took place in a detox center where the alcoholic had been confined for a couple of days. My brother Johnny was Intervened on in a hospital room. He was in traction when his friends came in. At first he thought, "This is great! All my friends are coming to see me here." But when the ninth arrival closed the door behind him, Johnny knew what was coming. "John," one buddy began, "we're real concerned about your drinking. Now that we've got you where you can't move, we decided to talk to you about it."

Even in neutral territory, you may run into some strange situations. Once a woman being Intervened on in an office excused herself to go to the ladies' room. After several minutes, someone went to look for her. She was gone. She was discovered trying to climb the fence that divided the building grounds from the adjacent freeway. (After witnessing that, I wonder if anyone could still believe she was just a social drinker.) The counselor did manage to get her back inside.

Do whatever you can to plan ahead. The Families in Crisis counselors tell about a number of awkward situations that resulted from a lack of planning. Once a tree surgeon who'd been expected for six months finally arrived on the date of the Intervention. When he began his work, the house shook so badly that the Intervention had to be halted until he was done. The flow of the process was ruined.

Make sure the coast is clear—no repairmen, deliveries, or IRS audits scheduled—when your Intervention is planned. Turn off the phone. Have a babysitter take care of the little ones. Put a DO NOT DISTURB sign on the front door.

Preparing for the unexpected

People often ask the counselor, "How are you going to introduce yourself? How will he know what we're going to talk about?" Not much introduction is necessary. The counselors say that people may be shocked by the number of people who are present and concerned, or they may be shocked by how organized the process is, but never once has anyone been shocked by the fact of the Intervention itself. They know exactly what everyone is there to talk about. Most everyone in the room has probably buttonholed the guy to talk about his drinking at one point or another, but never before have they gathered to talk to him as a group.

The first person to speak is the counselor. He explains that he's been working with the family and friends who have gathered today because they're concerned about the person's drinking. He will ask the person on whom they're Intervening to listen to their concerns because they love him and care about him.

The counselor will not mention anything about wanting the alcoholic to get help, since he'd probably tune out immediately. You'll have a much better chance of having him agree to seek help once he's seen his situation through everyone else's eyes.

Even though he's been asked simply to listen, the chances are pretty good that he'll dispute one point or another as the letters are read. The best response is to say, "That's the way I perceived it," or even "Perhaps you're right," and to continue reading. Bring up your mother and he may tell you she's a dingbat, but you just say, "We'll talk about her later" and continue reading. Acknowledge him, don't be rude, but don't take the bait. Avoid interruptions by never asking a question, even one that doesn't require an answer ("How could you do something like this?" "Don't you think your behavior is odd?"). Your only purpose is to continue reading.

If the person continues to interrupt, the counselor may gently remind him of his promise not to. If necessary, the counselor may explain to the alcoholic that his family is frightened or reassure him of their concern. The idea is not to allow the alcoholic to stop the Intervention or even to sidetrack it. Don't get suckered into this. Don't allow him to take control. Just keep focusing on him. He's so good at disrupting that focus. He'll try to turn the spotlight onto someone or something else, even to bizarre lengths.

One Intervention came to a halt when a son said, "Dad, whenever I'm around you I can smell alcohol on your breath." The man shouted, "Everyone is picking on me. It's not fair. I'll show you what's wrong!" He took out his dental plates and put them in his palm. "Smell them," he exclaimed. "They're what smells!" His wife told him to put his teeth back in, but of course by this time people were laughing hysterically, partly out of nervousness. They eventually regained control of the situation by sticking to their bottom lines and finally the man went into treatment.

One man waited until all the letters had been read and then said, "Now, it's my turn to say something." He looked toward his wife. "What about your weight problem?" She agreed that she had a problem, but added, "We are here today to talk about your drinking." "What about the phone bill?" he said to the daughter. "I'm here because I'm concerned about your drinking," she said. He tried to lock horns with every one of the ten people in the room in order to get the focus off his drinking.

During his Intervention, Sherm tried to do that with me. "You've accomplished a lot in your life," he said. "But you always fall short. You don't follow through on your commitments, and other people are saying the same."

I could understand his need to protect himself. Though I wasn't Intervened on, I went through Family Week in treatment during which people are equally candid. At first I was turned off, because people were saying things I had heard before. I was counting on my family to help me out. I thought, "When it's Sis's turn, she's going to set the record straight. She knows what a great gal I am and she's going to defend me." Instead, when Sis began talking, she nailed me. She wasn't hostile, just accurate. That helped me face reality.

Families in Crisis helped organize an Intervention at which the alcoholic said, "I'll sit here for this crap but I'm not going to do anything about it," turned his back on everyone and began to read a book. The family continued to read their letters. Their counselor had told them that as long as the alcoholic was in the room, they should keep talking since he couldn't avoid listening. He eventually agreed to go into treatment.

Another family that was very scared by the prospect of the father's reaction was shocked when, as they read their letters, he simply cried.

It's important to remember that a person doesn't have to come to his moment of truth in the Intervention, he just has to agree to be evaluated. If he's in a good treatment center, his problems will be addressed there.

If the person walks out

Although 95 percent of the time, the person will sit quietly through an Intervention, it is always possible that he won't. The room is set up so that there is only one empty chair left for the person to be Intervened on, and it is always located at the far end of the room. Psychologically, that makes it harder for him to leave, but some people will leave, either before the process starts or midway through. In either case, the person is asked to stay but is never physically restrained.

One woman bolted for the back door the minute she saw the eighteen people waiting for her. When her children followed her, she doubled back and went out the front door instead. Her son caught up with her on the lawn. "Please come in. I really love you," he said.

"No," the mother said. "I'll talk to you at my house and my house only."

The counselor advised him to come inside and let his mother go. The woman walked several blocks, called a taxi, went home and got drunk, just as the counselor had predicted. Within two hours she was phoning her friends, "How could you do this to me? How do you have the nerve to do this?" And the friends said, "We knew no other way to get help." They refused to support her. The only thing she had left was her alcohol. Within two days, the woman was in a treatment center.

When you see signs of surrender

If the person is ready to go with less persuasion than you had expected, you can cut short your original agenda. Take your clue to close the session if he or she says something like, "I didn't know I had hurt so many people." "What is treatment all about?" "Okay, I have a problem. What do I do now?" Or even, "Okay, I'll go." Stop reading the letters and give the person specific information about what to do.

You should be prepared to take the subject directly to treatment. Bags should have been packed and a room booked. If the treatment center is within driving distance, two people should be available to take him there. If not, plane tickets for him (and perhaps someone to accompany him) should be on hand. (Don't be surprised if he goes off for one last toot. If he's alone on a plane, he'll probably get loaded. I know people who have walked into a treatment center, dropped their bags and said, "I'll be back in five hours" and walked to the nearest saloon and gotten totally drunk. You're saying goodbye to a relationship. You're saying goodbye to an old friend. "One for the road," and all that.)

Asking for compliance

If the Intervention proceeds without interruption, the last person to speak will explain the goal. "We would like you to go into a treatment center for a professional evaluation and to follow through with the evaluator's recommendations. Will you go now?" That is the only question asked during the whole process.

Often what follows is silence. Don't be afraid of it, even though it will probably be uncomfortable. The person may be hoping that someone will bail him out. Also, he may need some time to absorb all that he's heard. Nels Schlander always times the silences. Recently everyone waited for a full minute and a half before they heard, "Yes, I guess I do need help." The family probably felt they'd been waiting for half an hour.

If the person being Intervened upon says something like "I'm not sure" or "Thanks for your concern; I'll think about it," the counselor may ask if he wishes to hear the letters again and will explain, "Your family needs to make some decisions based on your answer. They need it today."

Covering the bases

You should have reassuring responses to any legitimate reasons he proposes for delaying treatment. You should be able to tell him that you have checked out the insurance, that financial matters are under control, that arrangements are already made for the transportation to and the stay at the treatment center. You must be able to assure him that the family can manage without his presence. You should delegate jobs among the concerned persons—things that can be done in advance (such as going through his calendar to cancel or postpone appointments) and things to be done on the day of Intervention (such as gathering the letters to put them in an envelope for the treatment center).

If he says, "I have to go to work in the morning," I would hope you can say "Your employer is behind this 100 percent," but if you haven't been able to bring yourself to get the boss involved, then so be it. He will just have to take a leave of absence. What's at stake is his life. That's more important than any job, and the person he respects most in the group should make this point if necessary.

You should have worked with the counselor to anticipate any other possible concerns—weddings, graduations, holidays. If the person says, "I'll go after Christmas," you tell him that the greatest gift he could give you is going into treatment. Be firm. "Your bags are packed. The car is ready. We're going now."

If he won't go

What it comes down to is that you're asking him to choose: "Yes, I'll get help," or "My alcohol is more important to me than anything else." Some spouses fear that their mates inevitably will choose alcohol, but the fact is that until now, the spouses never were given any choice in the matter. Of course, it is probable that the alcoholic may say, in effect, "I'm glad you were concerned, but this is my life and I'm going to do what I want to do with it." He may even use words that aren't so pleasant. What do you do?

If he's willing to sacrifice his relationship with you and with your children in this fashion, you can see how far the illness has progressed. If you're willing to put up with a negative response, that's a sign of how far your illness has progressed, too. You must commit yourself to seeking treatment for the family with Al-Anon, Alateen, or another helping agency.

If there has been violence in the home, your family must move out to a place of safety.

Your final resort

Now, at last, you must give him some consequences of his behavior—what Families in Crisis calls "the bottom lines." If the person is still in the room after he has refused to go, you can read them to him. Even if he is not around to hear them, put them into effect right away.

The idea of the bottom line is to give the alcoholic no choice but treatment. I have heard an alcoholic say, "If they tried an Intervention on me, I'd tell the whole group to take a flying leap." But when you're told that you might not have a job left, and your wife doesn't want you around, and your friends aren't going out drinking with you anymore, and your kids are going to leave when they see you drinking, and so forth, you suddenly realize that all you're going to have left is your bottle. That may very well make you throw up your hands and say, "Okay, I'll go into treatment."

If you're a mother with an alcoholic spouse, you have to be very careful with the bottom lines. Don't try to put words such as "I won't see you if you don't quit" in the kids' mouths. Many kids love their alcoholic fathers too much to say that. Be aware that teenagers are particularly afraid of expressing their feelings because of the consequences: Suppose Dad doesn't go in for treatment? Then I'm in for it.

If Mom's bottom line is that she will take the family and leave him or insist that he move out of the house, she must really be able to follow through. If you are serious about this, tell your child just what you have in mind. The day before Sherm's Intervention, I had a long talk with Andrew. He and

I had had many chances to talk about how much happier I was now that I'd stopped drinking. I said to Andrew, "Here's what I'm going to do. Either Dad's going to get help tomorrow and go to school (that's how I explained the treatment center, as a school where you learn how to stop drinking), or he's going to leave home." Andrew looked at me very seriously and said, "I think that's a pretty good plan, Mom."

I wasn't making an idle threat, and neither should you. Say nothing unless you can follow through on it. If the boss has threatened to fire the dependent, he should do it. If separation is the answer, move out. If you want to get him out, you may have to get a court order. Some people have said, if you don't go into treatment, you can't come home and followed through by changing the locks and the bank accounts.

Alternative bottom lines

You do not have to go completely out on a limb. You can do an Intervention without your bottom line being that you will leave unless he goes into treatment. The bottom line is just something that you feel you must do for yourself until he gets some help. Instead of saying "I'm never going to see you again," you might simply say "I'm not going to be around you when you are drinking." The point is that at last you're taking back some power. Here are some other possible bottom lines:

· "I can no longer work for you under the existing conditions."

· "You aren't welcome at my house when you've been drinking."

· "You won't be served alcohol at my house."

· "Unless you get help, I won't take care of the shopping for you anymore."

· "I'll never drink with you again."

· "If you call when you've been drinking, I won't speak to you."

· "I won't go on that fishing trip with you."

· "I won't invite you to any family functions."

· "I won't go to social functions with you when you're drinking."

· "I won't call your employer anymore and lie for you."

· "I will not entertain for you and pretend everything is fine."

· "I'll leave if you start drinking."

· "I'm going to family counseling and to Al-Anon regardless of whether you get help."

One man who Intervened on his father said, "Dad, I was taught three things: to be industrious, to love my family more than anything, and to be honest. You taught me these values, but you're not following them. And until you get your value system back, I'm not going to listen to anything you say, because I don't believe you." He would continue to see his father, he said, but if the man began drinking, he would leave. Since this father got his self-worth from helping his children and giving them advice, this was a very significant bottom line for him, and it turned out to be the turning point to getting him into a treatment center.

Another family's effective bottom line was to deny visits with the grandchildren because "It's too scary to leave them with you." The grandfather didn't want to lose his relationship with his grandchildren. He was also very touched when his kids said, "We want our kids to know you the way we knew you when we were growing up." What a loving reason to Intervene on older folks.

A boss has bottom line options other than firing someone. He could say, "You're one of my most valuable workers. If you don't get help, I'm not necessarily going to fire you, but I'm going to start monitoring what you're doing very closely to make sure you're not doing anything detrimental. And don't expect a promotion. I can't give you more authority."

Sticking with your bottom lines

One man being Intervened on excused himself briefly after hearing the bottom lines. He returned with a letter that said, in effect, "I agree to go in for this evaluation in two weeks but I can't today because of business." The counselor had warned the family that if he didn't follow through, they should go right to the bottom lines, but they didn't. The wife was the first to give in. "You can still come back home," she said, "even if you don't get help." She set up the process for failure. Often a wife needs to look at why she wants to keep her husband sick. Perhaps she has to take a look at her own drinking. Or is she afraid he'll leave once he sobers up? Or is it simply that she's gotten so used to taking care of him that she doesn't want to give up the role? She thinks she's helping him but she's not.

If you are able to stick with your bottom lines, you will probably be amazed. I know of a seventy-two-year-old grandmother who had a glass of beer when she awoke every morning and then continued to drink all day. When her husband died, the adult children and grandchildren first tried at-home care, then put her in a nursing home, although the only reason the woman needed such care was because of her drinking.

Finally, and with many reservations, they decided to do an Intervention. "You don't understand what our mother is like," they told K.D., their counselor.

The family got the woman, in her walker, to the Intervention, but they were so frightened that the counselor had to start things off by saying, "Your family is scared, but they're here because they love you and they want you to hear some of their concerns about your drinking."

The woman screamed. K.D. told her family to keep reading, but she continued to make a commotion. Each time she heard the word "drinking," she moaned and rocked in her chair, clutching at her chest, saying, "You're killing me." Her response was the family's nightmare come true.

Finally K.D. said, "Take her home and leave her there," and, very upset, they did so. They told her they would leave fresh food for her but no alcohol. She kept calling with various excuses—the blinds needed fixing, the faucets were dripping—but the family said all they could do was take her in for an evaluation. Finally, she phoned and said, "Okay, come get me." They didn't believe her, but when they arrived she was sitting on the front step with her bag packed.

This woman was typical of powerful mothers who are used to getting their own way. The bottom line was very important to show her the family really meant business.

When my brother Johnny was Intervened on in the hospital, his wife and kids had never seen him drunk. Nor had many of his friends. He was a secretive drinker. Generally he'd excuse himself from gatherings and say he was going home early and instead go off to a haunt where friends weren't likely to appear. They were only able to nail him because his behavior had become erratic. He'd say, "I'll meet you at the game at 3:00," and not show until 5:00, or "I'm going to work tonight, so I won't be home" yet be unreachable at the office.

Johnny threw his friends out of his hospital room at the end of the Intervention, but not before they'd told him their bottom line: Unless he got help they'd never call him again. His wife was firm, too: "Go into treatment or don't come home."

"I did go home," he says, "and no one was there. I had no idea where my family was. My friends weren't talking to me. I thought, 'God, they really mean it.' It would have taken just one of them to break and say, 'I'm sorry, we've been too hard on you.' I'd have been out drinking like a wild man. But they were united. I didn't have any choices. When I went in, I said, 'Thank you, God, I'm in treatment. My family and friends are important. I don't want to go through life alone.'"

If you can hold onto your bottom lines, the Intervention will be successful. It is natural for the alcoholic to panic at the idea of changing his behavior. It just doesn't seem possible. An alcoholic considers treatment to be the enemy. But on some level he realizes that the people in the room aren't the enemy. You love the alcoholic, and he loves all of you. You have more power than you can imagine. Give him your support and be kind but firm. Don't buy into the self-pity, anger, and resentment he will feel as he hears the information. You are showing him that there is a problem, but you are also offering a solution—and hope.

If your goal isn't achieved

Most Interventions work. You will never know if yours will until you've done it. But in the rare case where you may not see immediate results, you may find it necessary to regroup and do another Intervention when a crisis occurs. That job will be much harder if you haven't followed through with the bottom line from the beginning. If you have, whether or not the alcoholic checks into a treatment center, you will see results from this Intervention. Now that you've gotten help and held to your bottom line, the alcoholic can't play the same games anymore. He will have to change in response.

You have planted a seed in his brain, too. My business associate's aborted attempt to get me into treatment stayed with me. Afterward, I was never as comfortable with the drinking. I always heard a little voice inside my head saying, "Maybe he's right. Maybe the drinking is causing me problems."

Whether it appears to work or not, the Intervention has done something terribly important. Your alcoholic will eventually be so full of pain he won't be able to take it anymore. Now he knows there is an alternative. It's easier to go for treatment than to live with the painful consequences of your drinking.

15/
The Treatment Period

Let's assume that everything went beautifully. The one you're concerned about is on his way into treatment. The rest of you are patting each other on the back, telling yourselves what a great job you did. You may even do an "instant replay" of the Intervention. You'll be feeling great, maybe even euphoric. But only temporarily.

Aftermath

Once the group has disbanded and you're back home, you may feel slightly let down, perhaps a bit lonely, even worried that you did the wrong thing. As you think back over what happened, you will probably need to talk further about your feelings.

Also, even though the counselors will tell you never to apologize for an Intervention—why should you apologize for being honest and helpful?—the fact is that everyone always feels some guilt. Even if you were at a point where you were willing to try anything, even if you felt you'd like to lock up the s.o.b. and throw away the key, by the time the Intervention is over you won't be angry anymore. You will have realized how you were affected and how you were suffering, but you will also understand your role in the situation.

You might go so far as to feel that had it not been for you, none of this would have happened. Parents who have learned about the possible genetic link in alcoholism start to take all the blame for their child's disease. A spouse may feel guilty because she's enabled the one she loves. A friend may feel guilty for having been the alcoholic's drinking buddy. A child may feel that he has betrayed his parent.

Perhaps you will have second thoughts about whether you needed such a dramatic solution to the problem. You almost certainly will wonder whether you did the right thing. In such a mood you're very vulnerable. If the one you love calls from a treatment center and sounds a little depressed or uncomfortable, your instinct is to rush over. This is absolutely the worst thing you could do.

The need for aftercare

It's critical that you and the other people involved in the Intervention regroup to talk things out. It's not unusual for a family to meet for aftercare and say, "How could we have done that to him?" You need to remind one another of the legitimate reasons for your concern and of the fact that unless you stick to your bottom line and listen to the counselors, you will fall into the same old traps. Whoever helps you with your Intervention must do follow-up sessions with the family. And if you still haven't become involved with Al-Anon, do it now.

Early in its history, Families in Crisis had a case in which the woman Intervened on called everyone from the treatment center to report that she didn't really have an alcohol abuse problem. When he investigated, the counselor learned that the center had not used the letters that were presented at the Intervention. The woman had given the center permission to interview only two people in order to assess her problem—her employer and a good friend, both of whom had drinking problems themselves. Based on their data, the woman was told she didn't need in-patient treatment.

Once she was out of the center, she visited her family and friends individually and spoke so persuasively that they began to question themselves. Eventually, they couldn't hold to their bottom lines. Finally, the family called Families in

Crisis for further counseling. Since then aftercare for the family has become routine.

One adolescent who went into a treatment center following an Intervention called his father to report that the nursing staff told him he could use pot responsibly. He walked out of treatment. Despite the fact that the father had been talking to the counselors directly and they advised him that the son needed to abstain, the father wanted to believe the son's story and to blame the treatment center for what happened.

If you have any questions about what's going on in treatment, talk them out in your group. Also, don't hesitate to call the director or staff at the center to make sure you're getting the story straight. Remember that anyone in the middle of treatment is still in denial and hasn't accepted the fact that he is alcoholic. (I personally didn't come to grips with my alcoholism until the fourth week. I knew I was alcoholic, but I couldn't accept the fact. Thank goodness I finally did.)

Your continuing concerns

You might still be in denial, too. You might want so badly to believe the one you love that you are still looking for a way to pin the problems on anyone—or anything—else. This is typical. He's scared, and so are you. He will usually give you plenty of reasons to be concerned whether you made the right choice.

I watched an episode of "Dallas" involving Sue Ellen, the family drunk. (It's amazing to me how much sympathy she gets for her drinking because she's married to J.R. If she sobered up she'd leave the jerk, take him for everything he's worth, and go live happily ever after.) In this particular show, she passed out in the punch bowl. It was amazing to watch people walk around her as if this were nothing unusual. In the next scene, she was in the hospital, looking like a mess. (Another fiction; lots of alcoholics look pretty good even when they're in treatment.) The doctor was speaking words to this effect: "We want to get you into a rehabilitation program because of your alcohol. Sue Ellen, this is going to be the hardest thing you've ever done in your life."

That show made me so mad! Treatment isn't a punishment, it's a wonderful experience. It wasn't the hardest thing I'd ever done, either; being a practicing alcoholic was a lot harder, but I couldn't have known that until I experienced sobriety. Don't feel sorry for the alcoholic in treatment even though it's very possible he'll call to say, "Get me out of here," or some variation: "Oh, my God, you don't know what they're doing here." "All these people are crying." "They're beating everyone up." "No one is nice to me." "It's terrible." "They're ganging up on me." "Wait till Family Week; they're going to get our whole family."

You'll also hear other complaints: that the staff is incompetent because they wear jeans with suspenders, for example, or that this center is not the right place because everyone else is a drug addict and he's an alcoholic. (It's very common for an alcoholic to call home and report for any number of reasons that he's not like everyone else at the center.) Remember that alcoholics in hospitals—like alcoholics who *should* be in hospitals—hear and see very selectively.

I know a fellow who came to the United States as a penniless concentration camp survivor. He was a great success and a wonderful role model for his kids. He taught them to work hard and be good to their family. But in the 1960s he started drinking and became a chronic alcoholic. The family put him into a treatment center—but only briefly. He complained that he couldn't understand what was going on because of the language barrier. They felt sorry for him and welcomed him home with open arms. It seems to me that in the forty years he has been in the U.S. he has managed to do a brilliant job of conducting his business dealings in English. I'm sure he could understand whatever was being said at the center. He was just handing his family a lot of baloney and they bought it. Now he's at home again, drinking. Drinking, and dying.

During aftercare, Families in Crisis prepares you for this kind of complaint and tries to give you the courage to stay firm. There have been instances in which a spouse was about to give in to a patient who wanted to be taken out of treatment and the rest of the family managed to stick by their guns. They told the spouse, "Do that and you're on your own."

Families in Crisis recommends you do one of two things if you are tempted to buy into the alcoholic's excuses. Either call other people who participated in the Intervention or call the treatment center and discuss your concerns with the staff. Chances are the wool is being pulled over your eyes. If you've seen the treatment center yourself, you should be re-assured that it's the right place for the one you love.

Judging the treatment center

I had a friend who led a very glamorous life as the wife of a world-class writer until she developed a major drug and al-cohol problem. Her friends were concerned but unwilling to do an Intervention. They wanted to leave things in her hands, despite the fact that she was completely deluded. One friend recommended a treatment center and my alcoholic pal decided to check it out. She felt the clientele wasn't chic enough for the doctors to have had experience dealing with her kind of problems. (What she couldn't get into her head was that if you're falling down stoned, it doesn't matter whether you live in a mansion or a tenement except that in the mansion you might fall on something softer.) Also, she didn't find the place up to the standards of the Beverly Hills Hotel.

The treatment centers I have seen are all very well kept, but I know that families who visit them tend to concentrate on things like how the mattresses feel or how the staff is dressed. I certainly advise you to look over the place and meet the staff, but don't get carried away if you see a speck of dust in a corner or you meet a member of the counseling staff who seems to be a bit of a character. (Chances are that you won't like everyone you meet in the treatment center. Do you like everyone you meet *out* of the center? The people who work in treatment centers are just as different from one an-other as are the alcoholics they treat.) What you should be thinking about is how the one you love will be helped and cared for here and recognize that the staff knows how to deal with his problems and you don't.

Families in Crisis had to deal with a professional man, very formal, always dressed in a three-piece suit, who was his wife's chief enabler. After visiting one treatment center, he said, "That's no place for Helen. She's got a serious addiction problem and she's in pain. Everyone there is walking around and seems to be in perfect health. And I don't see people in uniforms. I don't know if there are any professionals there." On top of that, judging from their appearance, he said, "The patients aren't my wife's sort of people."

The counselor told him that he didn't see the patients who were as ill as his wife because they were still confined to bed (few alcoholics go through withdrawal, but if so, the medical staff attends to them before they are assigned to a care unit) and that the doctors in that treatment center did not wear uniforms. As for appearances, only in his mind's eye did his wife look like Cinderella at the ball and seem out of place with what he perceived as commoners.

The worst thing in the world is to make comparisons with the other patients. People will say, "I saw he was in a group with someone who was shaking for three weeks after entering treatment, and gee, our alcoholic wasn't that bad. After all, he went to work every day. Maybe we were too quick to go for an Intervention. Maybe his case wasn't that serious. Maybe if we just talk to him, we can get him to stop drinking." That is the number one way to sabotage treatment. Avoid it by talking about your feelings with your Intervention group.

Someone is bound to say, "Remember how he went off the deep end that time?" and "Remember how you cried that night?" In a group, you won't be able to go back into denial and delusion. Furthermore, if you have some problems about the treatment center itself ("This place doesn't look so great," or "The person greeting the people at the desk is kind of punky looking"), they can help you put things into perspective.

Most important, those of you who were involved in the Intervention can reinforce one another and help prevent the alcoholic from manipulating you again. Once in treatment, the alcoholic gets his support from a group. You need a group of your own to help you with the healing process and give you strength. From now on both you and he will have to take care of yourselves.

What is the alcoholic going through?

You may wonder what really happens in treatment. I remember walking through the doors of Hazelden and thinking "My God, I hope I can live without alcohol." At the same time, part of me was saying, "I really don't need to be here. I'll stay a few weeks and get my act together and get people off my back. I can control my drinking if I really want to."

The first few days, I wanted people to know that I was a worthwhile human being. I had been judging myself for so long that I just wanted everyone to confirm that I was okay. So at first I gave out very little information about my illness, because the more I gave out, the more I felt someone would tell me I was no good. At the same time that I was looking for approval, I was also angry that I was alcoholic.

I suppose part of the anger was fear. I was afraid to hear about what was wrong with me and afraid of what was going to happen to me there. There were certain counselors who were rumored to be involved only in treating "really bad" people or mostly junkies, and if you got into their groups, those labels would be stuck on you. I know if they had put me in a certain wing at Hazelden I would have assumed that I had been diagnosed as in the chronic stage. If I'd been told I needed a single day of treatment more than the twenty-eight I'd gone in for, I would have been very fearful. I understand now that all of these were typical reactions.

Also, I was afraid of failing. Alcoholics are such people pleasers that they can't even talk about their fears, because they can't imagine saying, "What if I can't do this?" But that's what I was thinking: What happens if I have been screwing up so badly that I can never set things right? Where would I go from here? I'm sure that if they had changed my room at some point, I would have taken that as a sign I was failing. I understand this is pretty typical, too. Even if they didn't actually say so, I suspected that everyone was mad at me. I felt I deserved their anger. I knew I was screwing up in many areas.

During the admission procedures, I had a routine physical and I remember thinking how great I was and how different from everyone else because my blood pressure was normal and my vital signs were perfect. I had heard about the people in oxygen tents and the ones on medication for withdrawal, so I took pride in the fact that I wasn't as sick as any of them.

Also, I never did drink on a daily basis. Since I had my last binge several days before I arrived, I had time to get all the alcohol out of my system and so, when I checked in I felt I wasn't a mess. (I soon found my counselor and peers didn't agree.) I felt that set me apart from the great numbers of people who arrived totally bombed after one last fling. I thought, "Man, I am so much better than all these other people," which was of course a crock. The others were just a little farther down the very same road I was traveling. It was just a matter of time before I would be able to step into the shoes they'd fallen out of. But there I was, feeling so proud of myself because I had skipped the detoxification step.

In treatment centers, they consider compliance as another of the steps toward your goal. By compliance, they mean your acceptance of the fact that you need to be treated for your illness. (You might accept it as fact while not accepting it emotionally. That's the next step.) I think that some of the rules and regulations we had to live under during treatment were designed to help us reach the right level of compliance. Of course, there would have to be some rules and regulations just to keep order, but for most of us it was uncomfortable to surrender control over little things—like prescribing self-medication (such as aspirin) or signing out when you left the premises, too.

If your alcoholic calls to complain about the rules, don't pay too much attention. Just remind him that there isn't an organization in the world that doesn't have rules, including a country club. If it makes him feel like a child to follow rules, remind him they exist primarily to ease the operations of the center, not to harrass him.

The fact is that most of us entered with a self-centered attitude. Alcoholics have a rebellious spirit. They have a hard time following orders. We tried to find ways, even silly

THE TREATMENT PERIOD / 273

ways, to flout the rules. I had a friend who refused to wear her little plastic name tag. She said it put holes in her blouse. So they gave her tape, but somehow the name tag still fell off.

As I got deeper into treatment, I realized the world didn't revolve around me and that the rules, like being on time for meetings and signing out when we left the premises, made sense.

Spiritual healing in treatment

Before I left for treatment, a well-meaning friend told me, "Don't become one of those born-agains. You know, that's what they do to you in treatment. They brainwash you into becoming a religious zealot." Although I would recommend only a treatment center that followed the 12 Steps program, I would like to stress again that the program is simply a tool for living. Its only reference to God is indirect, as "a power greater than ourselves."

Some people hear the words "spiritual recovery" and, because they have been so abused in the name of religion, a wall goes up in front of their eyes. They think in terms of self-righteous religious types with phony smiles, judgmental or wrathful nuns, ministers, and priests. When I was a kid, I was very active in Sunday school. I once overheard my teacher say, "You know, her parents don't attend. I think her father drinks." That did it for me. From that Sunday on I played hookey. I took my offering money and skipped off to the nearest soda fountain to buy a sundae with it.

I've always been less interested in religion (for me that only means something formal and concrete, a building and people) than in spirituality. Spirituality involves hope and faith, and you don't have to be sitting in a church to find it. Personally, when I was out of treatment I had a real need to go back to church, to feel there was a God in control and to ask Him for help. I felt that overcoming my problem was a miracle, and that miracle was enough to create a spiritual reawakening in me.

I stopped drinking because I surrendered and went into treatment. Because I was willing to ask for help, I have experienced many miracles in the past two years (enough for a book in itself). They led me back to the church and to my higher power, God, who is love. He took me just the way I was. I had only to admit I needed help. Now I go to church to let Him know how much I appreciate all He has done for me through AA and the wonderful people I've met along the way.

The only way I know to return that help is to help others, and that's what this book is about. The staff at Hazelden gave me the tools to put myself back together and when I left, my faith was renewed, I had hope for a wonderful future, and I had a need to go back to the church.

Other aspects of recovery

Many people can maintain sobriety without a spiritual reawakening. Treatment is a spiritual recovery only in part. It is also a physical and psychological recovery. The treatment process teaches sick people to handle the problems of everyday life without booze and other drugs. The goal is to help you accept your disease and learn to follow certain steps to have a happy sobriety. The method is to break through denial so that you realize how powerless and unmanageable your life has become. It consists of attending lectures, reading selected materials, and attending group therapy sessions that help you get in touch with your feelings and break down your defenses. I like in-patient treatment because I feel that you recover best when you are removed from your daily activities and can face your problem in a controlled atmosphere.

Once you pass beyond the stage of compliance, you reach the stage of acceptance: taking personal responsibility for your recovery. Every day you seem to have a new insight. Something will come up that you did or said, and you'll recognize yet another example of inappropriate behavior or of the pain that the disease caused. As the cobwebs start leaving your head, you experience reality more and more.

The process is very painful at first because you feel that everyone is getting close to your secrets. You'll do anything to protect yourself. I was in treatment with a fellow who called his wife before she came up for Family Week and said, "If you bring up the boating accident, I'm leaving you." She called the counselor that day, and it was brought up in our group the next morning. No big deal was made out of it.

Still, the tendency is to avoid being put on the spot. I ran from the room during a counseling session early in my treatment. My brother Johnny started telling a lot of truths about my life. "You may think Mary Ellen's great. She's the kind of gal people really like. But let me tell you some things about Mary Ellen that you might not know," he said, or words to that effect.

I hid in bed and cried. And guess who I called? My mom. "Mommy, Johnny said all these horrible things about me." And she bought into it. What he said wasn't that horrible, but he let some monsters out of my Pandora's box. It was the first time any of those things had ever been discussed in the open—for example, the fact that I drank when I was pregnant.

One of the things you experience in treatment are grief sessions at which you have the opportunity to review things in your life that you didn't take time to mourn properly. I started thinking about my son's dog, Fritzi, whom Sherm and I had taken to a party with us. We had a few drinks first, or we probably would have left him home. During the party, he got loose, ran into the street, and was run over. And I knew it was because I'd been drinking and not paying attention. That knowledge just destroyed me. It was a hard thing for me to get over, a hard thing to admit to myself, that if I hadn't been drinking, my son's dog would not have died. I knew that Andrew knew it. He had to know it. He knew everything else that was going on, much as I tried to deny it.

But although I suffered pain, I didn't feel condemned or punished. I began to understand that some of what happened wasn't my fault, and better than that, maybe there was a way to stop the craziness in the future. I felt so relieved.

Beginning to feel well

Some alcoholics have gotten to the point where they feel, "I am totally useless. There is nothing good about me. I can't do anything anymore." If someone else isn't beating up on us, we do it to ourselves. Even if you're the most accomplished writer, the most productive salesman, the most convincing attorney, if you're an alcoholic, you always look at the down side. But when you arrive in treatment, all of a sudden, you're being built up.

Group sessions provide reality therapy. You can check with other people to find out if you're okay, and they begin to convince you that you are. They help you understand what behavior is getting you into trouble but also help you see what's terrific about yourself.

You connect with the others in a way that you will never connect with anyone in the outside world. You're with people who understand you deeply. Mary, one of the Families in Crisis counselors, recently ran into someone with whom she'd been in treatment for six and a half weeks ten years ago. She later said that as they talked, she realized that they shared something she didn't have even with people she is close to today.

In my opinion, there is as much worthwhile therapy that happens during the periods of socializing as during the official sessions. You're not judged. You can't help but start to feel good about yourself.

Learning to accept your illness

The most important thing that happens in treatment is that by the time you're ready to leave, you have an acceptance of the disease of chemical dependency. I can't tell you what an extraordinary relief it was for me to understand that alcoholism is an illness—that it wasn't something to blame myself for ("I shouldn't have drunk so much") or a moral issue. But, once you get all the data, you do become responsible for your own life. You're like a diabetic who is told that he must take insulin. If you're an alcoholic, you must stop drinking. You're not responsible for your disease, but you *are* responsible for managing it.

The role of family and friends during treatment

How should you act toward someone in treatment? For starters, lay off the phone calls during working hours. (Someone in treatment is working, too—working on himself.) The calls can be a real pain in the neck. The alcoholic is trying to concentrate on himself and his recovery. He needs uninterrupted time to think. I preferred to have people let me call them when I was ready and able. When I finally did phone a friend, I was thrilled when she simply asked, "Is there anything I can do to help?" I felt that someone really cared about me.

Feel free to send things like flowers and cards. Be as supportive as you would if anyone you cared for were in the hospital for any reason. Receiving flowers can make a patient's day. A friend told me that when she went into treatment the first time, she had dozens of cards and more flowers than anyone, but when she went into treatment the second time, she had none. To her that was a sign of how her disease had progressed. She'd lost her friends.

I got a lot of mail, but most of it consisted of notes from my attorneys and accountants saying, "We're all pulling for you, Mary Ellen." I realized that my life consisted of too many people surrounding me and trying to protect me (when possible) from myself.

Nels Schlander told me that what was most devastating to him when he himself went into treatment was to discover that all the people he had assumed were friends in fact were not. The only contact he had was from his parents and his wife.

Participating in Family Week

The real proof of caring is agreeing to be part of someone's treatment. I have a friend who's been in treatment a couple of times. Her mother sends gifts, but she's unwilling to be part of the process, which is what would really mean something. You will be asked to come to Family Week, and your participation is a critical part of the treatment.

Mine is a fun family. Everyone is comfortable and seems to be doing okay. Our lives appear normal to the outside world. We certainly weren't throwing pots and pans at each other or beating each other up. Still, drinking was the focal point of our activities and it did get us into a lot of trouble. Family Week helped make that clear.

The way Family Week works at Hazelden is that all the

alcoholics are in one unit and family members in another. I went through Family Week with Sherm's kids once he was in treatment, and I got to see how things worked from the family's side. I noticed that our group didn't say much in the morning session. Sherm's daughters were shocked by the other families, but I didn't see anything so shocking. I knew they were just being more honest than we were. Toward the afternoon, the trust level in the group got higher, and our family admitted that Sherm's drinking had affected each of them. Once the honesty starts, pretty soon you need a dumpster to handle all the garbage. But by the end of Family Week, a lot of the garbage has been covered over like new growth after an earthquake, and new shoots are starting to poke out of the shambles below. I know you will find Family Week a valuable part of your own experience.

At the beginning of treatment, the one you love may be depressed, but for everyone involved, treatment is the best thing that could ever happen. Once in a while, I pull into the parking lot of a treatment center near my home. Often I'll see people walking around with their heads hanging low. I know those are the newcomers, and I make a point of blowing my horn and waving at them. "Hi, how're you doing? My name is Mary Ellen and I'm an alcoholic. I went through treatment two years ago, and guess what? It's great!!" The twenty or thirty days I spent at Hazelden are much more meaningful and joyful than the most wonderful trip I ever took. I found myself. I found out that Mary Ellen Pinkham was okay just as she was.

You could give no better gift to the one you love.

16/
Aftermath

Like Intervention, recovery is a process rather than an event. Changes won't happen overnight. Nor will they be one-sided.

Your obligation to get help

In treatment, an alcoholic learns to be responsible for his recovery. During counseling, the family members should have learned to be responsible for changing their behavior, too. Alcoholism is a family disease, and getting sober is a family affair.

If you think you can send somebody off to treatment for a month to stop drinking and that's all there is to it, you aren't getting the message of this book and you're in for big trouble. You can't take the attitude, "I went through Intervention, I did my job, and now it's up to him." You've climbed the first mountain, but there are others beyond it. The best thing you can do for your alcoholic is go out and get healthier yourself and quit worrying about what he is or is not doing. Otherwise, he'll drink again. If the people around him change their behavior, an alcoholic has an 80 percent improved chance of becoming and staying sober.

The task will seem easier if you do it day by day and if you get help from Al-Anon and Alateen and, if you want more help, from one-on-one counseling. There is too much help available—and too much literature about relapse—for you to try and solve all these problems yourself. You have probably been trying to do so for years, and you know where that got you all—nowhere. Unless you are told how to make some changes in your life, you'll have the same old story (if not a worse one) at home.

Don't let the alcoholic continue to be in charge, either. Some are still running the show even from the treatment center. They tell the family not to come for Family Week, or they insist that the kids not be involved. No matter what your alcoholic says, go to Al-Anon. You've got to get help in order to give help.

The people who relapse are the ones who don't get themselves in AA (because they think that it's not for them, that they'll be associating with winos, or some other weak excuse) and the ones who don't get support because their families don't act. These alcoholics have a weak, sick support system, and once out of treatment they'll lead lives that are separate from the family. Most likely, they'll turn back to their chemical. Rarely, they manage to head off alone in their recovery. In either case, your relationship will break apart.

Why treatment fails

It's only because I feel so comfortable in my sobriety that I can publicly admit something I kept secret for years, which is that my month at Hazelden wasn't my first experience in treatment. I had been in treatment once seven years before that, shortly after Andrew's birth.

I came out of my first treatment without believing what I was told. I knew that nothing had changed. I had not really looked inside myself. I had not accepted the idea of a higher power. I had no realization that alcoholism was a disease, nor did I believe it was progressive. I learned different. That's why I had to go back. Believe me, I was in worse shape the second time around.

Since I wanted to drink, I had to persuade my family and friends that I was all right, and I managed that with hardly any effort. I had only to badmouth treatment and act very friendly. I did manipulate them, but it wasn't a major feat;

they were as sick as I was. They never gave me any bottom lines, so I could go back to my same old behavior. Two weeks after I came home, I was out drinking with another member of my family. The only one who really saw through me was my brother. And he alone couldn't make the difference.

I've discovered that it's not unusual to have to repeat treatment (and often the second course is the one that "takes"), but the first one can work if the patient follows his aftercare program and if the family gets involved and works on changing also. The people around me did not, the first time. I think that (like me) they didn't believe the disease was progressive and chronic, that it wouldn't get any better, only worse.

Eventually, of course, I found out that everything I had been told was true. The alcoholism doesn't go away no matter how much success you have nor how many people love you. I had to lose a lot more and hurt a lot more before I wound up back in treatment. The second time I had no choice but to listen. I listened, and I believed.

Some people never change. For them, treatment is like a revolving door. They start drinking again, and they come back. Most of them keep coming back—unless they die. If family members change, they can prevent such a thing from happening to the person they love.

When the family doesn't change

If you go back to an environment that supports your using, you're a dead duck. Shortly after completing treatment, a friend of mine returned home to find the living room filled with a group of friends smoking pot.

"What's going on?" he said to his wife. "I thought we agreed to keep our home chemically free."

She looked at him coldly. "I knew these friends before I knew you, and if you don't like it, you can get out." He'll never forget how badly she hurt him.

Fortunately, before being released from treatment, he had to choose a sponsor. When his wife disappointed him, something—he credits his higher power—moved him to call his sponsor. The fellow told him to drive right over. My friend stayed with his sponsor for two weeks, during which time he made arrangements to move out of his home. Not only has he stayed away from alcohol and drugs for years now, but also he's become a counselor in the field of chemical dependency.

He was one of the lucky ones. He somehow found the strength to get himself out of a situation that would only enable his using. During the difficult time of recovery, you need the support of your family. The sad thing is that sometimes they can kill you with kindness. Families in Crisis got a call from a woman who said, "My husband has had three treatments. He's drinking again and he wants me to get some Librium [a drug that's used in the detoxification process], and I want to know if you think I should do it."

The counselor realized the woman was waiting for her husband to make all the changes. She'd made none. She tolerated his drinking and kept accepting his promises to stop. There was a previous episode of her buying Librium for him. The counselor recommended an Intervention, but she backed off, saying, "I'll think about it if the situation gets really bad." It was "really bad" already, but she couldn't see it. Often you find that the same people who cry the blues about the person's drinking are the very ones who enable him to continue.

In my own family, my dad went in and out of treatment centers—in part, I'm sure, because there were never any changes at home. Treatment was something that happened to him but didn't affect the rest of us. I remember he used to complain about the coffee they served at the center, so my mom used to bring him coffee from home. What she should have been brewing at home was a plan to stop enabling my father.

I love my mother, and I know I could never find a better friend. She has stuck with me through thick and thin, and I'm sure she was as supportive of my father. She just didn't have the knowledge or the tools to give him some real help. I'm sure if she had it to do all over again, she would run her life differently. She wouldn't have enabled Al Higginbotham. Her love helped him tunnel deeper into his alcoholism, and all the while she believed she was doing the right thing.

Living with a recovering alcoholic

For a variety of reasons, life with the alcoholic just out of treatment may not be something out of "The Donna Reed Show." Naturally, you're a little tense. You're probably wondering if he's angry with you. You're on pins and needles wondering if he will stay sober. You're not sure what he's like when he's sober.

He has his own anxieties. He's worried about staying sober. He's uncertain of your love for him. He wonders whether he can fulfill all the new responsibilities he's taken on. As he got more and more out of it due to his drinking, he probably surrendered his natural roles to other members of the family. But if now Dad has returned to become a participating member of the household, he may want to make the decisions again, lay down the rules for discipline, handle the checkbook.

It's possible that he will take on the role of Superdad and expect the family to welcome him back with open arms when he starts planning all its activities. "Tonight, we're going to have dinner at 6:00 all together, and on Sunday, we're all going to church." The family may not be used to taking orders from him. The spouse may resent giving up the control she's assumed. On top of that, the kids don't believe in him or his plans. An alcoholic has a pattern of breaking promises. It will take a while for him to regain the trust of his family and for you to let go of those hostile feelings.

While the alcoholic and his family are trying to redefine their roles, you may be in for some weird times. My brother Johnny tells me that for the first year of my sobriety, every time he met me for lunch I'd be somebody else. He said he was tempted to greet me with, "Hi, Sybil." I was rid of all my past defensive behavior, and now I was trying on new hats to find out which one I could wear most comfortably. Similarly, the behavior the family has learned to adapt to life with the alcoholic must be unlearned. These habits don't go away magically. You must work at making changes. You must take risks. It takes time.

In treatment, you are asked not to make any major changes for a year. That means no moving residences, no quitting jobs, no new relationships, and no divorce. The sign of a really good recovery is when someone doesn't try to change things immediately. He should come back into the family, start taking care of himself, and give everyone time to gather round.

Marriages usually hold together for a while, but if they break up, it's because one person or the other admits, "I didn't know this person sober and he's not who I want to make my life with." If you're the sober one, I don't think you have to worry that you'll be unceremoniously dumped. If a breakup occurs, most likely you're the one who will initiate it.

Don't expect gratitude

What will be the general mood at home? Typically, there is a honeymoon period. The family is relieved that the hassles about chemical dependency are over, and everyone will try very hard to keep the peace. But things are probably not completely wonderful, and the surface pleasantness is just a cover-up for many underlying problems (such as money troubles, a job loss, children who are hurt and/or disgusted) and continuing anxieties.

There will inevitably be some kind of blowup, and when it happens, accept it without being too upset. Recognize that it's better for this phony honeymoon period to end before the disillusionment, hostility, anger, and sadness get completely out of hand.

You may still hold on to the idea that the alcoholic is the problem, not you. Meanwhile, he's got some grudges against you. If he's not exactly bitter at first, he'll certainly be reserved. If you're counting on a big pat on the back or a hug and a smooch, you may have to wait a while for it, as I learned with my sister Sue.

When Sue went to Hazelden, I was excited. I thought *I* would be the big event in her recovery. I waited in vain for the phone call to come up and help out. I later discovered that my sister had told her counselor to leave me out of it, that it was none of my business how she was doing.

When I called her, she was distant and cold. Finally I put myself in her shoes. She was dealing with a lot of hard issues, and I was the scapegoat. After all, I was the older sister, the one who was always telling her what to do, and she had had enough. She finally told me, "This will be my recovery, Mary Ellen, not yours."

Later, she and I were signed into the same aftercare program and she didn't show up. Even though I was finished with the process, I had come to lend a hand and introduce her around. It was then the counselor told me my presence made Sue uncomfortable. Angry, I told him that she was just using me as an excuse not to come.

Eventually, we went through a soul-searching together. I stopped telling her how to run her life. Although she wasn't too fond of me when she went into treatment (which I knew), I thought everything would be different in a couple of weeks. In fact, it took us several months to get back on track. As I got healthier, I realized I was trying to be my sister's caretaker. I'm not now, and good things have happened for both of us. Sue and Johnny are my best friends, and we share our crises and joys. We check in with one another out of concern, and I don't think any of us regards the other's phone calls as policing.

Sources of comfort

Some people come out of treatment like gangbusters. They start running, they begin physical fitness programs, they start looking really terrific. Then there are the others, like me. I was very, very lethargic for six months. I would drag to the office and have to leave in the afternoon and take a nap for an hour or two. I just couldn't stay awake.

I started smoking more and more. I craved sweets. I drank pots of coffee. All those things bothered me. My counselors told me, "Mary Ellen, you're a perfectionist." (Most alcoholics are.) They'd remind me that I was doing well, tell me "Let's just get through this" or "Take it one day at a time." They reminded me that the smoking, the sweets, and the caffeine weren't doing as much harm as the drinking and that, above all, I should try and learn to be good to myself. Recovery is a selfish process, and part of the selfishness means going to AA meetings as often as you need to. You're told to go to five meetings a week if necessary, even two a day. So while the one you love may not be spending hours hanging around bars, don't count on him to gather around the fire with the family just yet.

When I got out, I went to three meetings each week. Now I go once weekly. But there are times in my life when I feel stress and anger building up. I know that's a warning sign to go to a meeting. When my brother starts some of his old behavior, his wife suggests that he go to a couple more meetings a week. The people who get out of treatment and white-knuckle it, trying to go it alone, have a really hard time.

AA will help not only with the drinking but with the associated problems. Most people who are not alcoholic don't understand the disease and know little about it. If the alcoholic assumes that they understand, he will be disappointed and misled. If he tries to discuss the disease with people who know nothing about it, he won't get logical—or useful—responses. He needs to talk things through with someone who has been there.

Also, he needs role models. Who were the role models in his life to teach him to be a good parent or a good spouse? Chances are, they were missing. In AA he can find such people.

You, too, can find role models in Al-Anon, Alateen, and ACA. And there you will find support through difficult times such as those days when you will want to wring the alcoholic's neck. The idea of Al-Anon is to take care of yourself, not the other person. Al-Anon will help you realize that neck-wringing won't change a person. You can change only yourself, and to learn that, it is important to be around people who are learning that also. Good counseling and understanding friends will help you grow into the best person you can be.

Appropriate responses

How should you treat the person who's in recovery? From my own experience I can tell you several things to keep in mind. When you're recovering, you want people to listen. You don't want them to be judgmental. I gratefully remember one person saying to me, "Tell me where I can fit? What can I do to support you?" I have never forgotten that.

My sobriety meant a change in my life, and it was something I wanted to share, but often I wasn't invited to. It's spooky to walk into a roomful of people and realize the majority know you've been in treatment but no one is willing to talk about it, to ask, "What was it like? What happened?"

Some people make you feel as if you're a leprosy victim. They exclude you, they're uncomfortable around you, and they feel threatened. They don't want you at lunch because they're afraid they can't drink with you or in front of you.

I liked it when people came out and said what was on their minds instead of acting as if they were walking on eggs. I called a friend and said, "I'll meet you for a bump" (that's Midwesternese for a drink), and he blurted out, "You're not drinking, are you?" I started laughing because he was so upfront, and I told him I'd be having a "bump" of diet soda.

Occasionally I'd leave the office when I felt very lethargic and lonesome and scared, and someone finally said to me, "Mary Ellen, I care so much about you that the times you just take off, I get nervous." I preferred that to a reprimand or to being babied. I hated when people started calling around to find out where I was. I didn't want to be policed. I wanted compassion and understanding and appropriate cheerleading—a simple "I'm proud of you" once in a while or, better yet, "I see change and here's where I see it. You are so much more at ease. You're more fun to be around."

I had a hard time controlling some of my anger when I felt I was being treated like a three-year-old. There were several restaurants where I had made a habit of having my long drinking lunches, or "drunches," as I called them. One day after I'd returned from Hazelden I took a two-and-a-half-hour midday break in one of my favorite spots. As I walked back into work, one of the gals made a point of heaving a huge sigh of relief, presumably because I'd managed to return to work in the first place and I wasn't drunk besides. "Why would you go back there?" she asked.

"I like the food there," I told her. "I run into many people I like there." I resented having to defend myself. What I should have told her was, "I'll have to learn to handle my drinking no matter where I go," or, if I were feeling particularly put upon, simply, "I'll go to lunch wherever I please."

I want people to realize that I *choose* not to drink now. People say, "She won't have a drink because she can't." Well,

288 / MARY ELLEN PINKHAM

the fact is, I can. I can have a drink any time I want one. I choose not to: I'm a happier person when I don't drink, because I have a disease called alcoholism. A fellow who has diabetes can eat sugar, too, if he chooses. Like him, I avoid what's bad for me of my own free will.

I've told my friends that if any of them were to spot me drinking again, they should try to get AA involved immediately. And it's their choice if they want to be with me from that point on. Don't take care of me, I ask. Don't enable me. Get someone from AA.

What sobriety has done for me

I've changed so much in the last few years. I feel totally brand-new. Anyone who disagrees is seeing only what he wishes to see.

What I am is a result first of dealing with the drinking and then of practice. I started down the path by listening to what I'd been told in treatment. Then, I had to act on the advice I'd been given.

At the beginning of recovery, I'd find myself in discussions that didn't sit well with me, but instead of letting my old behavior take over—telling people what they wanted to hear or giving it to them straight between the eyes—I didn't say anything. Not a word. I just listened and tried to figure out where others were coming from instead of where I wanted things to go. I've become quicker to listen, slower to speak, and less apt to get angry. I handle myself differently when I have to face rough times. I don't see myself as a victim if things don't go my way. I don't demand instant results. I guess you might say I have learned how to be patient and developed perseverance.

I've also learned how to be honest. There were times I had to say things that scared the hell out of me. I had to tell people I loved that I didn't care for the way they treated me. That took so much effort. Looking back, I am still amazed to have discovered that when I spoke from my heart, not my head, people listened. The sky didn't fall. Often they agreed. And when they didn't, I had to learn not to take everything so personally.

Of course, none of this happened overnight. It won't with

your alcoholic either. Like me, he probably won't let go of all his delusions until some time has passed. Even two months after I came out of treatment, I was still denying that my alcoholism had any effect on my son. Andrew was having trouble in school and I never once connected it to my own behavior. Several more months of sobriety passed before the realization sank into my brain. Once the channels were opened and we began to have honest communications, Andrew told me a few things that made it clear he had been aware of all that was going on, and it had indeed affected him.

At this point, I was seeing a doctor regarding Andrew's problems. The doctor had advised me to give him Ritalin. I knew that he didn't need to be medicated—that, in fact, given his genetic predisposition to be adversely affected by mood-altering chemicals, the last thing in the world he needed was medication. He needed his mother.

Once I stopped denying my responsibility for his behavior, I could make an effective decision. I chose not to medicate Andrew but to move him to a school that would give him extra attention to make up for what he'd missed in the years when I wasn't available. I made the right choice. Andrew is doing beautifully these days.

One of the proudest moments in my recovery came when I was asked to speak at Andrew's Sunday School class. I asked Andrew what he wanted me to talk about. "How about your drinking, Mom? You will help a lot of these kids. Maybe they won't drink."

A final thought

I am so proud that I have passed some of the rewards of my sobriety down to my son. He isn't ashamed. He's proud. We've torn down the walls that kept us from one another in my family. That's what happens when you do an Intervention. It's the first step in opening up communications.

An Intervention is a miracle. I hope you will use it to stop the one you love from drinking.

And I want to remind you that, whether the one you love gets sober or not, *you* deserve a better life. How do you find it? Join a self-help group. Or call a treatment center and tell them you're living with an alcoholic and you yourself need counsel. It may not be easy, but I swear to you that if you follow through and start taking care of yourself instead of others for a change, you are in for a wonderful surprise. You'll find that you are worthwhile and that life can be fun. A better life is out there waiting for you to discover it.

I have tried to be completely honest in writing this book. I hope you can be honest, too. Don't live a lie. Don't turn away from the fact that alcoholism and other chemical dependencies are serious and that you and the one you love both need help. Get it—and you'll know what living is really meant to be.

Epilogue

Sherm Pinkham took ill on January 1, 1986, just as I was finishing the first draft of this book. On January 26, he went into the hospital, where he was diagnosed as having terminal cancer of the lungs. He died at home on February 23.

When I was in the hospital with Sherm, his longtime drinking friends, whom we both loved very much, would visit. Knowing he was very ill, they joked, "See what happens when you stop drinking?" At that point, the doctors had given him a year or two to live. Privately, our friends were concerned that he would hit the bottle again. "If I were sick," more than one of them told me, "that's what I would do."

Sherm was grateful for his sobriety, and I don't think that thought ever entered his mind. We took him home to die, and near the end he was terribly ill. One of the few things he could tolerate was orange juice. He loved it. Two or three days before his death, he held a glass of it and looked at me with such an expression of wonder it was childlike. "Why would anyone drink booze," he asked, "when he could drink orange juice instead?"

There's a prayer in AA that we all say—the Serenity Prayer: "God grant me the serenity to accept the things I cannot change, the courage to change the things I can, and the wisdom to know the difference." When Sherm was getting close to the end of his life, as his body started failing, his spirit and his faith grew tremendously. He was very silent. Few people knew what he was up to, but I knew that he frequently held onto the medallion he'd been given on his first year of sobriety and recited that prayer. He changed it a little: ". . . The things I cannot change, like my terminal cancer, and the wisdom to know the difference, so that I can still die with dignity and be at peace with myself." That simple prayer gave Sherm a great deal of strength.

Sherm had his share of painful problems. He had lost a ten-year-old son. When people hurt Sherm he never let them know. He was a typical Marine, a tough guy, recipient of a Purple Heart. He couldn't tell people what he needed or wanted. So they continued to hurt him.

Nobody was better than Sherm at turning the other cheek. He never said a bad word about his fellow man. He was not a gossip. Idle talk bored him. The only thing that was wrong with Sherm was his alcoholism. That's what this book is about—about being a good person who blows a lot of opportunities because of drinking.

Sherm read the first draft of this book, and he didn't find it painful to read the stuff about the two of us. He was very proud that our lives had gone in the direction they had recently taken. I'd looked forward to going on tour, maybe even making appearances with him. That might have been wishful thinking, because Sherm wasn't the kind of guy who talked a lot. But now it's all on the record. This book is my tribute to Sherm Pinkham.

They say you can't take anything with you, but you can leave lots behind. What Sherm left behind that meant the most to me and our son was that he was sober.

When it was obvious that Sherm was terribly ill, people thought, "Oh, oh, Mary Ellen's going to start drinking again." There's something I want to point out here. More than ever am I truly grateful for my own sobriety. If I had still been drinking, there would have been a lot of unfinished business, no opportunity to heal the wounds of the past. When I completed treatment, I was ordered not to make any changes, at least not right away. Otherwise, the first thing I would have done was leave Sherm.

Through our sobriety we found a common bond. We realized that our pain was due to our alcoholism, not some failing in our characters. I was glad I followed instructions and didn't act impetuously. By following instructions, I was taking care of myself. Ultimately, Sherm took care of himself, too. *By caring for ourselves, we wound up caring for each other.*

When he became sober, instead of seeing a person who was the source of a lot of my trouble, I saw in Sherm the man I had always loved, a man of gentle spirit, the man he was meant to be without this awful disease. I was so grateful that when my husband died, I loved him. I don't have any doubt in my mind about that.

Death—at least the way Sherm died—isn't peaceful. It's like being born. It's painful. You struggle. But nothing will stop it. Sherm fought so hard that last day. It was very, very tough for me. He couldn't even sip water but all he wanted to do was stand up. The next morning, after he died, I prayed for a sign that Sherm was okay. I went back upstairs and something told me to go into the bedroom. I pulled up the shade and looked around. No one would know that somebody had just died in here, I thought. It seemed so tranquil.

I moved closer to the bed. Cancer has an odor. The smell of it, the smell of death, fills the house. But on the bed where Sherm lay in agony, full of disease, the sheets smelled as if they had been laundered. They smelled of daisies, actually. All the bad odor was gone. A friend called that afternoon and said, "Mary Ellen, I've been through this and I should warn you. The house won't smell fresh again for weeks." I looked across the hall into the bedroom and silently said thanks to my higher power. That episode helped put me at peace.

Someone said to me, "You wouldn't have gone through this differently if you'd been drinking." I am amazed at how little people understand. I would indeed have done things differently.

Number one, Sherm would have died in a hospital. I couldn't have faced death. I'd have been too frightened. Instead of bringing Sherm home and spending the last days with him, I'd have paid him visits. They would have caused me great stress, and I would have handled the stress the only way I knew how. I would have gone to lunch and drunk my pain away, and then the next day I'd have felt too sick and too guilty to have been any help to Andrew or anyone else. Instead of serving my family, I would have been serving my disease.

Number two, my son would never have been able to do what he did, go to his father's deathbed and talk—tell him he loved him, that he was a great dad, that he was going to miss him. The old Mary Ellen would have felt that was too much for a child to handle. I would have protected him and taken him away from the sight of his dying father. As it turns out, one of the things Andrew is most content about is that he was able to talk to his dad before he died and tell him how he felt.

Number three, our family would not have been around us, nor would I have allowed them to help if they tried. When I recovered, I made my peace with everyone.

Number four, I wouldn't have had a circle of people around me like the people from AA, who knew, and helped teach me, what acceptance really meant. And since I no longer had the alcoholic's need to do everything my way or to do for others without allowing them to do for me, I was able to accept help from them, from family, from neighbors, from Sherm's friends, even from people I didn't know who reached out to me and Andrew and gave us unconditional love. They were all a part of what happened.

Number five, I would have had no church and no minister to lean on. I'd have been calling people up in the middle of the night asking where I could turn. Having a minister who knew me and a church where I felt truly at home gave me so much comfort.

Number six, I would have had guilt about my life with Sherm. If I hadn't stopped drinking, there would have been a tremendous amount. Instead, I felt okay about myself, very clean. My grieving was real and true but—let's put it this way—I wasn't throwing myself on the casket.

Finally, I would have reacted in a very self-centered way, telling myself that now I not only had all the business problems to deal with alone but also 100 percent of the responsibility for my son's care. I'd have been really frightened.

Instead, I know that I am not a victim, that I can do what is necessary, that all I must do is make good decisions. I will live my life as I have the last couple of years, a day at a time. Death is a part of life, it is an ending, but it is also, for me, a new beginning.

What a great gift it was for Sherm to die sober. His scores had been settled. He was at peace with his family, his friends, his God. He didn't have a lot of amends to make, but that last week at home, I saw a lot of people making their amends to him. I think he got a big bang out of that.

You come into life sober and you ought to leave it sober. It's painful to think about his friends' reaction to his final illness, wondering whether Sherm would start drinking again if the cancer had lingered on. I realize that they just don't understand. Drinking *means* lots of pain. Why would my husband have wanted to compound the pain of cancer with the pain of alcoholism?

After the funeral, what struck me was how differently people reacted. Some went home to their families and the people who loved them, others to the bars and their bottles. When I heard people were out drinking, I was appalled, and then it dawned on me that I would have done the same thing until a couple of years ago. Thank God I found another way to live my life. You have it in your power to help someone you love find another way, too.

Appendix: Recommended Treatment Centers

NOTE: Asterisks denote programs or facilities with which the author and the staff of Families in Crisis, Inc., are personally acquainted. All costs are approximate and subject to change. (When you look at costs, remember, health care today is expensive for every disease. A hospital stay runs upwards of $400 per day.)

ALABAMA

Decatur
Charter Retreat Recovery Center
P.O. Box 1230
Decatur, AL 35620
(205) 350-1680
Hospital setting

Program	Length	Cost
Adolescent Inpatient	8 weeks	approx $2,000/wk
Adult Inpatient	4–6 weeks	approx $2,000/wk

Tuscaloosa
Druid Oaks Addictive Disease Unit
1101 6th Avenue E.
Tuscaloosa, AL 35401
(205) 759-7380
Hospital setting

Program	Length	Cost
Adult Inpatient	3 weeks + detox time	$7,500

Adult Outpatient	3–4 weeks	$3,500/day program; $2,500/eve program
Co-dependent (with no involvement of dependent person)	as needed	$52.50/session

ALASKA

Anchorage
Charter North Hospital
Chemical Dependency Unit
2530 DeBarr Road
Anchorage, AK 99504
(907) 338-7575
Hospital setting

Program	Length	Cost
Adolescent Inpatient	6–8 weeks	$535/day
Adult Inpatient	3–6 weeks	approx $10,500 (21 days)
Adult Outpatient	5 weeks	approx $1,500

ARIZONA

Phoenix
St. Luke's Behavioral Health Center
1800 E. Van Buren
Phoenix, AZ 85006
(602) 251-8535
Hospital setting

Program	Length	Cost
Adolescent Inpatient	6 weeks	varies
Adolescent Outpatient	5 weeks	$1,585
Adult Inpatient (Acute)	21–28 days	$8,000
Adult Inpatient (Residential)	21–28 days	$5,700
Adult Outpatient	5 weeks	$1,595

Wickenberg
The Meadows
P.O. Box 97
Wickenberg, AZ 85358
(602) 684-2815
Freestanding facility

Program	Length	Cost
Adult Inpatient	approx 6 weeks	$266/day

NOTE: No aftercare provided, but counselor at facility assists client in finding aftercare upon return home.

ARKANSAS

Ft. Smith
Sparks Regional Medical Center
Care Unit Hospital Program
1311 So. I Street
Fort Smith, AR 72901
(501) 441-5500
Hospital setting

Program	Length	Cost
Adolescent Inpatient	30+ days	$1,500/wk
Adult Inpatient	1 month	$1,500/wk

CALIFORNIA

La Jolla
Scripps Memorial Hospital
The McDonald Center
9888 Genesee Avenue
La Jolla, CA 92037
(619) 458-4300
(800) 382-HELP
Hospital setting

Program	Length	Cost
Adolescent Inpatient	45 days (average)	$17,000
Adult Inpatient	30 days	$12,500
Adult Outpatient	6 weeks	$1,920

Rancho Mirage
*Betty Ford Center
39000 Bob Hope Drive
Rancho Mirage, CA 92270
(619) 340-0033
Freestanding facility (medical care available if needed)

Program	Length	Cost
Adult Inpatient	4–6 weeks	$6,000
Adult Outpatient	6 weeks	$2,300

San Diego
Villa View Community Hospital
5550 University Avenue
San Diego, CA 92105
(619) 582-3516
Hospital setting

Program	Length	Cost
Adult Inpatient	26 days	$5,600
Adult Outpatient	8 weeks	$1,200

COLORADO

Arvada
Cottonwood Hill, Inc.
P.O. Box 427
Arvada, CO 80001
(303) 420-1702
Residential facility

Program	Length	Cost
Adult Inpatient (includes teens 16+)	30 days	$210/day
Adult Outpatient	6-week program (5 nights per week, 6 P.M.–9:30 P.M.)	$1,200

DELAWARE

Delaware City
L.K.E.C./Delaware Addiction Services
Box 546
Delaware City, DE 19706
(302) 834-9201, ext. 211
Residential facility
NOTE: Private, not-for-profit program.

Program	Length	Cost
Adolescent Inpatient	28 days	$100/day
Adult Inpatient	28 days	$100/day

FLORIDA

Avon Park
Florida Alcoholism Treatment Center
100 W. College Drive
Avon Park, FL 33825
(813) 453-3151
Residential facility
Note: Pro-rated for Florida residents if unable to pay (sliding scale).

Program	Length	Cost
Adult Inpatient	28 days	$110/day

Miami
South Miami Hospital Addiction Treatment Program
(305) 662-8118
Hospital setting
NOTE: Families receive counseling for 3 months after client's discharge.

Program	Length	Cost
Adult Inpatient	4–7 weeks	$7,200

West Palm Beach
Hanley Hazelden Center at St. Mary's
901 45th Street
West Palm Beach, FL 33407
(305) 844-8558
Freestanding facility

Program	Length	Cost
Adult Inpatient	28 days	$4,200
Adult Outpatient (daytime)	11 days full-time; 10 weeks aftercare	$1,200

GEORGIA

Atlanta
West Paces Ferry Hospital
Addictive Disorders Unit
3200 Howell Mill Road
Atlanta, GA 30327
(404) 351-0351
Hospital setting

Program	Length	Cost
Adult Inpatient	2 weeks min + eval	$2,500/2 wks
Adult Outpatient	2–4 weeks + eval	$1,000/2 wks

Valdosta
Green Leaf Center
2209 Pineview Drive
Valdosta, GA 31602
(615) 870-5110
(800) 247-2747 (GA, FL, TN, NC, SC, AL residents)
Freestanding facility
NOTE: Senior citizens unit; substance abuse unit; co-dependency.

Program	Length	Cost
Adolescent Inpatient	4 weeks average	$350/day (varies)
Adult Inpatient	4 weeks average	$350/day (varies)

IDAHO

Coeur d'Alene
Pine Crest Hospital
Lifeworks Center
2301 N. Ironwood Place
Coeur D'Alene, ID 83814
(208) 666-1441
(800) 221-5008
Hospital setting
NOTE: For aftercare, contractual arrangements made with outside centers and counselors.

Program	Length	Cost
Adult Inpatient	21–28 days	$380/day

ILLINOIS

Chicago

*ARC (Addiction Recovery of Chicago)
1776 Moon Lake Blvd.
Hoffman Estates, IL 60194
(312) 882-0070
(800) 942-0541 (Illinois residents)
Freestanding facility

Program	Length	Cost
Adolescent Inpatient	approx 42 days	$225/day
Adult Inpatient	approx 28 days	$245/day
Adult Intensive Outpatient	5 weeks, 20 sessions	$1,600
Cocaine Intensive Outpatient	5 weeks, 25 sessions	$2,000

Martha Washington Hospital Treatment Center
4055 North Western Ave.
Chicago, IL 60618
(312) 583-9000
Hospital setting (unit is freestanding)

Program	Length	Cost
Adult Inpatient	26 days average	$9–12,000
Adult Outpatient	20 days/eve long-term/day	$1,500

Springfield

Sangamon-Menard Alcoholism & Drugs Council
723 South Fisk
Springfield, IL 62703
(217) 544-9858
Freestanding facility

Program	Length	Cost
Adult Inpatient	28 days	based on income and number of dependents
Adult Outpatient	1 year	based on income and number of dependents

INDIANA

Terre Haute
Hamilton Center, Inc.
620 Eighth Ave.
Terre Haute, IN 47804
Alcohol & Drug Services
(812) 231-8350
Hospital setting

Program	Length	Cost
Adult Inpatient	10 day detox only	Title 20 funded
Adult Outpatient	varies	subsidized fee scale based on ability to pay

LOUISIANA

New Orleans
Counterpoint Center of New Orleans
3601 Coliseum Street
New Orleans, LA 70115
(504) 897-9700
Hospital setting

Program	Length	Cost
Adolescent Inpatient	40 days	unavailable
Adolescent Outpatient	varies	unavailable
Adult Inpatient	28 days +	unavailable
Adult Outpatient	varies	unavailable

Shreveport
Charter Forest Hospital
9320 Linwood Avenue
Shreveport, LA 71106
(318) 688-3930
Hospital setting

Program	Length	Cost
Adolescent Inpatient	5–7 weeks	$14,700 approx.
Adult Inpatient	30 days	$10,600 approx.

MAINE

Lewiston
St. Mary's General Hospital
Chemical Dependency Unit
45 Golder Street
Lewiston, ME 04240
(207) 786-2901
Hospital setting
NOTE: Intensive aftercare 14 days post-discharge. Regular aftercare 2 years post-discharge.

Program	Length	Cost
Adolescent Inpatient	28 days+	$195/day
Adult Inpatient	21–28 days variable	$195/day

MARYLAND

Baltimore
University of Maryland
Alcohol and Drug Abuse Program
721 W. Redland
Baltimore, MD 21201
(301) 528-6800
Freestanding facility

Program	Length	Cost
Adolescent Inpatient	program in development	sliding scale (depends on income)
Adolescent Outpatient	individualized	sliding scale
Adult Inpatient	28 days	sliding scale
Adult Outpatient	6 months	sliding scale

MASSACHUSETTS

Worcester
Doctors Hospital of Worcester
107 Lincoln Street
Worcester, MA 01605
(617) 799-9000
Hospital setting

Program	Length	Cost
Adult Inpatient (15+)	varies	varies
Adult Outpatient (15+)	varies	$55.00 individual session; $27.00 group session
Naltrexone Outpatient	6 months to 1 year	varies

MICHIGAN

Monroe
Alcohol & Substance Abuse Center
528 N. Telegraph
Monroe, MI 48161
(313) 243-5483
Freestanding facility

Program	Length	Cost
Adolescent Outpatient	varies	sliding scale
Adult Outpatient	varies	sliding scale

MINNESOTA

Center City
*Hazelden Foundation
15245 Pleasant Valley Road
Center City, MN 55012
(612) 257-4010
Residential facility

Program	Length	Cost
Adolescent Inpatient	30–45 days	$4,150–$5,850 (approx)
Adult Inpatient	30–35 days	$4,150–$4,700 (approx)
Adult Female Outpatient	15 weeks	$1,272 (approx)

Minneapolis
*Abbott–Northwestern Hospital
Chemical Dependency Program
1800 1st Avenue S.
Minneapolis, MN 55403
(612) 874-5510
Hospital setting

Program	Length	Cost
Adult Inpatient	21–28 days	$170/day
Adult Outpatient	20 days	$96/day for day program; $64/day for evening program

* St. Mary's Rehabilitation Center
Chemical Dependency Services
2512 South Seventh Street
Minneapolis, MN 55454
(612) 338-2234
Hospital setting

Program	Length	Cost
Adolescent Inpatient	35–40 days	$259/day
Adult Inpatient	approx 28 days	$165/day
Adult Outpatient	4 weeks, 20 sessions	$65/session

St. Louis Park
* Parkview Treatment Center
3705 Park Center Boulevard
Minneapolis, MN 55416
(612) 929-5531
Residential facility

Program	Length	Cost
Adult Inpatient	4 weeks	$5,000
Adult Outpatient	4–6 weeks	approx $2,500

St. Paul
* New Connection Programs
73 Leech Street
St. Paul, MN 55102
(612) 224-4384
Freestanding facility
Note: Many additional programs offered—evening for adolescents, families of prechemically dependent, extended residential program (2–6 months, $86/day for adolescents with multiple problems.)

Program	Length	Cost
Adolescent Inpatient	28 days average	$165/day
Adolescent Outpatient	4–6 weeks (days)	$76/day

* St. John's Hospital
Chemical Dependency Program
403 Maria Ave.
St. Paul, MN 55106
(612) 772-2600
Hospital setting

Program	Length	Cost
Adolescent Inpatient	varies	$158/day
Adolescent Outpatient	6 weeks	$63/day
Adult Inpatient	5–28 days	$158/day
Adult Outpatient	15–20 days	$63/day

MISSISSIPPI

Jackson
Brookwood Recovery Center
5354 Interstate 55 South
Jackson, MS 39212
(601) 372-9788
Freestanding facility

Program	Length	Cost
Adult Inpatient (17+)	30 days (alcohol); 40 days (alcohol + drugs)	$6,800–$7,500
Adult Outpatient (17+)	varies	varies

MISSOURI

St. Louis
St. John's Mercy Medical Center
The Edgewood Program
615 S. New Ballas Road
St. Louis, MO 63141
(314) 569-6500
Hospital setting

Program	Length	Cost
Adolescent Inpatient (with adults)		
Adolescent Outpatient	6 months	$1,600 ($26 per hour)
Adult Inpatient	25 days	$195/day
Adult Outpatient	6 months	$1,600 ($26 per hour)
Co-Dependent	10 days	$800

MONTANA

Billings
Rimrock Foundation
Box 30374
Billings, MT 59107
(406) 248-3175
Freestanding facility

Program	Length	Cost
Adolescent Inpatient	35 days	$7,595
Adult Inpatient	28 days	$5,900

NEBRASKA

Omaha
Immanuel Alcoholism Treatment Center
6901 North 72nd
Omaha, NB 68122
(402) 572-2016
Hospital setting

Program	Length	Cost
Adolescent Outpatient	6 weeks	$1,600
Adult Inpatient	21–28 days	$5,500–$6,000
Adult Outpatient	8 weeks	$1,600
Co-Dependent	6 weeks	$630 (1st member; $250 for each additional)

Scottsbluff
West Nebraska General Hospital
Chemical Dependency Unit
4021 Avenue B
Scottsbluff, NB 69361
(308) 632-0282
Hospital setting

Program	Length	Cost
Adult Inpatient	30 days	$4,800
Adult Outpatient	9 weeks, 32 sessions	$1,545
Co-Dependent Outpatient	2 weeks, 10 sessions	$420
Co-Dependent Inpatient	30 days	$4,800

NEW HAMPSHIRE

Dublin
Beech Hill Hospital, Inc.
New Harrisville Rd.
Dublin, NH 03444
(603) 563-8511
Hospital setting

Program	Length	Cost
Adolescent Inpatient	21–28 days	$210/day
Adult Inpatient	21–28 days	$210/day

NEW JERSEY

Princeton
Princeton House (Princeton Medical Center)
905 Herrontown Road
Princeton, NJ 08540
(609) 734-4631 (information)
(609) 734-4636 (admissions)
Freestanding facility (but affiliated with Princeton Hospital)

Program	Length	Cost
Adult Inpatient	28 days	$2,000/wk
Adult Outpatient	6 weeks	$75/day

NEW YORK

New York City
Beth Israel Medical Center
Chemical Dependency Treatment Program
10 Nathan D. Perlman Place
(212) 420-2900
Hospital setting

Program	Length	Cost
Adult Inpatient	approx 28 days	$340/day

St. Vincent's Hospital and Medical Center of New York
Alcoholism Treatment and Education Program
203 West 12th Street
New York, NY 10011
(212) 790-8273
Hospital setting

Program	Length	Cost
Adult Inpatient	28 days	$485/day
Adult Outpatient	varies	$15–65 session

Syracuse
Benjamin Rush Center
672 S. Salina St.
Syracuse, NY 13202
(315) 476-2161
Hospital setting

Program	Length	Cost
Adolescent Inpatient	8–10 weeks	$390/day + physician cost
Adult Inpatient	6 weeks	$370/day + physician cost

Yorktown Heights
*ARC Westchester
P.O. Box 37
Yorktown Heights, NY
(914) 962-5000
(800) 942-2200 (New York)
(800) 431-4545 (CT, NJ, PA, D.C.)
Freestanding facility

Note: Family in-patient therapy for five days at no cost; room and board charges only.

Program	Length	Cost
Adult Inpatient	30–35 days	$288/day

NORTH CAROLINA

Raleigh
Wake County Alcoholism Treatment Center
3000 Falstaff Road
Raleigh, NC 27610
(919) 821-7650
Hospital setting

Program	Length	Cost
Adolescent Inpatient (with evaluation can be admitted to adult program)		
Adolescent Outpatient (with evaluation can be admitted to adult program)		
Adult Inpatient	10 days (average)	$15–30,000
Adult Outpatient	varies	adjustable

Winston-Salem
Alcoholism Program of Forsyth County
725 Highland Ave.
Winston-Salem, NC 27101
(919) 725-7777
Hospital setting

Program	Length	Cost
Adult Inpatient	30 days–6 weeks	sliding scale; county assisted
Adult Outpatient	3–6 months	

NORTH DAKOTA

Grand Forks
United Recovery Center
860 South Columbia Road
Grand Forks, ND 58201
(701) 780-5900
Freestanding facility

Program	Length	Cost
Adolescent inpatient	6–8 weeks	$185/day
Adult inpatient	4–5 weeks	$143/day
Adult outpatient	20 sessions	$86/session

OHIO

Cleveland
St. John & West Shore Hospital
Alcoholism Unit
29000 Center Ridge Road
Cleveland/Westlake, OH 44145
(216) 835-6059
(800) 345-LOVE (Ohio residents)
Hospital setting

Program	Length	Cost
Adult Inpatient (adolescents may be admitted)	28 days (2 wks inpatient, 2 wks outpatient)	unavailable
Adult Outpatient	4 weeks	unavailable

OKLAHOMA

Broken Arrow
12300 E. 91st Street
Broken Arrow, OK 74012
(918) 252-2541
Freestanding facility

Program	Length	Cost
Adult Inpatient	28 days	$7,000 (contract basis EAPs; $8,000–$8,200 non-EAPs)
Adult Outpatient	8 weeks	$1,500
Family Program	varies	varies

Tulsa
Brookwoodhaven Hospital
201 S. Garnet
Tulsa, OK 74128
(918) 438-4257
Licensed psychiatric hospital (with special cocaine withdrawal program)

Program	Length	Cost
Adult Inpatient (16+)	25 days	$240/day
Adult Outpatient (16+)	individualized	$40–60/hr indiv; $25/hr group

OREGON

Portland
Providence Medical Center
Alcoholism Treatment
5104 N.E. Hoyt
Portland, OR 97103
(503) 230-6119
Hospital setting

Program	Length	Cost
Adult Inpatient	30 days	$4,200 approx
Adult Outpatient	25 days	$1,600 approx

PENNSYLVANIA

Aliquippa
Gateway Rehabilitation Center
Moffett Run Road
Aliquippa, PA 15001
(412) 766-8700
Freestanding facility

Program	Length	Cost
Adult Inpatient	28 days	$4,480 (detox: $220/day; treatment: $160/day)
Adult Outpatient	15 days	$1,200

Bensalem
Livengrin Foundation
4833 Hulmeville Road
Bensalem, PA 19020
(215) 639-2300
Freestanding facility

Program	Length	Cost
Children's program (7–12 years)	3 session increments each Saturday morning	$10/session/child
Adult Inpatient (18+)	21 days	$3,360/21 days; $950/5 days detox
Adult Outpatient (18+)	varies	$40/hr indiv; $15/½ hour group (per person)
Residential Family Program	5 days	$500

Ephrata

ARC (Addiction Recovery Corp.)/The Terraces
1170 South State Street
Ephrata, PA 17522
(717) 627-0790
Freestanding facility (with separate cocaine program)
NOTE: Relapse program of 42 days + detox ($8,300); Cocaine Chronic Relapse program.

Program	Length	Cost
Adolescent Inpatient	49 days + detox	$14,000
Adult Inpatient	28 days	$6,700
Family Program	6 days	$550

Pittsburgh

South Hills Health System
Jefferson Center Hospital
Chemical Abuse Services
(412) 664-5386
Hospital setting

Program	Length	Cost
Adult Inpatient	detox only	
Adult Outpatient	varies	sliding scale

SOUTH CAROLINA

Travelers Rest
North Greenville Hospital
Alcoholism and Drug Treatment Program
807 N. Main St.
Traveler's Rest, SC 29690
(803) 834-5131
Hospital setting

Program	Length	Cost
Adolescent Inpatient	6–8 weeks	$223/day, $915/6 weeks + physician fee
Adult Inpatient	4–6 weeks (drugs 6 wks)	same as above

SOUTH DAKOTA

Aberdeen
Worthmore Care Unit
400 15th Avenue, NW
Aberdeen, SD 57401
(605) 622-3425
(800) 952-2250 (S. Dakota residents)
Hospital setting

Program	Length	Cost
Adult Inpatient	28 days average	$195/day

TENNESSEE

Harriston
Addiction Recovery of Chattanooga
8614 Harrison Bay Road
Harrison, TN 37341
(800) 233-3737 (out-of-state residents)
(800) 821-2914 (Tennessee residents)
Freestanding facility

Program	Length	Cost
Adolescent Inpatient	45 days	$11,895
Adult Inpatient	35 days	$8,965

Memphis
Methodist Outreach, Inc.
2009 Lamar Avenue
Memphis, TN 38104
(901) 276-5401
Freestanding facility

Program	Length	Cost
Adolescent Inpatient	40–60 days	$400/day (approx)
Adolescent Outpatient	6 weeks minimum	$400/wk (approx)
Adult Inpatient	28 days	$9,800 (approx)
Adult Outpatient—partial hospitalization (3 hrs/day Mon-Fri)	5 weeks	$100/day (approx)

TEXAS

Houston
Brookwood/Parkside Recovery Center
Parkside Lodges of Texas, Inc.
5638 Medical Center Drive
Katy, TX 77450
(713) 392-3456
Freestanding facility

Program	Length	Cost
Adult Inpatient	28 days/alcohol	$8,300
	42 days/drug	$12,400

Liverpool
Parkside Lodge
638 Harbor Road
Liverpool, TX 77577
(713) 393-2023
Freestanding facility

Program	Length	Cost
Adolescent Inpatient	7–10 days (evaluation)	$335/day
	28 days (treatment)	unavailable
Adolescent Outpatient	6 months	$20/session

VERMONT

Brattleboro
Brattleboro Retreat Addictive Disease Center
Linden Street
Brattleboro, VT 05301
(802) 257-7785
Hospital setting

Program	Length	Cost
Adolescent Inpatient	45–60 days	$375/day
Adult Inpatient	1 month	$199/day

VIRGINIA

Arlington
Arlington Hospital
Alcoholism Treatment Program
(703) 558-6536
Hospital setting

Program	Length	Cost
Adolescent Inpatient	28 days (alcohol only); 42 days (alcohol + drugs)	$10,000/42 days
Adolescent Outpatient	7 weeks	$1,150
Adult Inpatient	28 days	$7,000
Adult Outpatient	7 weeks	$1,150

Harrisonburg
Arlington Treatment Center
Route 3, Box 52
Harrisonburg, VA 22801
(703) 434-7396
Freestanding facility

Program	Length	Cost
Adult Inpatient	28 days	$6,000

WASHINGTON

Tacoma

Puget Sound Alcoholism Center
215 S. 36th Street
Tacoma, WA 98408
(206) 474-0533
Hospital setting

Program	Length	Cost
Adolescent Inpatient	6 weeks	$8,640 + $120 for doctor
Adult Inpatient	21 days	$4,480 + $120 for doctor
Detoxification program	3–5 days	$250/day

WISCONSIN

Fond du Lac

Fond du Lac County Alcohol & Other Drug Abuse
  Information and Referral Center
459 E. First St.
Fond du Lac, WI 54935
(414) 929-3565
Freestanding facility

Program	Length	Cost
Adolescent Outpatient	open-ended	$35/hr max (based on ability to pay)
Adult Outpatient	open-ended	same as above

Port Washington

DePaul Port Washington Unit
743 N. Montgomery Street
Port Washington, WI 53074
(414) 284-5872
(800) 242-2112 (Wisconsin residents)
Hospital setting

Program	Length	Cost
Adolescent Inpatient	28 days	$7,500
Adolescent Outpatient	15 weeks	$500 avg/15 weeks
Adult Inpatient	28 days	$7,500
Adult Outpatient	15 weeks	$500 avg/15 weeks

| Co-Dependency Outpatient | 28 weeks | $2,000 |
| Children's Program (ages 6–12, outpatient) | 8 weeks | $200 |

Prescott
Riverwood Center
445 Court Avenue North
Prescott, WI 54021
(715) 262-3286
(612) 437-2133
Hospital setting

Program	Length	Cost
Adolescent Inpatient	open-ended	$325/day
Adult Inpatient	21 days	$115–$210/day
Adult Outpatient	10 weeks	$1,075

WYOMING

Cody
Chemical Dependency Center
707 Sheridan Avenue
Cody, WY 82414
(307) 525-7501
Hospital setting

Program	Length	Cost
Adult Inpatient (16+)	28–30 days average (may be longer for adolescents)	$172.50/day
Adult Outpatient (16+)	12 weeks minimum	sliding scale

Kemmerer
SWARA Outreach
922 Cedar Street
P.O. Box 807
Kemmerer, WY 83101
(307) 877-4780
Freestanding facility

Program	Length	Cost
Adolescent Inpatient	28 days	sliding scale
Adolescent Outpatient	open-ended	sliding scale
Adult Inpatient	28 days	sliding scale
Adult Outpatient	open-ended	sliding scale